THE JOYCE OF EVERYDAY LIFE

CONTEMPORARY IRISH WRITERS

Series editor: Anne Fogarty, University College Dublin

Irish studies is currently being vigorously rethought, not only in connection to major figures such as James Joyce, W. B. Yeats, Eva Gore-Booth, Flann O'Brien, Samuel Beckett, Elizabeth Bowen, and Mary Lavin but also within a larger framework, with particular attention to feminist issues, the environmental humanities, the perspectives of migrants in Irish society, nationalism and transnationalism, Northern Ireland and its writers, the Irish language, and the lively and often genre-crossing fiction, poetry, drama, and film of contemporary Ireland.

This series brings theoretically informed perspectives to a consideration of the work and lives of Irish writers. The volumes provide general discussions of interpretive issues and offer varied strategies for understanding them, with the intention of appealing to an informed audience—advanced undergraduates, graduate students, and general readers as well as scholars of Irish literature and culture.

Recent titles in the series:

The Joyce of Everyday Life
Vicki Mahaffey

Edna O'Brien and the Art of Fiction
Maureen O'Connor

John Banville
Neil Murphy

Medbh McGuckian
Borbála Faragó

Eavan Boland
Jody Allen Randolph

Bernard MacLaverty
Richard Rankin Russell

For more information about the series, please visit bucknelluniversitypress.org.

THE JOYCE OF
EVERYDAY LIFE

VICKI MAHAFFEY

BUCKNELL
UNIVERSITY PRESS

Lewisburg, Pennsylvania

Library of Congress Cataloging-in-Publication Data

Names: Mahaffey, Vicki, author.
Title: The Joyce of everyday life / Vicki Mahaffey.
Description: Lewisburg, Pennsylvania : Bucknell University Press, [2024] |
    Series: Contemporary Irish writers | Includes bibliographical references
    and index.
Identifiers: LCCN 2023054363 | ISBN 9781684485277 (hardcover) |
    ISBN 9781684485260 (paperback) | ISBN 9781684485284 (epub) |
    ISBN 9781684485291 (pdf)
Subjects: LCSH: Joyce, James, 1882–1941—Criticism and interpretation. |
    Life in literature.
Classification: LCC PR6019.O9 Z72527 2024 | DDC 823/.912—dc23/eng/20240530
LC record available at https://lccn.loc.gov/2023054363

A British Cataloging-in-Publication record for this book is available from the
British Library.

References to internet websites (URLs) were accurate at the time of writing.
Neither the author nor Bucknell University Press is responsible for URLs that may
have expired or changed since the manuscript was prepared.

⊖ The paper used in this publication meets the requirements of the American
National Standard for Information Sciences—Permanence of Paper for Printed
Library Materials, ANSI Z39.48-1992.

bucknelluniversitypress.org

Distributed worldwide by Rutgers University Press

For J.E.R. and Conor Jack Mac, for their love of wordplay and aptitude for puzzles

CONTENTS

THE JOYCE OF EVERYDAY LIFE

INTRODUCTION

On Living and Reading

The Joyce of Everyday Life was designed to open the door to a different—more collaborative and social—way of reading and revitalizing lived experience. By transforming the dominant understanding of words, it celebrates the power of non-instrumental language to remove the shroud of habit from the everyday, exposing the hidden wonders of the here and now and infusing routine experience with pleasure, laughter, and joy. As Joyce's friend Frank Budgen explained, Joyce understood words as alive, as "with radium, or coal with human flame. They have a will and a life of their own and are not to be put like lead soldiers, but to be energized and persuaded like solders of flesh and blood. The commerce of life new mints them every day and gives them new values in the exchanges."[1] Words preserve concrete meanings in an almost archeological way; they also resonate with other words through similarities of sight and sound. As Budgen puts it, they are "mysterious means of expression as well as an instrument of communication" (175). Curiosity and attentiveness to the histories and interconnectivity of these dynamic and colorful words spark delight, amusement, and a livelier awareness of the self and its surroundings.

One overarching idea behind this book is that everyday life is akin to everyday reading: both can be deadened by habit. Children find each discovery delightful because of its novelty. At four or five, my daughter Laura loved for me to read *Finnegans Wake* aloud. She would ask, "Mom, can we play that game where you tell me a word and I guess what it is? I think it's called Femagains Wake." Both daily life and ordinary reading are conditioned by rules, rules that serve the important function of structuring lived or imagined experiences and making them easier. Over time, though, that very ease makes life and reading predictable or dull. Everyday life is almost inextricable from the language we use for it. By naming things, we (like Adam) gain dominion over them and they lose their power over us—power to make us see, or startle, or reflect. Words harden into tools with no value beyond their use. It is no longer easy to see a table as a marvel, such as it becomes in the "Oxen of the Sun" episode of *Ulysses,* where it is described as "a board that was of the birchwood of Finlandy and it was upheld by four dwarfmen of that country but they durst not move more for enchantment."[2] Unlike Joyce's table, instrumental objects and the language used to designate them have been drained of their capacity to surprise and imaginatively delight.

Joyce's earliest published fiction is peopled by characters who have become estranged from imagination and creativity by habit, familiarity, vanity, education, thoughtless obedience, or self-interest. *Dubliners* is an anatomy of everyday life gone flat, instrumental language grown stale. The characters seek adventure, love, or freedom but cannot achieve it, and they do not know why. One by one, they fail to communicate or to achieve communion with others. In "A Painful Case," for example, Mr. James Duffy lives a tightly ordered existence by design: "His life rolled out evenly—an adventureless tale."[3] Joyce drily captures the uneventful regularity of Duffy's austere existence: "His father died; the junior partner of the bank retired. And still every morning he went into the city by tram and every evening walked home from the city after having dined moderately in George's Street and read the evening paper for dessert" (*D* 108). Duffy's life is devoid of both grief and sweetness; his postprandial treat is the utilitarian language of a newspaper. His punctilious schedule allows him to distance himself from other people while insulating him from feeling—anger or loneliness. Most importantly, although he reads Nietzsche and is translating Gerhart Haupt-mann's play *Michael Kramer* (something the author James had also done), James Duffy cannot see himself objectively from the outside, with humility to leaven his self-approval; he lacks the capacity for self-reflection.

Mr. Duffy has formed a judgment—"every bond . . . is a bond to sorrow" (*D* 108)—that for him has hardened into fact. That fact precludes him from forming attachments, not only with people (Mrs. Sinico being the most prominent example) but also with objects or his environment ("The lofty walls of his uncarpeted room were free from pictures" [*D* 103]; his room is spare and purely functional). His focus is invariably outward rather than inward, and he has carefully curated what can reach him from the outside. He doesn't see family except on holidays, has no friends, lives "at a little dis-tance from his body" as well as "the city of which he is a citizen," and even thinks of himself from time to time in the third person (*D* 103–105). Ironi-cally, Mrs. Sinico suffers from precisely the same kind of isolation that Mr. Duffy has proudly and defiantly chosen; hers, however, is circumstan-tial rather than self-imposed. In their separate prisons, they are unexpect-edly united by a love of Mozart's music.

Mr. Duffy's life, both before and after he knew Mrs. Sinico and "entan-gled his thoughts with hers" (*D* 106), is an example of the "bad everyday": a sharp and in this case contemptuous awareness of the deficiencies of the world has left no room for him to learn about *himself*.[4] He is encased, pain-fully,[5] deadened to the unpredictable and transitory nature of life and obliv-ious to his own rigidity of mind. Most of the characters of *Dubliners* share Duffy's lack of self-awareness (not to be confused with self-consciousness, which connotes embarrassment rather than acceptance). Only the boy at the beginning of *Dubliners* and Gabriel in "The Dead" have moments in which they can see their errors or defects from a nondefensive perspective, one that might inspire a change of course. Even Stephen Dedalus in *A Por-trait of the Artist as a Young Man* struggles to see himself objectively, achiev-ing it only in flashes. Near the end of the book, he records in his diary that he "unluckily" made "a sudden gesture of a revolutionary nature" when talk-ing to the woman he had idealized. He reflects, "I must have looked like a fellow throwing a handful of peas into the air."[6] As this moment illustrates, the movement from subjective passion to objective vision can be humor-ous, and it can prompt a change of heart as well. After this encounter, Stephen reflects, "I liked her today. A little or much? Don't know. I liked her and it seems a new feeling to me. Then, in that case, all the rest, all that I thought I thought and all that I felt I felt, all the rest before now, in fact . . . O, give it up, old chap! Sleep it off!" (*P* 213). Leopold Bloom asserts the value of self-awareness more soberly in *Ulysses* when he thinks, channeling Robert Burns, "See ourselves as others see us" (*U* 13.1058; 8.662); for more on this, see chapter 9, "On Glass").[7]

The everyday—whether in living or reading—need not resemble Duffy's, with its self-protective indifference tinged by hauteur. Through his intelligence, though, Duffy has taken the first step toward a state of mind that might possibly produce self-awareness: he has removed the shackles of immaturity, which Immanuel Kant defines as needing to seek and obey guidance from others.[8] But Duffy's understanding is independent to a fault, which suggests that something more than independence of mind is needed to achieve insight into *oneself*: it is also necessary to live in (and react to) a responsive environment. Such an environment is essential for sustained human development: it allows an individual to get to know and feel who she is by encountering multiple mirrors, both human and material, in the surrounding world. Duffy's creation of surroundings devoid of anything that might trigger or constitute response—his room has only one "adornment," a lamp—helps to predict his reaction to Mrs. Sinico's passionate expression of feeling for him: disgust and disillusionment. Duffy has successfully weaned himself from needing *guidance* from others, but, unfortunately, he finds *response* to be intolerable, at least until it is no longer available after Mrs. Sinico's untimely death.

The reason Joyce is the central focus of this book is because of the high value he placed on insight into the self: not only for him personally, but for his readers. His books (despite their reputation as obscene) encourage not voyeurism but self-reflection. One often-quoted letter he wrote to the publisher of *Dubliners,* Grant Richards, refers to the collection as a "nicely polished looking-glass" in which he hopes readers will have the opportunity to see themselves. The understandably angry tone of the letter has sometimes prompted critics to underestimate the seriousness of what Joyce is saying: his works are designed, above all, to stimulate readers to see themselves as they are, in reality rather than fantasy. They do that by unsettling the reader's presuppositions (or prejudices, a word that literally means "prejudgments"): about themselves, others, books, and society. Joyce made himself a character in his own fiction to show how fiendishly difficult it is to achieve accurate, balanced self-awareness. In *Dubliners,* the autobiographical first-person narrator is thrice spurred to question himself, to recognize and reevaluate his prior assumptions, as is Joyce's fictional avatar Gabriel Conroy in "The Dead." Their self-revelations about the limits of one's self-understanding, although painful, are shot through with possibilities for clearer and more honest future perception. Joyce suggests that accurate self-knowledge makes people more capable of love as well as communal connection.

Gabriel Conroy best exemplifies how fresh self-awareness can foster a greater capacity for love. Near the end of "The Dead," when he catches a glimpse of himself in a mirror, he sees himself as a fatuously self-important man acting as pennyboy for his aunts, an image that stands in sharp contrast to his earlier vision of himself as a generous, highly educated man of letters (both are caricatures). But in "The Dead," the story continues beyond Gabriel's sudden shift in self-perception to show that his self-questioning has produced a different view, not only of himself but of his wife as someone he has not yet learned to love ("He had never felt like that himself towards any woman but he knew that such a feeling must be love" [*D* 224). That in turn produces a tentative and shadowy freedom, both imaginative and emotional. His mind's eye takes him out the window of the Gresham Hotel into the falling snow, moving all the way to the west coast of Ireland where the ghost he imagined as a rival lies buried, leading him toward a new compassion and awe for the fates of "all the living and the dead." One important question remains, though: How can a character—or writer—experience or stimulate new angles of vision for viewing the self and others? How can self-serving projections and deceptions be sympathetically punctured so as to allow room for change?

If *Dubliners* lays out problems Joyce wanted to solve for himself and others through his writing, the rest of his corpus antically beckons readers toward new ways of reading and living that don't produce such stalemates. Readers of this book will discover, for example, how sleeping resembles reading, and how washing the dirt out of sheets and clothing while gossiping resembles publishing a book. It argues that the Odysseus of *Finnegans Wake* is a salmon, and that Finn MacCool's legendary wisdom is that of a child. *Huckleberry Finn* rides divisions such as black and white as if they were the Mississippi River bisecting the United States. Readers will learn how young women are like margarine in a world where men are the genuine dairy products. Adultery is reviewed through the lens of adulteration, and virgins are comically recast as commodified idols who must suppress awareness of the animality of their bodies if they are to be "purchased" in the marriage market. Words are broken down into their alphabetic components, then whimsically "decorated" and recombined in ways that intertwine the sacred and the profane. Books are reclassified as windows, mirrors, and doors.

For the remainder of this introduction, I will not try to anticipate the wildness and meaningful fun of the chapters that follow. Instead, I would like to recount a few of the writing techniques Joyce used to jostle his readers out of boredom and complacency. The first technique is to turn the narrative from a window into a mirror that reflects the reader at strategic points. Joyce does this by bringing words to life so they can "talk back" to (as well as reflect) the reader. Another technique is to deploy multiple perspectives and to direct attention to etymology as a way of accessing the vitality of words. Openness to the obsolete meanings of words as impactful, if ghostly, depends on a nonlinear view of time. Time in Joyce must be anachronistic, with multiple layers that reference past and future from the vantage point of the present. Finally, I suggest a variety of contexts for understanding Joyce's revised view of the everyday in an epilogue. The perspectives recounted there come are those of Xavier de Maistre, whose book *A Journey around My Room* Joyce owned in Trieste, Sigmund Freud (especially *The Psychopathology of Everyday Life*), Henri Lefebvre, and Maurice Blanchot.[9]

SILVERING THE NARRATIVE

Turning a work of fiction into a mirror at key moments is an art, one likely to be met with resistance. In the "Telemachus" episode of *Ulysses*, Joyce alludes to Oscar Wilde's quip about how readers are never satisfied with representations of themselves when Mulligan holds his cracked looking glass up to Stephen with the command, "Look at yourself, . . . you dreadful bard!" (*U* 1.134). Stephen looks, thinking, "As he and others see me." Mulligan, however, positions Stephen as Wilde's Caliban, enraged "at not seeing his face in a mirror" (*U* 1.136, 143). In the preface to *The Picture of Dorian Gray*, Wilde used this image to illustrate the dislike of *romanticism*;

readers don't want to see representations of themselves as better than they are, or romanticized. Wilde pairs the dislike of romanticism with a dislike of realism, which he describes as "the rage of Caliban at seeing himself in a mirror." [10] By implication, readers are Calibans who do not want to see themselves at all. Wilde presents Caliban as the ordinary, well-socialized reader, enraged at any attempt to represent or ignore him.

Another signature feature of all Joyce's books is his refusal to focalize his narratives through the eyes of an omniscient narrator. Such narration is arguably a crutch for readers that relieves them from having to interpret the events for themselves. It paternalistically guides them through conflicts and difficulties only to reassure them that everything will be wrapped up in the end. A narrator provides all the context that is necessary for readers to follow events without stopping to puzzle things out. It also keeps the reader invisible, giving him or her the structural position of voyeur. Instead of relying on a single omniscient narrator, Joyce makes frequent, judicious use of free indirect discourse, a form of third-person narration colored (and limited) by the thoughts, perceptions, and idioms of the character it is describing.[11] In *Ulysses*, "The doorway was darkened by an entering form" is arguably Stephen's idiom, although presented in the third person (*U* 1.386). In the *Dubliners* story "Clay," the third-person narrator replicates what Maria sees and hears while blindfolded, adopting her perspective while recounting it, a technique that simultaneously blindfolds the narrator-dependent reader. The different chapters of Stephen's life in *A Portrait of the Artist as a Young Man* are governed by a sequence of narrative styles consistent with Stephen's own point of view at each stage. *Ulysses* is famous for its style-per-hour structure. In every work, Joyce nudges readers to remember there is no such thing as omniscience. Every individual point of view is partial, which necessarily entails distortion. It is always up to the reader to ascertain what is missing.

What is most unique about Joyce's fiction—experienced by many readers as difficulty—is its capacity to read the *reader* better than the reader can read *it*. The rules of interpretation, like the rules of genre, are easy to discern, which allowed Joyce to subvert them. Less well understood, however, is how Joyce uses words and objects to "talk back" to anyone who interrogates them. Sometimes, especially in the phantasmatic "Circe" episode, this happens literally, as when Lynch's cap speaks, satirizing Stephen's paradoxical reasoning: "Ba! It is because it is. . . . Jewgreek is greekjew. Extremes meet.

Death is the highest form of life. Ba!" (*U* 15. 2097–2098). Less surprisingly, the gramophone sings (*U* 15.2170–2173, 2211–2212), the gas jet says "Pooah! Pfuiiiiiii!" (*U* 15.2280), and the moth recites a poem (*U* 15.2469–2477). The doorhandle echoes "Theeee!" (*U* 15.2694), and Bella's fan flirts with Bloom (*U* 15.2754–2803). She is replaced by Bella's hoof, who also speaks (*U* 15.2820, 2824). Even the nymph in the oak-framed picture and the yews that surround her can talk, as they step out from the art print that hangs over Bloom's bed at home (*U* 15.3232–3470). Art, like objects, can come alive and converse with (or reflect something to) its viewers or users.

WORDS AND THINGS ARE AUTONOMOUS, IF NOT ACTUALLY ALIVE

In *Aesthetic Theory*, his last, posthumously published work, Theodor W. Adorno further develops a theory of art that is "autonomous," something he differentiates from "committed" art, or openly political art with an agenda (such as the plays of Bertold Brecht). Autonomous art gains its autonomy by seeming to split itself off from reality as we know it and yet engaging with it dialectically, through its contradictions and refractions. Such art has the potential to expose the aporias or blind spots both in the reader and in the society it reflects by drawing attention away from the ordinary to the extraordinary. So, "what is unreal and nonexistent in art is not independent of reality."[12] Literature can reflect or talk back to its reader or viewer because the richness and historical depth of the language it relies upon is not bounded by the form or the author's intention. That very excess can help the reader see beyond what he has been trained to "know." As Adorno explains in the draft introduction to *Aesthetic Theory*, "Art does not exist as the putative lived experience of the subject who encounters it as a tabula rasa but only with an already developed language of art. Lived experiences are indispensable, but they are no final court of aesthetic knowledge. Precisely those elements of art that cannot be taken immediately in possession and are not reducible to the subject require consciousness and therefore philosophy" (447). In Joyce's works, it is the elements of art that cannot be immediately possessed that make the reading experience seem difficult, but those are the same elements that invite the reader to enter the work at a deeper level. They stimulate critical reflection that produces a new and more comprehensive self-awareness, allowing the reader to enter into a dialectical relationship or dialogue with the work. The object, which Adorno calls "objectified spirit," is once again "rendered fluid through the medium of reflection" (453).

As he continued to write, Joyce evinced a greater and greater respect for the material world as potentially conversant with the human, even to the point of imagining things as alive and capable of speech, but Joyce's view of the object is closer to Adorno's concept of autonomous art than it is to the ecologically motivated, postmaterialist theories of things as actually alive. Both perspectives represent attempts to undo the human subject's subjugation of the other as an object, but the advantage of seeing things as exercising a kind of autonomy is that it emphasizes the power of the individual's imagination to access hidden truths. (Adorno would attribute the occulting of such truths to the false consciousness produced by social conditioning.) In "Circe," the lemon soap that Bloom has carried in his pocket all day rises into the sky like a yellow sun and sings a song about the virtues of cleaning things up. Although it's funny and literally impossible, that very impossibility is also meaningful in that it draws a reader's attention to the ways that Bloom's interest in reform resembles the power of soap to cleanse and freshen. Earlier in the day, Bloom registers the communicative power of things in the "Aeolus" episode, as he listens to the machines sliding out folded newspapers along with the creaking of a door: "Sllt. The nethermost deck of the first machine jogged forward its flyboard with sllt the first batch of quirefolded papers. Sllt. Almost human the way it sllt to call attention. Doing its level best to speak. That door too sllt creaking, asking to be shut. Everything speaks in its own way. Sllt" (U 7.174–177).

In the "Sirens" episode, things not only speak but also make music, from the sound of a garter being snapped on a barmaid's thigh to a seashell roaring in the ear to the tap tap of the blind piano tuner's cane to the jingle of Blazes Boylan's carriage as it drives him to the similarly jingling bed of Molly (and Bloom). This is also, not coincidentally, the episode in which the narrator starts to address and even parody the confusion and dawning comprehension of the reader, as in the following parenthetical asides when Lenehan is looking inside a piano: "he (who?) gazed in the coffin (coffin?) at the oblique triple (piano!) wires" (U 11.291–292). In Finnegans Wake, to cite just one of many examples, a bag full of 111 presents is isomorphic with three children in their mother's womb (at different times) and the hump on their father's back.[13]

The capacity of things to act (if not to speak) has been explored somewhat differently by Jane Bennett, who presents a thing not as inert and merely useful, but as an "actant" (a term she borrows from Bruno Latour): "a source of action that can be either human or nonhuman; it is that which has efficacy, can *do* things, has sufficient coherence to . . . produce effects, alter the course of events."[14] Inanimate matter is reconfigured as something magical (it is significant that Bennett's previous book was *The Enchantment of Modern Life: Attachments, Crossing, and Ethics*). Bennett builds on a concept that W.T.J. Mitchell explains as follows: "Objects are the way things appear to a subject—that is, with a name, an identity, a gestalt or stereotypical template. . . . Things, on the other hand, [refer to] the moment when the object becomes the Other, when the sardine can looks back, when the mute idol speaks, when the subject experiences the object as uncanny" (quoted in Bennett, *Vibrant* 2). The power of a thing to take on the wildness of an animal, the expressive agency of a living creature, resisting its own instrumentalization or mechanization, is the possibility Bennett expands and develops.

For Joyce, things can assume what is almost an alternate form of subjectivity in their capacity to reflect or serve or resist the viewer. The line between art, function, and humanity becomes blurred in ways that feel both delightful and unsettling. Jean Cocteau visually captures this diverse power of things in his 1947 film *La Belle et La Bête*, in which gloves and mirrors come to have magical properties. Candelabras have human arms and bust-topped pillars have living eyes, all of which move in response to human subjects. (The Disney animated version of *Beauty and the Beast*, with Lumière the candelabra and Mrs. Potts the teapot, seems indebted to Cocteau in this respect.) In *Finnegans Wake*, Joyce modifies Beauty and the Beast to "booty with the bedst" (*FW* 560.20). Here, the objectifying power of female beauty (which turns her into property) is underscored by her new name, "booty" (both treasure and a boot), and the relation of the Beast to an object turns him into a "bed" that is also the "best." What is happening here is that language is not only revealing the hidden link between living beings and things, it is also resisting its own instrumentalization: it refuses to let its significations be confined to those assigned by convention or intention. It is like the Beast's magic mirror: it shows hidden or suppressed meanings; language becomes an actant. It mediates between the object and the idea of the object through the phenomenology of how words look and sound. Joyce's sensitivity to the objective dimensions of the subject—its capacity to be reduced to furniture—and to the wayward aliveness of objects may well have been primed by the experience of having been a "subject" in a colonized country that contested his autonomy and humanity.

Some of the chapters that follow focus on "things," such as beds, sheets, fat, and letters, whereas others focus on broad topics—love, adultery, religion. For Joyce, though, the thing does more than look back at its human user, it also "speaks." Attentiveness to the materiality of language allows us to see a word as a "thing," too, with its multiple alternate forms of agency. It turns the collection of letters in individual words into an epistle, sent to a living, responsive recipient who may well "write" back. No longer are these dead letters, like letters collected in a room because they have no recipient.

WORDS ARE THINGS TOO

As he writes successive books, Joyce attends less and less to language as a tool for expressing conscious intentions and more to its material agency, its potentially broadening, prismatic effects upon thought. Words are doors that can be opened—wormholes into the experiences of other times and places—but they can also seem closed. When a reader picks up a work of Joyce, s/he must immediately wrestle with the fact that Joyce's language *obstructs* the reader's view of the characters' lives as often as it enables it. Joyce's language draws attention to itself as a "thing" with the capacity to divert focus from the fictions it purports to tell. A word or phrase becomes obscure rather than transparent, causing the reader to stop and wonder, most often (initially) about Joyce. Is he flaunting his erudition at the reader's expense? Sometimes, though, the reader interrogates his or her own expectations and reactions, which can offer unexpected reconfigurations of the reader's own self-image.

Joyce gives a visual image of how the mirroring of readers can work in the "Circe" episode of *Ulysses*. Stephen and Bloom (literary characters who are also readers) look into the same mirror and see an image of an author, Shakespeare (beardless, horned—perhaps emasculated?) reflected back at them (*U* 15.3821–3824). The mirror talks back to them, but what does it say? One of the many implications of this literally impossible and thereby magical reflection is that spectators or readers do not typically understand that authors reflect *them* through the mirrors of the authors' own experience and language. Hamlet is aware of the power of art to reflect, which lies behind his plot to trap Claudius's conscience in the "mousetrap" of the play within the play of *Hamlet*. He tells the players that the purpose of playing is to "hold the mirror up to nature to show virtue her own feature, scorn her own image," but he also wants to do something more practical: to make Claudius see his own action as treacherous. What he doesn't anticipate is that Claudius can interpret the play in more than one way, that he might understand the play as a threat to *himself* from Hamlet. Spectators (or readers) often don't *want* to see themselves, warts and all, in what they read, which makes interpretation a crucial art.

The materiality of language, then, turns a word into a "portal of discovery" (*U* 9.229). In addition to being a portal, a word can also act as a porter, carrying other words or meanings packed up in it the way a suitcase carries clothes. The idea of a "portmanteau" word dates from 1871, when Lewis Carroll in *Through the Looking-Glass* puts it into the mouth of Humpty Dumpty. He explains the word "slithy" (from "Jabberwocky") to Alice as a blend of "lithe" and "slimy": "You see it's like a portmanteau: there are two meanings packed up into one word." Joyce takes this even further. For him, a portmanteau can be not only a word like "bedst" (combining "best," "bed," and "beast" while suggesting the beginning of "bedstead"), but also an ordinary word that hides other words or associations inside it. An example might be the word "evil," which is not only part of the word "devil" but also an inversion of the word "live." Moreover, its sound could suggest "Eve's ill," the cause of the Fall. Since the name "Eve" comes from a Hebrew word for "life," her ill brought about death. The word-portmanteaus of some writers have unusually revelatory properties; their words may look ordinary enough, but when "opened" they reveal things about mundane life that readers never knew, or had learned to ignore. Everyday life then loses some of the banality thrown over it by habit and familiarity; it becomes newly estranged, uncanny, even communal. The "non-human, thingly power" that Bennett theorizes as a nascent "political ecology" may be extended from matter to the image and the word; images and words become living "things," taking on a life of their own through their nontransparency and their power to move through time and space, accreting meaningful connections that purely rational readers have learned to ignore (*Vibrant* xiii).

However, as Claudius's strange reaction to Hamlet's "Mousetrap" suggests, a word (or work of art) might appear more like a Trojan horse than a suitcase or door. Hugh Kenner once wrote, "Language is a Trojan Horse by which the universe gets into the mind."[15] Kenner's metaphor captures the deceptiveness of words, their capacity to contain a host of hidden meanings, and it also presents the (conscious, deliberate) mind as a walled citadel designed to keep such things out. Additionally, Kenner's conceit implies that the hidden meanings of words can be dangerous, since the Greeks who hid inside the Trojan horse sacked the city that took them in. And they are dangerous, but only to the exercise of rational, conscious discourse; to art, they are crucial.

Joyce began his investigation of the "living" nature of things as early as *Stephen Hero* and *Portrait* through Stephen's aesthetic theories. The goal of apprehension, according to Stephen's formula (repurposed from Thomas Aquinas) is to apprehend the "soul" of an object. The method is to perceive an object's wholeness (*integritas*) by first separating it from its context. The next task is to examine the object's formal components (*consonantia*), including the relation of those parts to the whole. The final result is *claritas*, when the object is returned to its context and becomes radiant (*P* 178–179). The effect on the perceiver of seeing "the scholastic *quidditas*, the *whatness* of a thing*,*" is a "luminous silent stasis of esthetic pleasure . . . [an] enchantment of the heart" (*P* 179). The thing has come to life as that which it is. The moment when a perceiver apprehends the beauty of something can simultaneously be understood as an act of "reading" (defined as highly analytical and sensual observation performed with acute self-awareness) and the beginning of artistic expression. Reading and writing are collapsed into this moment, as the culmination of the act of apprehension results in a "conception" that can develop into a new work of art.

An example of Joyce's treatment of things—here an ordinary piece of furniture—as "alive" in time and space may be found in the chapter 1, "On Beds." The vibrancy of the bed is accessible primarily through the word, its etymology, and even the bedlike appearance of the word itself (a one-word concrete poem of sorts). It achieves agency partly through its relation to lived experience (recorded in the bodily impressions made upon it) and partly through verbal associations (such as "beast"—"bedst" in *Finnegans Wake*), history, and even philosophy. The buried history of the word takes us back through underground tunnels to writing tablets and graves, to the intersection of sleep, death, sex, reading, eating, and birth in a single verbal-material conjunction. Seen as a vital word, a bed, such as the one most of us return to every night, gives rise to ideas of resurrection through the association of sleep with death. Writing, too, as something that was once "engraved," becomes another kind of bed in which readers put their immediate experience to sleep in order to "dream" or imagine experiences that never actually took place, but that can alter their mood and even their habitual mode of relating to their daily lives.[16] If we define enchantment as Thomas Moore does in The Re-Enchantment of Everyday Life as involving "both a dulling of the mind and a sharpening of perception," that happens whether the head is on a pillow or in a book.[17]

Words, then, have a latent vitality or agency comparable to that attributed to inanimate matter by recent "Thing Theorists." As vital things, they can also "propel ethics," or greater personal awareness and social connection (Bennett, Enchantment 4–5).[18]

ETYMOLOGY AND ASSOCIATION, OR METEMPSYCHOSIS AND PARALLAX

It is a critical commonplace to regard two Greek words, "parallax" and "metempsychosis," as the "crossed keys" of Ulysses. "Parallax" is "the difference or change in the apparent position or direction of an object as seen from two different points of view."[19] Because of that difference, more than one perspective is required for accuracy. "Metempsychosis" is the word Molly asks Bloom to define in the "Calypso" episode. From ancient Greek philosophy, it refers to the transmigration of souls after death, thereby suggesting that souls have more than one existence in time. These two keys, when considered together or "crossed," represent the path to self-determination for the reader as they once were political symbols for Home Rule on the Isle of Man (the lower house of the Manx parliament is called the "House of Keys"). When Bloom wonders about the word "parallax," it cues the reader to ponder its significance for the use of different perspectives in Ulysses. The styles keep changing throughout the book in part to give the reader multiple points of view on the day as it changes through light and time and location and weather.[20] Similarly, metempsychosis is also used to signify the uncanny similarities that span change, this time across time rather than in space. The most well-known example is Joyce's juxtapositions of characters from different time periods: Bloom and Odysseus, or

Bloom and Shakespeare (along with King Hamlet, whom Shakespeare was believed to have played).

A fine-grained, language-oriented interpretation can supplement and extend these large-scale relocations in time and space. One of the ways Joyce crafts his book to reflect the reader (and to prompt the reader to entertain new reflections) is by making it rewarding to read words across time (metempsychosis) as well as to explore their connections with other words in the present (parallax). Derek Attridge quotes Ferdinand de Saussure's assertion that "etymology is before everything the explanation of words by research into their connections with other words."[21] This diachronic, prismatic reading of a word across time makes it comparable to synchronous word play: "In both devices the same process occurs: two similar-sounding but distinct signifiers are brought together, and the surface relationship between them is invested with meaning through the inventiveness and rhetorical skill of the writer. If that meaning is in the form of a postulated connection between present and past, what we have is etymology; if it is in the form of a postulated connection within the present, the result is word-play" (Attridge 108). The value of the connections readers are able to make is self-confirming: it affects the way they think and feel.

Attending to the associative connections between words, then, is another way of correcting for parallax: it affords more than one perspective on a word. Joyce's distinctive, carefully tuned language confronts the reader with alternative ways of connecting individual units of thought into patterns of "meaning" by changing the reader's awareness of how words vibrate against one another. In music, such effects are labeled "sympathetic vibration," produced when the sustain pedal on a piano is pressed. The pedal lifts all the hammers so that the strings vibrate together in a way that enriches the tone.[22] In *Ulysses*, Stephen is highly attuned to the possible interconnections between words, as we can see when he wonders if rhymes have reasons in "Aeolus": "Is the mouth south someway?" (*U* 7.714). *Finnegans Wake* works almost exclusively through association. Two of the names of the main protagonist, HCE, help to illustrate this. One of his names, Earwicker, suggests "earwig." Earwigs were thought to crawl into a sleeper's ear and lay eggs in his brain at night.[23] In a way, that is how Joyce's night language works. But the ear also has wax in it, and by replacing "wig" with "wick," Joyce suggests that Earwicker can facilitate both better hearing (by removing wax) and creating illumination in the night by wicking the wax into flame. The word "wick" is also associated with "wicked," or morally bad, which is applicable to Earwicker as a fallen man (he is also Adam).

One of his other names is "Porter," a dark, bitter beer like stout, as is appropriate for a man who owns a bar. As a black beer that forms a white head when poured, porter is both dark and light, like HCE himself. A porter is also someone who carries burdens, such as suitcases, and HCE appropriately has a hunch on his back. The oldest meaning of "porter" is door- or gatekeeper, and HCE is above all that. He, and the language he emanates in sleep, works as a portal between different worlds—different languages and different eras. I explore the various meanings of another of HCE's names, Tim Finnegan, in chapter 3, "On Salmon."

Etymology (the "metempsychosis" of a single word) works in a special way: to undo the linearity of time by making connections across it. It does not privilege original meaning, which would make it, comically, a "false-meaning adamelegy" (etymology is false when it takes the form of nostalgia for Adam, the original man [FW 77.26]). For Joyce it is not a nostalgic exercise but a guide to the concrete particulars packed inside words that have become abstract and isolated over time. It collects lived experiences from different temporal moments, restoring historical and imagined life to things. Joyce's interest in etymology was long-standing, if we read as autobiographical his account of Stephen walking around with a copy of Skeat's *Etymological Dictionary* under his arm in *Stephen Hero.* Importantly, through their histories, words retain traces of older, *collective* experience. I will give a fuller account of Joyce's nonlinear model of time in the next section.

Joyce directs the reader to appreciate (or even ingest!) the entire history of a word in *Finnegans Wake,* when a narrator enjoins, "pleasekindly communicake with the original sinse" (FW 239.1–2). The reader is being asked to "eat" words—semi-cannibalistically—as they were before another fall, the fall into babble (or the fall of the Tower of Babel), to find their lost, obsolete, or obscured meanings. To read with a feel for the original "sinse" is to channel Adam and Eve while "communicating" in the sophisticated Eucharistic sense of the term, which involves communing with others while experiencing the pleasure not only of hearing but also of *digesting* the word, incorporating it into one's body and life (etymologically, "to digest" is to "separate, divide, arrange)."[24]

To see the material and human world freshly refracted through the lens of language is to experience both mourning ("elegy," as in the rendering of etymology as "adamelegy," discussed above) and pleasure ("cake"). It feels simultaneously like sin (defined as exile or separation[25]) and connection (a shared meal). The recovery of lost meaning produces pleasure, but the recognition of irreparable loss is painful as well as humorous.

Communication (understood through the sacrament of communion) is one response to the proliferation of languages that resulted after humanity tried to build the Tower of Babel (the babble that resulted from Babel is one of the running themes in *Finnegans Wake*).[26] The erection of this tower (representing the attempt to climb too high, to be as gods, a replication of the original sin) produced a fall (very much like the fall of Tim Finnegan/Humphrey Chimpden Earwicker from a ladder in *Finnegans Wake*). The result of both efforts was exile, pain, misunderstanding, and division among peoples. Joyce's references seem to be urging the reader to "eat" words as they were before the fall into babble, to find their lost, obsolete, or obscured meanings. This must be an active effort, not the passive receipt of impressions characteristic of most reading. Joyce, then, might be said to be advocating a view of language as meaningful babble—babble with the power to alert us to the layers of buried historical and spiritual meanings that subtend what we normally understand as sense.

An example of how we can see parallax and metempsychosis working in Joyce's language is apparent in the phrase that haunts Stephen's mind in *Ulysses*, "agenbite of inwit," a Middle English phrase meaning remorse of conscience. Arguably, Joyce uses the older form because "agenbite" (again bite) allows readers to hear the etymological meaning of "remorse," to bite again. Stephen's inner thoughts bite him, again and again, when he thinks about his treatment of his mother. Here, the conversation between words is a reverberation across time designed to uncover the sensual concreteness of a metaphor that has morphed into an abstraction, although that metaphor is still lodged in the etymology of "remorse." Joyce's use of an unfamiliar phrase (a "word-thing") is designed to make the reader wonder what it means, and perhaps even to find out, which may well lead to a discovery of the history of "remorse." That is how the word talks back. Joyce challenges and potentially reshapes the reader's assumptions about a word and its meaning by interfering with his or her desire to concentrate on the story rather than the medium through which such stories are told.

LAYERED TIME

Joyce relies upon an unusual "chronosophy" (wisdom about time), not only in his use of etymology but also in his approach to a day. Joycean time becomes more than mere sequence because of the attention it pays to the historical "deposit" of past experience that can be excavated from words. The best tool I have found for illustrating Joyce's deployment of non-chronological time is the nonlinear model developed by the Belgian historian Berber Bevernage. What he attempts to do is establish a model of time that accommodates anachronism, something that Joyce achieved in practice both in *Ulysses* and *Finnegans Wake.*

In his article on "Time, Presence, and Historical Injustice," Bevernage offers a critique of the view of time as "an infinite continuum of fleeting presents."[27] He labels this model of time "pointillist," a term derived from painting, because it resembles a series of dots arranged in a line, each dot devouring the one before it. (151). Bevernage's reasons for challenging common presuppositions about the linearity of time and history are as intriguing as his conclusions. He posits that history and justice both depend upon the notion that the past is distant or absent, which makes the past ontologically inferior to the present. He then identifies two opposing responses to this ontological inferiority, epitomized by Friedrich Nietzsche and Walter Benjamin, respectively. Bevernage argues that for Nietzsche, history must "serve life and the future; it should not strive to achieve historical justice," whereas Benjamin advocates solidarity between the living and the dead, "arguing that living generations should not aim at the future but at preceding generations in their striving for justice"—the living have a power, however "weak," to redress the injustices of the past (Bevernage 150). In short, Nietzsche counsels us to forget, Benjamin to remember. We are caught in the crosshairs of two incompatible directives, directives that amplify a fundamental conflict between two different views of time.[28]

Bevernage proposes what he calls an "alternative chronosophy" based upon the unlikely mating of Althusser and late Derrida. What this alternate conception of time amounts to is a "layered conception of history" in which the past continues to live in the present, spectrally, and in which histories are seen as plural, fragmented, antagonistic, and yet still present (Bevernage 157).[29] Jacques Derrida takes up the notion in *Specters of Marx* (1994), associating this new conception of spectral time with Hamlet's declaration that the time is "out of joint."[30] The living present is mottled; two "nows" can impossibly coexist. The present is shot through with the past, which "makes the present waver" (Bevernage 162); contemporary time bears an "untimeliness" that is important because, he argues, such untimeliness bears within it the seeds of justice, which Derrida associates with anachronism.

It is only through a vision of the moment as fissured—as bearing within it the spectral presences of the past—that we can experience the past as not fully absent, that we can hear its ethical claims for justice. The past loses its ontological inferiority through anachronism, because "spectrality cannot be *dated*—in a chain of presents, according to a calendar—but it surely is historical" (Bevernage 164). The embeddedness of the past in the present is a "firmly historical (while non-historicist) phenomenon" (Bevernage 165). The past can never be *fully* present, however, or it is no longer past. The choice between a living present and a dead and absent past is therefore a false one. Instead of finding ourselves caught between the "tyranny of 'everlasting pasts'" and "triumphalist 'eternal presents,'" we enlarge "the area of structural undecidability," which allows for a greater degree of personal choice.

Bevernage's critique of chronosophy illuminates an important facet of Joyce's epiphanies, which valorize the moment when different, often incompatible times and realizations converge in spectral illuminations. Mr. Deasy triumphantly celebrates history as progressive and teleological: "All human history moves towards one great goal, the manifestation of God" (*U* 2.380–381), but Stephen recoils from such a view, defining God as "a shout in the street" (*U* 2.386) and history as "a nightmare from which I am trying to awake" (*U* 2.377). Why is it a nightmare? Because a lockstep succession of moments arranged in a chain creates a weight on the chest, a nightmarish determinism, that inhibits movement. Yeats, too, claims, "a mind that grasps objects simultaneously according to the degree of its liberation does not think the same thought with the mind that sees objects one after another."[31] Yeats spent his life at war with chronological time, daring the shadows to whom he writes to bid him "strike a match / And strike another till time catch" ("In Memory of Eva Gore-Booth and Con Markievicz").[32] He relished the prospect of the end of the world, willing the "Boar without bristles" to come from the West" and root "the sun and moon and stars out of the sky" and to lie "in the darkness, grunting, and turning to his rest" ("He Mourns for the Change . . ."). Sequential thinking constitutes its own conceptual limit, and for Yeats it is the violence of history itself that exposes the impoverishment of mere chronology. T. S. Eliot, too, proclaims in *Four Quartets* that "all time is eternally present."[33] Discovering the etymology of a word brings its meanings at different times into the present, layering different points in time instead of allowing each point to devour the one before it.

CAVEATS FOR THE READER

Joyce's great subject is human self-deception: its mechanisms, its value as a defensive strategy, and its costliness. He is as interested in the self-deceptions he knows readers will resort to as those that comfort, frustrate, and blind his characters, because his anatomy of self-deception grew out of autobiographical self-examination. Joyce traps his readers, making it difficult for them to make sense of his fiction in habitual ways, but he does so with deep sympathy and uncompromising honesty. What is the solution to the problems of everyday life? Obviously, there is no solution, but Joyce does offer his readers a strategy: to recognize and accept—with laughter rather than lacerating self-criticism—disavowed and habitual contributions to those problems. First-time readers will reveal their potentially paralyzing habits of mind—the psychopathology of everyday life—in the way they read. Joyce's books invite the reader to discover that process at work in the moment of reading.

One difficulty of Joyce's writing comes from the fact that he respects the reader's freedom to an unusual degree; he is as dedicated to the value and mechanisms of mental and emotional liberty as his more militant Irish compatriots were to political and economic freedom. In this respect, Stephen Dedalus does speak for Joyce when, in *Ulysses*, he points to his brow and says, "In here it is I must kill the priest and the king" (*U* 15.4436–4437). When Joyce gives the reader freedom to construct meaning, however, it is always within definite parameters, otherwise the experience would be little more than a Rorschach test. For many readers, however, the unfamiliar responsibility of actively constructing the meaning of what they read is more unpleasant than joyous.

Joyce's carnivalistic embrace of multiple perspectives (on the self as well as others) is not primarily a means of displaying his stylistic virtuosity; it is done to promote social justice by reminding everyone of the limits of what any individual can see or know. A renewed appreciation of one's own limits confers value on gathering a variety of other perspectives, which is how the practice of seeing a given problem or person from several different angles initiates movement toward a more just and enlightened society. What is surprising about how Joyce renews such awareness is that his methods are not at all moralistic; instead, they are designed to enhance the reader's own enjoyment of (and insight into) everyday life, an enjoyment that may spill over into a new understanding and acceptance of human foibles, including our own. Learning to read in less conventional ways can unlock the humor as well as the latent vitality of ordinary activities while also sparking a Bloomian interest in and compassion toward others. It accomplishes what W. H. Auden gloriously commanded that poetry do in his elegy for W. B. Yeats: "In the deserts of the heart / Let the healing fountain start, / In the prison of his days / Teach the free man how to praise."[34]

Arguably, most reading practices are obedient rather than free. Interpretation is a conditioned—or learned—activity governed by predictable rules. In a sense, the common reader is under a spell. Readers' conditioned assumptions about life, language, meaning, and even themselves are the products of a "normalizing" spell that tends to render these things instrumental, stable, familiar, legible. Joyce reveals the hidden magic of everyday life by disenchanting, or unspelling and respelling, language. And that magic has the potential to change the reader's conception of the strangeness of the world outside and within her. The "spell" (a set of words with supposed magical or occult powers to cause harm) is social, and by the end of his career Joyce associates its constrictive power with that of orthography, the grammatical convention that binds a word's power to a single order of letters and an agreed-upon set of meanings (often abstract). Joyce's arch and joyful practice is to break the spell by artfully manipulating the reader to occupy new and different positions in relation to the words on the page. In *Finnegans Wake*, comprised of deliberate misspellings (or respellings), Joyce does this with every word, thereby releasing and celebrating that word's other potential meanings and associations, its power to form connections, to multiply perspectives.

Readers are challenged to unspell or scramble their vision of reality, but another challenge comes from the limitations of individual temperament. Through the words of Stephen Dedalus, Joyce suggests that an individual's experience of the world is predicted by the range of his or her imagination:

no one can accept "in the world without as actual" anything that he or she has not previously imagined "in his world within as possible" (*U* 9.1041–1042). In the "Scylla and Charybdis" episode of *Ulysses*, Stephen paraphrases a passage by Maurice Maeterlinck to propose that the world we traverse is only as large as the self at which such journeys begin and end: "Maeterlinck says: *If Socrates leave his house today he will find the sage seated on his doorstep. If Judas go forth tonight it is to Judas his steps will tend.* Every life is many days, day after day. We walk through ourselves, meeting robbers, ghosts, giants, old men, young men, wives, widows, brothers-in-love, but always meeting ourselves" (*U* 9.1042–1046). It isn't immediately clear what Stephen means, but Maeterlinck's *Wisdom and Destiny* (1898) helps to contextualize it. When introducing the examples of Judas and Socrates, Maeterlinck explains: "Nothing befalls us that is not of the nature of ourselves. . . . If Judas go forth tonight, it is towards Judas his steps will tend, nor will chance for betrayal be lacking; but let Socrates open his door, he shall find Socrates asleep on the threshold before him, and there will be occasion for wisdom."[35] According to Maeterlinck, an individual's relation to the world proceeds from his or her values, attitudes, and expectations: Socrates and Judas will exhibit wisdom and betrayal, respectively, regardless of what they find. Maeterlinck claims, for example, that if Judas or Socrates had been in the positions of Orestes or Hamlet, they would have committed no murders, and there would have been no tragedy (35, 46). In his view, what makes heroes tragic is resistance to wisdom (defined as self-knowledge and self-acceptance [27–80]), which is why Judas and Socrates are not tragic despite the fact that they were killed (38). The hallmark of wisdom, then, is a capacity for accepting reality, regardless of its implications for the self or ego. As Maeterlinck explains, the difference between sorrow and joy is the difference between "a gladsome, enlightened acceptance of life and a hostile, gloomy submission; between a large and harmonious conception of life, and one that is stubborn and narrow" (8–9). For Maeterlinck, an individual's fate is the consequence and expression of his or her relative openness of heart and mind; it is an individual's realistic awareness and acceptance of his or her limitations that produces wisdom and deflects tragedy. What this means for the reader of Joyce is to be careful with the impulse to resist new perspectives, or to hold too tightly (and unconsciously) to a static, unified, idealized, or diminished view of the self.

An extraordinary effect of Joyce's restructuring of literary norms is that it takes an act that is often isolated and individual and turns it into something communal. The main precedent for such writing is sacred scripture, but Joyce's work is decidedly profane, although shot through with spiritual bullets. When a reader accepts the limitations of his or her perspective and current understanding, it creates an impulse to ask others for supplemental knowledge or insight. Those who are importuned need help too, however, which results in a collaborative act of making (and remaking) meaning. The implications of this will be addressed more fully in the conclusion.

When we put all the pieces of Joyce's writing together—the depiction of himself as a talented yet limited literary character, the concern with how such "characters" can live their lives with greater freedom and meaning, the desire to shape his fiction into a looking glass that promotes new self-awareness on the part of the reader together with the equally strong impulse to put language through a prism to illustrate the hidden beauties of everyday life, and finally the elaboration of a method for perceiving the *quidditas* of each word and thing in the book or world in which one finds oneself—we are left with a kind of fiction that operates according to very different rules than the ones readers are used to following. Readers' habitual expectations, shaped by past experience and by the laws of genre, are thwarted. The question is, will they then experience that uncertain glimmer of a new perspective? That is up to them.

1 ▸ ON BEDS

One of the objects we physically use every day (or every night) is a bed. For Joyce, the bed (not the hearth) emerges as the center of domestic existence. Unexpectedly, it also serves as a counterpart to the book: both are places where people go for renewal and even for transformation, where they may experience pleasure and a release from consciousness that is either temporary (in the case of sleep) or permanent (in death). The bed is also a site of intimate sexual connection. The sexual frankness of Joyce's books may be understood partly as stemming from the kinship between books and beds: Joyce's books were put on trial as "dirty sheets." In the "Anna Livia Plurabelle" episode of Finnegans Wake, we see two washerwomen air and discuss these dirty sheets. These women are, on one level, death and love, respectively; at the fall of night they devolve into a tree and a stone on either side of the river of life.

What emerges when we read a real thing—here a bed—through language, using a method modeled by Joyce? The bed becomes more than a piece of furniture entered nightly without thought; it is reconfigured as a repository of lived history. Recalling the bed's history recontextualizes it, stripping away its mere functionality and reinvigorating one's sensual experience of it; similarly, the history of the word "bed" adds a poetic dimension to the word, making it more than just a useful sign. History is deposited in language, where it is preserved as layers of meaning. One's conception of the nature, function, and interrelation of things expands when they are reviewed through the history of language, philosophy, and literature.

Joyce liked to say that every room should have a bed in it.[1] To contemplate a bed is to align oneself not only with Joyce, but with Homer, Aristotle, Plato, Shakespeare, Proust, and Emily Dickinson, to name only a few. It is helpful to begin by thinking, not of a bed, but of a related everyday object, a table, that has a comparable capacity to mediate between the ordinary and the philosophical. In Virginia Woolf's To the Lighthouse, when Lily asks Andrew what his father's philosophy books are about, he replies, "Subject and object and the nature of reality."[2] To illustrate what he means, he tells her to "think of a kitchen table . . . when you're not there." So when Lily thinks of Mr. Ramsay's works, she sees, lodged in the fork of a pear tree, "a phantom kitchen table, one of those scrubbed board tables, grained and knotted, whose virtue seems to have been laid bare by years of muscular integrity, which stuck there, its four legs in the air" (23). Joyce uses the more comprehensive image and material reality of a bed (which sometimes serves its occupants as a table as well, as it did Molly and Boylan in Ulysses) to do something similar to what Andrew says his father tried to do in To the Lighthouse: to figure subject and object and the nature of reality, but also to identify a material place that serves as a nexus of life, death, sex, and writing, where extremes meet and fantasy and reality commingle. Any time one puts a collection of words and letters—or even one or more human beings— between two covers, that "frames" a set of interconnections that has the power to extend itself beyond that frame (one could also compare the bed frame to a picture frame). The bed illustrates not only the nature of reality, but the beginnings and endings of life—human, floral, and vegetable—as well as the unstable overlapping of art and nature.

The part of Ulysses concerned with the Blooms begins and ends with a bed. As something that contains blooms, it is comparable to a flower bed, but it also resembles Homer's Ithaca as the first and last point of an odyssey. It is a loose or broken bed, and in its brokenness it makes music: "He heard then a warm heavy sigh, softer, as she turned over and the loose quoits of the bedstead jingled. Must get those settled really. Pity. All the way from Gibraltar. Forgotten any little Spanish she knew. Wonder what her father gave for it. Old style. Ah yes! Of course. Bought it at the governor's auction. Got a short knock. Hard as nails at a bargain, old Tweedy" (*U* 4.58–64). Bloom associates the bed with Molly, moving in thought from it to her without a hitch ("All the way from Gibraltar [the bed]. Forgotten any little Spanish she knew [Molly]"), but we as readers know that Bloom sleeps in the bed as well. He left it before we tuned in that morning, rising from the "wrong side" ("Got up wrong side of the bed" [*U* 4.233–234]), and he will enter it at the end of the day, with his head at its foot ("He . . . removed a pillow from the head to the foot of the bed, prepared the bed-linen accordingly and entered the bed" [*U* 17.2112–2113]). This bed is not only a flower bed and a grave: as the first bed was the earth, theirs provides the reader with a picture of how they are grounded, where they came from, and where they will end. It is the alpha and the omega of an epic day, and when occupied it "sings," making a jingle with the potential to jangle. (A jingle anticipated by the jingle of Boylan's carriage as he rides to occupy it.) Fitted with sheets, bearing flakes of the potted meat eaten there as well as the imprint of another (strange, male) body, the bed is also an unexpectedly mundane version of the book itself, haunted by encounters we did not witness, and bearing the traces of ongoing consumption: food (in the case of the Bloom's bed, that food is Plumtree's Potted Meat, with its overtones of both sex and an occupied coffin: dead meat in a tin). What is a bed? Joyce thought a lot about the nature and form of the bed as a refuge, resource, inevitable resting place, and work of art or craft. He thought it through Homer, Plato, Aristotle, Shakespeare, and above all through language. For Joyce, the bed serves as a material place where opposites conjoin—life and death, male and female, birth and death—but it is also an artistic construct where the circle can be squared, the stone made to move, the mute to sound, the inanimate to germinate. The Blooms' bed, like the bed of the River Liffey it would become in *Finnegans Wake*, is musical, discordant, stained, and everchanging, a microcosm of Joyce's books of the day and the night.

In the "Aeolus" episode of *Ulysses*, under the headline "Rhymes and Reasons," Stephen wonders if rhymes rhyme for a reason: the bed, in both *Ulysses* and *Finnegans Wake*, is importantly connected with several words that rhyme with it: "dead," "wed," "fed," "read," and "said": the relations among birth, death, writing, and eating are multiply determined. Another cluster of words reinforces the first: "litter," "letter," "literature," "*letto*" (Ital. "bed"), "*lit*" (Fr. "bed"; also "reads," third person present indicative, as in "il/elle/on lit", or "he is reading").[3]

What sex, death, sleeping, procreation, eating, and writing all seem to have in common is a relation to "digging." According to the *OED*, the word "bed" comes from an Indo-European root, *bhodh*—, which in turn produced the Latin *fodere*, "to dig," referring to a dug-out place or lair (for sleeping). The first and last beds are the earth ("grave" comes from an Old English word meaning "to dig," and in Latin, the word for grave is *fossa*, stemming from the same root as the Latin word for bed). The symmetry of first and last is reproduced typographically in the lowercase appearance of the word "bed," with the "b" mirroring the "d" and the shape of the whole resembling a bed viewed from the side. Digging, of course, is also associated with agriculture and therefore with food; moreover, insofar as human sexual procreation resembles planting (a digging with the penis to implant *semen*—which means "seed"—inside a female body), sex and birth also form part of this constellation of related activities. Joyce demonstrates his awareness of the connection between sexual intercourse and planting in the "Penelope" episode, when Molly thinks about the Prince of Wales's visit to Gibraltar in 1876, imagining that he might have been her father. She muses that he, who had found lilies and planted trees through his love for the aptly named Lily Langtry, probably "found lilies there too where he planted the tree he planted more than that in his time he might have planted me too if hed come a bit sooner then I wouldnt be here as I am" (*U* 18.501–503).

If making a bed, a grave, food, or a child all involve "digging," then so does literature: "letters," too, were something originally dug, or engraved, on writing tablets (Charles Onions associates the word "letter" with the Greek *diphthera*, meaning "writing tablet" or "table").[4] The connection of reading and writing with sleeping, childbirth, and dying is further underscored through the web of words that includes *litter* (a group of animal offspring but also a disorderly accumulation of things, and finally a portable bed); the previously mentioned French *lit*; Italian *letto*; *literature* (written works to be read and/or slept through), and also *littoral*, pertaining to the shore (as of a river bed, something else that is *dug*). The word "book" itself stems from an Old Teutonic word meaning "writing-tablet, leaf, or sheet," and it is also related to the Gothic *bôka*, or letter of the alphabet (*OED*). It is easy to see how a collection of sheets protected by covers suggests a potentially productive bed in which one alternately "digs" or labors, and rests.

The subterranean connection between books, beds, impregnation, and graves is tacitly acknowledged in "Scylla and Charybdis," when Stephen looks at the books in the National Library, thinking of them as "coffined thoughts around me, in mummycases, embalmed in spice of words," thoughts "once quick in the brains of men" (*U* 9.352–353; 356). The pun on "mummy" as both mother and corpse economically underscores the rhyme of "womb" and "tomb" while applying both to a literary "corpus," or body. Joyce's awareness of writing as an activity closely connected to the earth and to beds is also reflected in "Nestor," when Stephen identifies the ink stain on Sargent's cheek with a "snail's bed": "On his cheek, dull and bloodless, a soft stain of ink lay, dateshaped, recent and damp as a snail's bed" (*U* 2.126–127; "a stain of ink, a snail's bed" is repeated at ll. 139–140). In Stephen's thoughts, the "snail" that has bedded on Sargent's cheek and guided his "crooked signature" is an image of Sargent himself, whom Stephen reads like a book, contemplating his vulnerability and slowness, imagining that his mother alone had saved him from "the race of the world," which but for her "would have trampled him underfoot, a squashed boneless snail" (*U* 2.141–142).

The Blooms' bed produced both life (their daughter Milly) and death (their dead son Rudy). Once again, it is a place where opposite extremes meet, comparable to that of Odysseus and Penelope in the *Odyssey*. In Homer's epic, the bed is the quick or life of the home: a *telos* for Odysseus's journey and a secret Penelope protects; a symbolic representation of their marriage. Like the "quick" of flesh, the bed is secret, sensitive, and alive, yet it is also rooted in the earth, which connects it with the earliest meanings of a bed and makes it immovable. Odysseus's bed is secret in that no one knows how it was constructed except Odysseus, Penelope, and a servant. The nature of this secret reflects a truth about the marriage of Odysseus and Penelope: their bed—like their marriage—is a living thing, with a bedpost made from an olive tree. That association with the tree and the earth gives the bed stability while maintaining a contrary association with productivity and growth. For Homer, long before Joyce, the "secret" bed was a carefully crafted place quite literally associated with roots and the family tree.

In book 23 of the *Odyssey*, after Odysseus has revealed himself to Penelope, the two test one another through a discussion of beds. First, each accuses the other of being mysterious, until Odysseus asks to have a bed made up for him alone, "since her heart is a cold lump of iron."[5] Penelope seems to concur, telling the nurse to bring out "the bedstead he made himself" (23.185). Odysseus then shows he knows "their old secret" (23.213), roaring:

> Who moved my bed? It would be hard
> For anyone, no matter how skilled, to move it. (23.190–191)

He tells how he built the bed out of a living olive tree (which in English reinforces the suggestion of the tree's vitality through its two parts "O, live"):

> There was an olive tree
> Growing on the site, long-leaved and full,
> Its trunk full thick as a post. I built my bedroom
> Around that tree, and when I had finished . . .
> I lopped off all of the olive's branches . . .
> until
> I had myself a bedpost. I bored it with an auger,
> And starting from this I framed up the whole bed,
> Inlaying it with gold and silver and ivory
> And stretching across it oxhide thongs dyed purple.
> So there's our secret. (23.196–209)

Penelope's heart is melted by his revelation of "the secret / Of our marriage bed, which no one has ever seen" (23.232–233):

> And they went with joy to their bed
> And to their rituals of old. (23.302–303)

Having "come to the bed/ [They] have long desired" (23.368–369), after making "sweet love," Penelope and Odysseus take "turns / Telling stories to each other" (23.306–308), and the *Odyssey* winds to a close. Clearly, the bed is the place of storytelling as well as lovemaking.

Joyce, while respecting the ingeniousness of the way the Homeric bed was constructed, changes the emphasis and expands the various ways in which the bed is connected with the earth, birth, death, and flow. First of all, by naming his protagonists "Bloom," he obliquely associates their bed with a flower bed (in *Finnegans Wake*, the bed of the Porters is similar, a fragrant strawberry bed beneath its strawberry coverlet). The Blooms' bed, unlike Odysseus's, is far from unmovable: it has in fact been brought from Gibraltar, where Bloom thinks Molly's father bought it at the governor's auction (Molly, while knowing what Bloom has been told, suggests it had actually belonged to "old Cohen" [*U* 18.1213]). In "Eumaeus," Bloom recollects "the morning littered bed etcetera" (*U* 16.1472), the description of the bed as "littered" reinforcing the connections between beds, birth, and waste or disorder. But the most important feature of the Blooms' bed is its "brass quoits and pendent viper radii loose and tremulous under stress and strain," "the snakespiral springs of the mattress being old." The bed's association with snakes is reinforced by the subsequent reference to it as "a lair or ambush of lust or adders" (*U* 17.2116–2118). If the bed is an Edenic flower bed, that makes it attractive to snakes.

What Molly calls "the lumpy old jingly bed" (*U* 18.1212) jingles because its brass quoits are loose. These quoits actually speak during the "Circe" episode: "Jigjag. Jigajiga. Jigjag" (*U* 15.1138). "Jig-a-jig" is listed in the *OED* as an imitative word "expressing reiteration or alternation of light, short, jerky movements." The bed, then, tells the story of the sexual trotting that has taken place upon it.[6] The jingling of the bed establishes it as a place of music and harmony, while simultaneously suggesting a more threatening "dance" (or "jig") that resembles the noise made by a trotting horse (jigajiga), reminding Bloom that Molly, like *Finnegans Wake*'s ALP after her, will "ride a cock horse to Banbury Cross."[7] "Loose quoits" are not generally associated with beds. What the word introduces are subliminal reinforcements of the bed with female sexuality and death, as well as a suggestion that Joyce's bed is linked to stones rather than the tree of Odysseus's bed.[8] Eden, to Bloom, is an innocent obliviousness to the way that sex and death are entwined; the "snakespiral" mattress springs and "pendent viper radii" that resemble a lair of adders together with flakes of partly consumed food indicate that Bloom's perspective is decidedly postlapsarian: the forbidden food—here "potted meat," with its suggestions of sexual intercourse and buried corpses—has been eaten, the snake has entered the garden, and Adam and Eve are aware of their own nakedness and lust. The mirage of the Promised Land as a fertile garden has been challenged by a vision of "a dead sea in a dead land, grey and old. . . . Now it could bear no more. Dead: an old woman's: the grey sunken cunt of the world" (*U* 4.221–228).

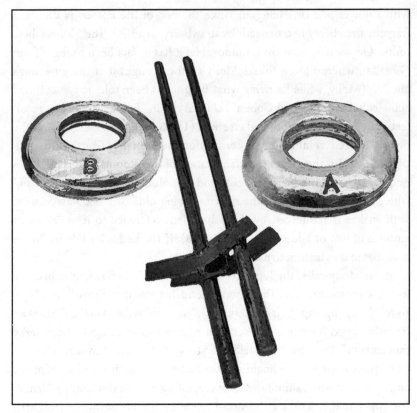

FIGURE 1. Brass quoits game. Illustration by Dennis Haugh. Used by permission.

The word "cunt" has an important connection with the "quoits" that cause the bed to jingle. First, consider the shape of a quoit, which is a metal ring that is thrown at a peg in a game that resembles horseshoes.

The shape is that of the vaginal opening, and the fact that a quoit is thrown onto a peg stresses its playful association with sexual intercourse more strongly. However, the word "quoit" is also akin to "cunt" (as well as "queen" and Chaucer's "queynte"). Etymologically, "quoit" seems to be related to "prick" or "spur," like the word "quicken." An alternate spelling is "quna," the root of "queen." Gloria Bertonis associates both words with cuneiform, the most ancient form of writing. She relates that "'cuneiform' derives from Sumerian 'kunta,' meaning female genitalia. It survives in the patriarchal slur, 'cunt.' Cuneiform consists of arrangements of pubic triangles or 'V's, which is the ancient Paleolithic symbol for woman."[9] Matthew Hunt argues that the

FIGURE 2. Stones of the Lanyon Quoit, a neolithic tomb in Cornwall, England. Lukassek/Shutterstock.com.

"cu" prefix—"cw" in Irish and Welsh, "co" in the Romance languages— signifies female sexuality in Indo-European languages as well as Hebrew, Arabic, and Irish (the "cu" prefix is also discernible in "cow" and "cunning," both words related to femaleness).[10] The "loose quoits," then, suggest sexual consummation and transgression, but "quoit" also has another meaning: it is the large covering-stone on a cromlech (lit. "arched flat stone") or dolmen— believed to be burial markers—in Celtic areas (by extension, the term often refers to the whole structure of three or more standing stones topped by a flat stone in the shape of a bed or table [*OED*]).

The secret of the Blooms' bed, now known to Molly's lover Boylan as well as Bloom, is not the same as the secret of Odysseus and Penelope's: it is not immovable, rooted in the earth. What is special about the Blooms' bed is not its connection to a tree but to stones: it has quoits or "stones" that move and even speak. Like Odysseus's, Bloom's bed is strangely alive, but in a discomfiting rather than reassuring way. It tells in the language of sex and death what Odysseus's bed tells through immobility and growth: that a bed is a place where opposites meet, where "death is the highest form of life" (*U* 15.2099). This is perhaps the most significant resemblance between a bed and a book: since the earliest "books" were essentially tablets, those tablets were slabs of stones, like the quoits or stone tops of cromlechs, or grave beds. Beds and books are both paradoxically "engraved" with life through the digging that produced them and that continues to be enacted *in* them, by its occupants and readers: "Each one who enters imagines himself to be the first to enter whereas he is always the last term of a preceding series even if the first term of a succeeding one, each imagining himself to be first, last, only and alone whereas he is neither first nor last nor only nor alone in a series originating in and repeated to infinity" (*U* 17.2127–2131).

Near the end of the book, the narrator evinces an exquisite awareness of the multivalent functions of the Blooms' bed when he describes how Bloom enters that bed at the end of the day: "With circumspection, as invariably when entering an abode (his own or not his own): with solicitude . . . ; prudently . . . ; lightly, the less to disturb: reverently, the bed of conception and of birth, of consummation of marriage and of breach of marriage, of sleep and of death" (*U* 17.2115–2121). Stephen's consciousness in "Proteus" is equally alive to the wide-ranging human meanings of the bed, which he associates closely with women. When thinking of the "handmaid of the moon," rising from sleep, he ponders: "Bridebed, childbed, bed of death, ghostcandled. *Omnis caro ad te veniet* ["all flesh comes to thee"] (*U* 3.396–397). Bloom is less willing to associate the bed so one-sidedly with women, however. Unlike Stephen, haunted in a macabre way by his dead mother, Bloom appreciates his dying father's practical enthusiasm for "animal heat." He tells Bella Cohen's fan in "Circe" about how his father prepared his deathbed, inspired by the Hebrew Scriptures: "Near the end, remembering king David and the Sunamite, he shared his bed with [his dog] Athos, faithful after death" (*U* 15.2785–2786). This memory recurs more soberly in "Ithaca," where Bloom's father's bed becomes an image of the death inside life, of depression and mortality locked in stubborn resistance to the transcendental. Bloom glimpses the first five words of his father's suicide note to him when he opens the second drawer, which evokes the following "reminiscences of a human subject suffering from progressive melancholia": "An old man, widower, unkempt of hair, in bed, with head covered, sighing: an infirm dog, Athos: aconite, resorted to by increasing doses of grains and scruples as a palliative of recrudescent neuralgia: the face in death of a septuagenarian, suicide by poison" (*U* 17.1887–1892). Bloom associates his dead father with the bed in Queen's Hotel where his corpse was found next to his mourning dog. He also, however, imagines the bed as a nest

FIGURE 3. The merchants break the roc's egg, an episode from the fifth voyage of Sinbad the Sailor in *One Thousand and One Nights*. Illustration by Gustave Doré from "Les Mille et une nuits," Le Magasin pitoresque, Paris, 1865. Wikimedia Commons.

as well as a grave, for men as well as women, as we see when an egg fantastically appears in the bed as Bloom falls asleep at the end of "Ithaca."

Bloom's bed has the power to lay an egg: not just any egg, but the huge roc's egg (the size of 148 hens' eggs) from one of the Sinbad tales in the *Arabian Nights*. According to Arabic tradition, the roc never lands on earth, but only on one mountain in the center of the world, a mountain that, by implication, is associated with Bloom's bed. As we see at the end of "Ithaca," when Bloom goes to bed he finds Sinbad's egg. Joyce seems to identify the unconscious mind with the bed of all the auks and rocs of night and day: "Going to dark bed there was a square round Sinbad the Sailor's roc's auk's egg in the night of the bed of all the auks of the rocs of Darkinbad the Brightdayler" (*U* 17.2328–2330). The egg is simultaneously identified as that of a roc and an auk, but rocs and auks—despite the rhyme—have very different characteristics. A roc is a huge mythological bird who became a means of rescue when Sinbad was stranded in the roc's nest. When the bird returned, Sinbad strapped himself to his leg with his turban and escaped. The auk, in contrast, is a real but flightless bird that is now extinct (it is related to the penguin). Here, the language of the book mingles the fantastic and the real, the square and the round, the bright and the dark, the good and the bad in a representation of Bloom's liminal consciousness as he drifts into sleep. That power to produce a state of altered consciousness is one of the magical properties of the bed, a power generated not only in sleep, but also in birth, death, sex, and reading.

Joyce underscores the idea of a bed as a sacred place that is both good and bad in *Finnegans Wake*, where the entire book (being a dream) takes place in bed. Joyce uses the word to denote "best" (spelled "bedst" [*FW* 356.26 and 531.5]) as well as "bad" (as in "bed minners" for "bad manners" [*FW* 444.26]). Sleep reveals sides of the dreamer that are highly admirable and sides that are despicable: as Bloom insists in "Circe," "Sleep reveals the worst side of everyone, children perhaps excepted" (*U* 15.3272–3273). On the one hand, Moses was found in a "bed of fasciated wattles" (*U* 14.394–395); on the other, as the boatswain's chanty insists, *"Pope Peter's but a pissabed"* (*U* 14.649). Whether we're talking of a "luteofulvous bed" of water or the "bedded pears" in the fruit basket Boylan brings to Molly, the good, the bad, and the ugly are all intertwined in bed.

Joyce's fiction could practically be told from the point of view of its beds, beginning with the bed in which Stephen's sister Isabel dies in *Stephen Hero* and progressing through *Dubliners*, which begins and ends with a bed. The first bed is the one on which Father Flynn's corpse is laid in "The Sisters," the last the bed of Gabriel's unconsummated lust, on which Gretta sobs herself to sleep in "The Dead." The bed is a major player in such stories as "A Boarding House" and "Grace," and references to beds range from coffins (the coffins that the monks use as beds "to remind them of their last end" in "The Dead") to the creased paper strewn with parsley that serves as the "bed" of the fat brown goose on the Morkans' table. The occupied bed probably deserves its own category, since the question of whether a bed's occupant provides "calefactory" comfort or maggoty horror is a real question in the "Hades" episode of *Ulysses*. From Bloom's appreciation of Molly's "ample bedwarmed flesh" in "Calypso" (*U* 4.238–239) to his affirmation of "warm beds: warm fullblooded life" in "Hades" (*U* 6.1005), from his fear of death as a state in which he will "lie no more in her warm bed" (*U* 6.554–6555) to his sense of the advantages of an occupied as opposed to an unoccupied bed in "Ithaca," Bloom registers a lively sense of the attractions of Molly's presence in bed. The narrator lists those advantages as "the removal of nocturnal solitude, the superior quality of human (mature female) to inhuman (hotwaterjar) calefaction, the stimulation of matutinal contact, the economy of mangling done on the premises in the case of trousers accurately folded and placed lengthwise between the spring mattress (striped) and the woolen mattress (biscuit section)" (*U* 17.2037–2041). Although Bloom considers using an automatic bed as a means of exposing Molly's adultery and exacting retribution (as Hephaestus once did by trapping Aphrodite and Ares[11]), considering "exposure by mechanical artifice (automatic bed)" and concluding "not yet" (*U* 17.2202–2203), he is nonetheless able to reenter his bed, where his "antagonistic sentiments and reflections... converge" in a "final satisfaction" with Molly's "adipose anterior and posterior female hemispheres, redolent of milk and honey and of excretory sanguine and seminal warmth" (*U* 17.2227–2233). Unlike Saint Kevin in Glendalough, who is supposed to have thrown a woman out of his cavelike bed in the side of a rock to her death in the lake below (see *FW* 600.36–601.01),[12] Bloom neither rejects human company in bed nor does he demand an unsullied virtue in himself or in his bedfellow.

In *A Portrait of the Artist as a Young Man*, Stephen writes his only piece of literature—the villanelle of the temptress—in bed, heavily influenced by sleep and desire. Joyce is already exploring the relationship between literature, sex, death, and sleep, what in *Finnegans Wake* will be called "his litterery [littered, literary] bed" ([*FW* 422.35). That understanding of the bed as a site of writing, sex, and temptation emerges in *Ulysses* through Stephen's argument that Anne Hathaway was unfaithful to her husband (William Shakespeare), an infidelity that Stephen sees as reflected in Shakespeare's bequest to her of their "secondbest bed" in his will (*U* 9.680–719). For Stephen, the wife's betrayal is one stimulus that, combined with the death of his father and son Hamnet, resulted in Shakespeare's creative potency: as she disports with "a dullbrained yokel" in a bed in Stratford, Shakespeare works to express his sense of loss through his writing in London. Death, sex, and writing all transpire in bed. The narrator in the "Scylla and Charybdis" episode mockingly plays with the language of Shakespeare's will to accent the action of leaving:

Leftherhis
Secondbest
Leftherhis
Bestabed
Secabest
Leftabed. (*U* 9.701–706)

It is illuminating to contrast Stephen's argument that Anne and Shakespeare were engaged in a "contest" of beds with the analogous but more harmonious view of a contemporary British poet, Carol Ann Duffy, who presents Anne and Shakespeare as lovingly writing "romance and drama" with their bodies in their second-best bed. Stephen reads Shakespeare's writing as a reaction to Anne's activity in their bed at home, which allows readers to see his situation as analogous to Bloom's in *Ulysses*. Although Bloom doesn't write to process his cuckolding, he does, like Shakespeare, become more capacious or myriad-minded in an effort to comprehend it. Duffy, on the other hand, identifies the Shakespeares' bed as the book in which they wrote his plays through their lovemaking. In her sonnet "Anne Hathaway," Duffy treats Anne and Shakespeare not as bed-competitors, but as collaborators, composing his works together with their bodies in their second-best bed while guests sleep nearby in their best one. It isn't until the final couplet that we learn that Shakespeare is dead and that Anne is remembering their loving bedplay:

The bed we loved in was a spinning world
of forests, castles, torchlight, clifftops, seas
where we would dive for pearls. My lover's words
were shooting stars which fell to earth as kisses
on these lips, my body now a softer rhyme
to his, now echo, assonance; his touch
a verb dancing in the centre of a noun.
Some nights, I dreamed he'd written me, the bed
a page beneath his writer's hands. Romance
and drama played by touch, by scent, by taste.
In the other bed, the best, our guests dozed on,
dribbling their prose. My living laughing love—

I hold him in the casket of my widow's head
as he held me upon that next best bed.[13]

Anne is now a widow, and her head is now the "bed" in which she contains their lovemaking; the rhyme of "head" and "bed" gently suggests that her "head" is now their second-best bed; it has become a casket or coffin that holds their living love.

Surrounded by books that he sees as thought-coffins ("Coffined thoughts around me, in mummycases, embalmed in spice of words" [U 9.352–353]), Stephen hammers home his argument that Shakespeare's bequest showed no solicitude for his wife's well-being after his death: "He was a rich country gentleman. . . . Why did he not leave her his best bed if he wished her to snore away the rest of her nights in peace?" (U 9.710–713). This prompts Eglinton, "bedsmiling," to recall that "antiquity mentions famous beds" (U 9.718). In an episode in which Aristotle and Plato are two of the opposites in the position of Homer's paired dangers, Scylla and Charybdis, Eglinton's remark encourages a closer look at the discussion of beds in both.

Plato, in book 10 of the *Republic,* and Aristotle, in book 2 of the *Physics,* both interrogate the nature of material reality as artistic creation through an investigation of the bed.[14] They disagree about whether the process of making is bottom up (starting with matter) or top down (beginning with the idea). Aristotle asks whether the "bedness" of a bed is due to the material of which it is made, or to its form. He concludes that it isn't the material composition of a bed that makes it what it is because "if you planted a bed and the rotting wood acquired the power of sending up a shoot, it would not be a bed that would come up, but wood." Therefore, the bed's real nature has to be that which "persists continuously through the process of making." Moreover, although the "nature" of a bed inheres in its form, a bed cannot be said to be a work of art until it achieves its potential in matter. Interestingly, Joyce seems to have wanted to craft art that balances nature (or motion toward the realization of form) with stasis (that which is immobilized in matter), creating books that have the contradictory characteristics of a bed as Aristotle describes it: a work of art in which form and matter complete one another. For Aristotle, in creation (whether natural or artistic) it is the result or purpose of the process that matters most:[15] the product is the fulfillment of the creative process, a paradoxical balance of opposite forces, such as matter and form.

Plato, in contrast, argues that the "bedness" of a bed exists before the construction of any actual beds; it inheres in the formal idea or concept of a bed. For Plato, artists can do no more than reproduce or reflect those pre-existing concepts or forms, which is why Plato devalues human artistry as derivative and mechanical. Joyce implicitly situates these differing views of beds—as a priori template or as final cause—behind Stephen's discussion of the second-best bed Shakespeare wills to his "unfaithful" wife. Shakespeare's best bed was his work, which exquisitely balances movement and rest, life and art, object and concept, in the effort to create something new, as Plato argued only God could do, or as Aristotle suggested only the material could accomplish.

How can a book do what, on the one hand, God can do—create a fresh template or form—while also approximating what a woman in childbirth does, give birth to a new life out of the lives other people? The idea that the book is a product of labor is memorably demonstrated in the "Oxen of the Sun" episode, where Mrs. Purefoy lies "groaning on a bed with a vinegared handkerchief round her forehead, her belly swollen out" (*U* 8.373–374), as English literature gestates through the narrative. Sex, birth, death—these are all signs of the principle of motion Aristotle associated with nature. The book serves as womb *and* tomb, a place where the reader's awareness of the world around her goes to "sleep" and a kind of dreaming takes its place. To read a book is to simulate—temporarily—one's own death, with the hope of "waking" at the end transfigured: resurrected and changed. When we are "above ground," we are bedded in a "Book of Breathings" in an effort to "kick time" (*FW* 415.23–24). Joyce's books help in "blessing the bedpain" (*FW* 328.36); they lead us into the "bed of trial, on the bolster of hardship, by the glimmer of memory, under coverlets of cowardice" (*FW* 558.26–27) to that glorious and ignoble place where life begins and ends, where motion and rest meet "spancelled down upon a blossomy bed" (*FW* 475.8).

Beds, especially when framed by Plato and Aristotle, encourage reflection about self-awareness and its optimal relation to the subconscious. Whether considered in relation to books, gardens, sex, adultery, graves, or the process by which they were made, beds anticipate heads, which alternately accommodate states of alertness and those of rest. Creativity, love, and life are all informed by a tension between knowing and not knowing, seeing and not seeing, the conscious mind and the obliviousness of an unconsciousness that may well be partly communal in that it rescrambles or

FIGURE 4. Garden bed. Photo by Morgan Gerace. Used by permission.

respells the social as well as the individual. Imagination and dream are as vital as reason, and perhaps more so because they tend to be devalued or discounted. In our age of artificial intelligence, though, it is more important than ever to remember the renewing power of a bed or a book to re-order one's thoughts and feelings. As Joyce puts it in *Finnegans Wake*, his "night-book" that takes place entirely in a head in bed, "Only is order othered. Nought is nulled" (*FW* 613.13–14).

The multivalent meaning of a bed as flower bed, marriage bed, and grave is hauntingly illustrated by a brass bed in the garden of one of my neighbors, pictured here. It was her marriage bed, and after her divorce she put it in her garden so her ex-husband would have to drive by it every day. It is simultaneously a memorial to the productivity of their marriage and a tribute to the children conceived there and a marker commemorating the death of that connection.

Perhaps the most fitting tribute we can offer Joyce's "allaphbed" (*FW* 18.17), his "clay book," his bed of engraved and littering letters, is to approach his books not only with a determination to dig, with all the effort and pleasure digging implies, but also contemplatively, thoughtfully, as one would enter a sacred place. This is how Emily Dickinson greeted what was probably a grave:

Ample make this Bed—
Make this Bed with Awe—
In it wait till Judgment break
Excellent and Fair.
Be its Mattress straight—
Be its Pillow round—
Let no Sunrise' yellow noise
Interrupt this Ground—[16]

2 ▸ ON DIRTY SHEETS

When we enter the night world of Finnegans Wake, Joyce's language becomes more obscurely layered with multiple meanings, and every story calls up varied frames of reference: mythical, folkloric, factual, geographical, and autobiographical. In the "Anna Livia Plurabelle" episode, Joyce returns to the subject of the book as a bed, in which lifestories are written by the body. Two washerwomen near the River Liffey "read" the lives of Dubliners through the dirty clothes they are washing, "publishing" their secrets in the oral form of gossip. The focus in this episode is not on the book/bed, but on the sheets within both: how they are stained (and made colorful) by living, and how such public expression helps to clean or whiten them; publication serves as the social analogue to the Catholic practice of private confession. What the moralist calls "dirt" is, seen from another angle, living color.

In "Anna Livia Plurabelle," Joyce relates the mundane act of washing to the sacred history of God's cleansing of the sinful world through the flood. One important difference between this cleansing and profane "laundry" is that God's action was destructive but limited; He promises never to destroy the world again through the covenant He makes with Noah, sealed by the sign of the rainbow in the heavens. Daily washing, however, renews the material world, and it is something that

must be repeated over and over again. What is written on the sheets through liv-
ing and "published" through town gossip are simply the surprising, unexpected,
private but also communal facts of life, sex, and death. The washerwomen suggest
that the most private acts of the body are also ones in which everyone (separately)
participates.

In a poetic prose that seems musical nonsense on first reading, but which
is gradually revealed as multiply layered and exquisitely precise, Joyce presents
publication as a "cleansing" conversation between two laboring women, perhaps
like Sylvia Beach and Adrienne Monnier (Beach published Ulysses, *and Monnier*
was her partner, a bookseller and the editor of a journal that once published an
episode of Finnegans Wake*). At the end of the chapter the gossiping washer-*
women merge into the landscape, becoming a tree and a stone on the two banks
of the river (Beach's name evokes a tree—beech—and meunier *is the French*
word for "miller," one who works with a stone). The washerwomen/publishers
are reclaimed as part of the environs of Dublin; writing and publishing, like liv-
ing and loving, are two phases of the natural and civic rhythms of life.

There are two ways to blacken sheets of paper: by writing on them (manually or with bodily fluids) and by printing them as part of the publication
process. Writing, then, is on one level a spoiling of "purity," and is sometimes represented as a dubious art form verging on the criminal. Ibsen, in
his agonized last play, *When We Dead Awaken,* emphasizes how his sculptor-
protagonist's art had hurt the woman he had "used" as a model. Wilde, in
"Pen, Pencil and Poison," considers the kinship between crime and culture
more broadly, arguing that crime and art develop out of a similarly autonomous or resistant attitude to prevalent social norms. Yeats approaches this
idea by admiring the loveliness and innocence of a blank page, the image of
which is evoked by the stormy white of flying swans in "Coole Park and
Ballylee, 1931." Yeats writes that such whiteness could set aright what
"knowledge *and its lack* had put awry" (my emphasis). Interestingly, Yeats
arraigns ignorance and knowledge as equally responsible for producing
inscriptions that kill a reader's receptiveness. He describes the unmarked
page as "So arrogantly pure, a child might think / It could be murdered with
a spot of ink." Yeats imagines the ink of a writer as something that can *mur-*
der the purity and loveliness of an unwritten page (even as reading accultur-
ates and thereby ages a child); on the other hand, there is something
arrogant about such whiteness that may justify its staining.

Yet there is more to writing (and publishing) than sullying pages. It also is a way of bringing dirty secrets to light. That process of revelation may also constitute a reparation, a removal of dirt by exposing and agitating it. Darkness made visible is no longer "dark," in the sense of "secret." This is an important reason why Joyce wrote so truthfully and matter-of-factly about sexuality, even aberrant forms of sexuality: openness is cleansing, akin to Catholic confession, although when done publicly rather than in private it can also be scandalous. The banning of *Ulysses* for obscenity is often alluded to in *Finnegans Wake,* but it is an especially important subtext for the "Anna Livia Plurabelle" episode (I.8), which is about washing dirty laundry while simultaneously airing the "dirt."

The pure white page, a crisscross of soaked, bleached, and beaten tree fibers, is appropriately called a "sheet"; the word "sheet," which was first applied to paper in 1510, comes from the Old English "cloth, covering" (*OED*). Bed sheets, like their paper equivalents, may also testify to "sins" or physical deeds that have left traces on them. Think about Joyce's handkerchief, and what Nora helped his body "write" on it when they first "walked out" together;[1] Wilde's bed sheets, which served as evidence of "gross indecency" in his trials when the chambermaid at his hotel was called to the stand; the infamously stained blue dress that led to President Clinton's impeachment in the United States, or, in a different vein, Veronica's napkin, which bore the imprint of Jesus's face after she wiped it (Joyce calls her napkin "Veronica's wipers" [*FW* 204.30]; see also Yeats's poem "Veronica's Napkin").

The close connection between the sheets of a book and a bed is reinforced by the similarity between the production of paper and the manual laundering of a bed sheet. Before the advent of the steam laundry, a bed sheet was washed with a mixture of wood ash and animal fat, rubbed and beaten with a wooden baton, rinsed in the running water of a river, twisted or wrung out by hand, then dried in fresh air and sun.[2] Similarly, paper was produced by obtaining fibers from trees or plants by beating or boiling them, adding water and possibly sizing or bleach, pressing them and letting them dry, as one would dry a bed sheet. The similarity between laundering and papermaking is also apparent in the terms they share ("sizing" may be added to vegetable fibers when making paper or to bed sheets as starch), but a deeper and less obvious connection between the different kinds of "sheets" is their common position as a surface where a white and dark work together to produce a reflection of life.[3] Unexpectedly, the "Anna Livia Plurabelle" episode, like so much of *Finnegans Wake,* ends up investigating the nature of writing; here, writing is presented as a bodily act as well as a mental one (see the discussion of writing with the body in chapter 1, "On Beds"). The episode turns on what we might call the paradoxical relation of dirt and cleanliness: cleanliness emerges as the women *admit, discuss, even publish* (rather than ignore or deny) the "dirt"—or byproducts—of being human. Laundering in this episode is not a "whitewash" but a revelation of bodily and mental waste that is simultaneously a textual "baptism" that cleans, renews, and refreshes. Literary writing is portrayed as another kind of stain produced on sheets by the body, with much labor (see chapter 4, "On Writing by Hand"); its status as a bodily product is part of what makes it so potentially intimate and revealing: carefully crafted words, like bodily fluid on sheets, or even like pottery shards in an archeological site, offer glimpses into an everyday life that is normally hidden from view.

Writing about reality involves both author and scribe in an intimate relation to bodily waste and human error, which Joyce represents as what the writer uses to stain the page (a story is only possible if something has gone wrong). In "Shem the Penman" (I.7), the episode that precedes "Anna Livia Plurabelle," ALP's son Shem combines feces and urine to make ink, which he uses to write on "the only foolscap available, his own body," producing "from his unheavenly body a no uncertain quantity of obscene matter" (*FW* 185.35–36, 29–30). Shem writes deliberately, self-consciously; he is acutely conscious of how his own body provides materials for writing. In "Anna Livia Plurabelle" it is not merely the hand but also the torso that writes, confessing its dirty secrets to the "cloth" so that they may be published and cleansed. Writing seen from this angle is simultaneously dirty and clean, legible and cryptic, secret and public, conscious and unconscious. It cannot justly be put on trial to be judged admirable or despicable; it is merely a material testimony to a vital, true-to-life conjunction of the intersection of embodied truths, both fair and foul.[4]

The body writes on clothes—especially sheets and undergarments—in many ways, typically without calculation or deliberation. Despite this fact of everyday life—which children intuit when they snigger at the relation of the "pen" and the "penis"—most people picture writing as a cerebral activity rather than as a more complex interplay between body and mind, in which unconscious revelation is mixed with intentional, manual labor.

Readers familiar with Joyce's works know about his erotic interest in women's soiled underwear, without necessarily realizing that he regarded these "understandings" as a kind of text that corresponded with those he constructed deliberately. That Joyce regards sex and writing as closely akin is figured in his various spellings of literature in *Finnegans Wake* (as containing litter—rubbish—and a litter—the offspring of an animal, as well as a bed, *lit*, and letters).[5] Joyce even presents the human spirit as something that may be enriched by dirt, as he shows by evoking Margaret Mary Alacoque ("mathared mary allacook" [*FW* 214.23]), the saint who protected her humility by cultivating thirst, sometimes refusing to drink water unless dirty laundry had been washed in it.[6]

One of the washerwomen's imprecations to "ptellomey soon" (*FW* 198.2) helps illustrate how narration in time can help the speaker map her location in the world. The River Liffey, which Joyce refers to as "Geoglyphy" (*FW* 595.7) and which babbles or speaks "nonsense" as it moves through space, is one of the many models for the book itself, as it takes its readers through rapidly changing places and times. The washerwomen's portmanteau word "ptellomey" packs "tell me" together with "Ptolemy," thereby concisely reflecting Joyce's intention to entangle narrative with time, space, and history. Narration, like geography, facilitates travel, whether actual or imagined. "To ptellomey" is to act as a kind of Ptolemy, the name given to Claudius Ptolemaeus, the celebrated second-century Greco-Egyptian mathematician, astronomer, and geographer who mapped Ireland ("Hibernia") with surprising accuracy despite never having been there. According to P. W. Joyce, Ptolemy's description of Ireland—which is more accurate than his account of Britain—probably owes its greater accuracy to the fact that he got his information from Phoenician traders.[7] HCE emerges as one of those traders/traitors (see the reference to HCE as "the trader" [*FW* 198.6]): "In a gabbard he barqued it, the boat of life, from the harbourless Ivernikan Okean" (*FW* 197.28–29), the Ivernikan Ocean being the name Ptolemy gave to the Irish Sea. Geography, like narrative, uses a journey in time to draw the contours of a place, so that space and time become as interdependent as black and white on the page.

Another phrase urges us to regard narrative as a liminal form, moving like a jack-o'-lantern between good and evil, life and death. One of the washerwomen asks about a bit of gossip: "Who sold you that jackalantern's tale?" (*FW* 197.26–27). The jack-o'-lantern originates from an Irish legend about

FIGURE 5. Jack and his lantern. Illustration by Dennis Haugh. Used by permission.

living between heaven and hell, light, and darkness: Jack was a miserly, lazy man who was about to be taken away by the devil until he tricked the devil into giving him more time. In different versions the trick takes various forms: Jack traps the devil in a tree, taunts him into becoming a sixpence and holds him in his hand, which is marked with a cross, or beats him at a game of dice. When Jack finally dies, St. Peter won't let him into heaven and the devil won't allow him into hell; when he complains about wandering in the darkness between the worlds, the devil throws him a firebrand and Jack carries it inside a hollowed-out turnip, thus becoming Jack of the Lantern or Jack O'Lantern.

Finnegans Wake implies that everyday life is " jackalantern's tale" in which people are neither clearly good nor bad, and the world is neither completely dark nor light. The bodily and earthly (represented by the turnip, gourd, or other root vegetable) and the spiritual or divine (represented by fire) exist in eerie proximity. To put it another way, the jack-o'-lantern is a representation of what it means to be human: a burning spirit incarnated in a root vegetable, wandering between heaven and the grave.

In *Ulysses,* Bloom thinks about the paradox that "dirty cleans" (*U* 4.481). What we learn when we trace the webs of verbal association through a single chapter of *Finnegans Wake* is that laundry washed in a river is a figure of life, which is defined by opposite extremes (or banks) that mirror each other while cradling a musical, moving current between them. Washing is a simultaneous act of whitening and darkening: the clothes are whitened while the water is darkened ("He has all my water black on me" [*FW* 196.12]); the unceasing movement of the river disperses the dirt and deposits it on (in) the river's "banks." If we consider the momentary equipoise of light and darkness in a running stream, we can understand why this chapter about washing takes place at twilight, or "evening," when light and dark are momentarily evened. Here, gossipy moral judgment about good and evil actions is as briefly impartial as the light and darkness; the result of such evening is a text that is both colorful and musical, and never static or rigid. Through the voices of the two washerwomen, "two belles that make the one appeal" (*FW* 194.26–27), Joyce gives us a representation of the "gossipaceous" River Liffey "chattering to herself" and "running with her tidings [tides, news]" (*FW* 195.4, 2; 194.23). Her job, like that of the washerwomen on her banks or that of a journalist, is to make HCE's "private linen public" (*FW* 196.16), a job that is joyful as well as painful and unrewarding (although ALP is "happy as the day is wet," one washerwoman complains about the discomforts of "scorching my hand and starving my famine" in order to "publish" HCE's "dirt" (*FW* 195.1, 196.15–16). Women's labor and literary texts are presented as moving in similar ways, producing comparably paradoxical effects. In reading as in publishing, illumination is a function of obscurity: as paper is meaningless without the blackening effects of type, so is the workaday legibility of the conventional word rendered fresh and surprising by mechanisms that at best seem illegible or nonsensical, at worst obscene. Joyce's method in *Finnegans Wake* is to publish the unconscious, "dirty"—or bodily—secretions/secrets of language, thereby renewing communication. "Wring out the clothes! Wring in the dew!" (*FW* 213.19–20). The wringing of laundry—like the ringing of a bell—signals a celebration of renewal. Appropriately, "new" is transformed into something that involves freshness and moisture ("dew"), signaled by sound: a bell, as in "plurabelle."

When we turn to the two washerwomen, we see that they operate symbolically on several different levels: topographically, they are both the two banks and the river that runs between them. As something that is both two and one (in that they reflect one another), the women are versions of ALP, or the river of Liffey/life, as well as ALP's daughter Issy and her reflection in the mirror. Finally, they become ALP's twin sons, Shem and Shaun, the "rivals" who are also, as the word suggests, embodiments of the river's banks ("rivals" derives from the French word for "banks," *rives*). As penman and postman, her sons write and deliver her news. This connection is reinforced when the washerwomen devolve into a tree and a stone at the end of the episode, making them "tree-stone," or Tristan, yet another emblem of the combination of Shem and Shaun. The washerwomen's position as "tree-stone" opposites is again underscored when ALP refers to them in her final soliloquy as Mrs. Quickenough (i.e., alive enough, but also a reference to the quicken tree) and Miss Doddspebble (i.e., dead people, but also pebble, or stone) (*FW* 620.19). These names identify the women with the forces of life and death, light and shadow, between which we eke out an everyday existence.

Historically, the washerwomen evoke Irish working-class female laborers. Biographically, they are associated with Sylvia Beach and her partner, Adrienne Monnier, as touched on above. Beach is a homonym for beech, and Sylvia—a name Beach chose for herself to replace her given name, Nancy—means "woods or forest," like her father's name, Sylvester). Monnier, as noted above, is a variant of *meunier,* a miller who mills with a stone. Beach is well known as the American woman who published *Ulysses* in Paris, despite it already being scandalous, and Monnier, also a bookseller, published part of *Finnegans Wake* in her French language review, *Le Navire d'Argent,* three years later (October 1925).[8] As washerwomen cleansing sheets in the river of life, they are also publishers and sellers of dirty books, which in the episode take the oral form of rumor and gossip.

FIGURE 6. The Bunworth Banshee. Illustration by W.H. Brooke, in *Fairy Legends and Traditions of the South of Ireland* by Thomas Crofton Crocker, 1825. Alamy.

Mythologically, the washerwomen are not only banshees (what the Norse would call Valkyries), but also the (black) raven and (white) dove from Noah's Ark, humankind's emissaries to test the waters after that extreme laundering of the world, the flood.[9] Like the Anna Livia whose internal conflicts they dramatize, they represent all polar oppositions, even frost and fire: ALP is described as someone whose "*frost*ivying tresses [are] dasht with *virev*lies" (*FW* 199.36, my emphasis; although a fiery insect who also vies and lies, she above all lives—*virev* is an anagram of *vivre*, the French verb "to live"). Together, HCE and ALP constitute the Tower of Babel—he the tower, she the babble—built by Noah's descendants, the erection that marked the boundary between linguistic unity and disunity, human collaboration and dispersal ("She'd bate the hen that crowed on the turrace of Babbel" [*FW* 199.30–31]). ALP's babbling, like that of the river she embodies or the multilingual referents of *Finnegans Wake*, only *sounds* like nonsense to those who lack the gift of tongues. After the fall of Babel, which is at once a tower and a universal language, we have to work hard to understand one another. Finally, the two washerwomen represent the romantic union and feisty disunion of HCE and ALP, their similarities and differences captured in their respective roles as hunger striker ("hungerstriking all alone" [FW 199.4]) and famine victim ("starving my famine" [FW 196.15–16]), sometimes replayed as a hungry man and his wife/cook (FW 199.4).

Margot Norris has given a thorough account of the realistic background against which the washerwomen are drawn, emphasizing the social work they perform through their female labor.[10] While engaging in one of the two oldest jobs of women (cooking and washing), they talk in a way that constitutes a kind of song, which Norris rightly calls a work song, that serves to recover the complex doubleness of ALP as "desirable nymphet and rag-picking hag, clear rivulet and polluted harbor" (141). Norris argues that Joyce is here working to recover an understanding of social and utilitarian labor, countering the usual artistic effort to sublimate that labor in order to produce beauty in art. She traces the ancestry of ALP-as-washerwoman to two of Joyce's earlier characters: Nausicaa washing her finely embroidered trousseau in the Odyssey (resurrected by Gerty displaying her private linen a little differently in Ulysses) and Maria working at the Dublin by Lamplight Laundry—in reality a Magdalen's home for fallen women—in the Dubliners story "Clay" (D 147–148). Washing, by implication, is both a penance for sexual errancy and a privilege associated with the power of baptism (literally the act of dipping in water), which is both a cleansing of sin and the right to name or christen.[11] Norris astutely brings up Samuel Butler's argument that Nausicaa was actually the author of the Odyssey, which reinforces the implicit connection between writing and the cleansing/blackening process of washing. She also stresses the biographical resonance of Joyce's interest in laundry, since as Brenda Maddox has documented, Nora was employed to do washing and ironing for Livia Schmitz in Trieste, the wife of Italo Svevo who was one of the models for ALP (Nora had earlier worked as a laundress in Galway before leaving home to become a chambermaid, which Joyce renders in "ALP" as "shamemaid" [FW 212.17]).[12]

It is hardly surprising that Joyce depicts washing not only as paid servitude for women of the working class, but also as part of the drudgery of marriage for women without the money to send their laundry out. He stresses the connection between marriage and manual labor by describing the movement of the Liffey in the ironic language of the marriage vows: "to wend her ways byandby, robecca or worse [for better or worse, for richer

FIGURE 7. Banshees. Illustration by Dennis Haugh. Used by permission.

or poorer], to spin and to grind, to swab and to thrash, for all her golden lifey in the barleyfields and pennylotts of Humphrey's fordofhurdlestown [Dublin as Baile Átha Cliath: Ford of the Hurdles]" (*FW* 203.4–7). Not only was washing associated with poverty in Joyce's own family, it was also linked more generally with poverty in Ireland, especially during the famine, when women took in laundry to get food. As ALP sings in the song the two washerwomen are trying to "lerryn" (*FW* 200.36), "*Is there irwell a lord of the manor or a knight of the shire at strike, I wonder, that'd dip me a dace* [penny] *or two in cash for washing and darning his worshipful socks for him now we're run out of horsebrose* [oatmeal] *and milk?*" (*FW* 201.13–16)[13]

Norris writes compassionately about the labor of real Irish washer-women, but she gives less attention to the mythological function of the two narrators of the episode as figures who, like the midwives Stephen imagines in "Proteus," wield the power of life and death, light and darkness. The Scottish cousin of the banshee, the Bean Nighe, is found at the side of desolate streams and pools, washing the bloodstained clothes of those about to die. Some describe these banshees as small, with webbed feet; other accounts attribute to them one nostril, one long protruding tooth, and one long, withered, dangling breast. If you get between the banshee and the water, or (alternatively) grab her breast, she will grant you three wishes. According to legend, these washerwomen at the ford are the spirits of women who have died, some say in childbirth. Like Jack O'Lantern, the banshees mark a location between life and death.

The activity of doing laundry also reenacts the meaning of the Irish phrase from which the name "Dublin" derives: *Dubh lionn*, or "black pool." As night falls and eve dies and the river babbles and women scrub, the water blackens. When the water gets black, it's clear we're in Dublin: "She . . . lay and wriggled in all the stagnant black pools of rainy [Erin]" (*FW* 204.17–18).

Although they can exchange roles, when ALP is the cleansing Liffey, HCE plays the part of the sinful marauder whose story she tells, an incarnation of Dear Dirty Dublin, "duddurty devil" (*FW* 196.13), or "dear dubber Dan" (*FW* 199.14). HCE's blackness, or dirtiness, is produced by soil ("saale" [196.15]), which is a word linked to the word for pig (*sus*), like "dirt," which is related to "dung." Dirt, soil, and defecation are all verbally connected; HCE has written on his shirt in soil or excrement. His bodily "writing" on clothes, then, is not dissimilar to Nora's, as Joyce indicates in his 1909 letters to her, when he describes his interest in her brown-stained drawers as dirty and filthy. On the one hand, he argues that "the dirtiest are the most beautiful" (*SL* 186); on the other, he says that her drawers are "as spotless" as her heart (*SL* 189). Both statements are true by the contradictory truths that meet when something is washed, baptized, or written: in the black and white of material textuality, purity and dirt are held in momentary balance so as to reflect the fullness of a contradictory reality.

Joyce situates the everyday labor of washing against the biblical background of the Flood, which cleansed the entire world of evil, saving only one large ark. HCE is a mariner, like both Noah and Odysseus, as well as a

Scandinavian marauder and a "gran Phenician rover" (FW 197.31). He also bears a resemblance to Joyce when he took Nora to Italy by boat, and the Romans who abducted the Sabine women at a feast in honor of Neptune ("he raped her home, Sabrine asthore" [FW 197.21]). Described as "eld duke alien" (FW 197.2–4), or Deucalion, the Greek Noah, he sails from the Irish Sea (Ivernikan Okean) on "the boat of life . . . till he spied the loom of his landfall and he loosed two croakers from under his tilt" (FW 197.28–30). Several things are going on at once in this heavily layered "history": if we read it through the lens of Noah's story, HCE's triumph is to ride "the wash" (FW 197.34) and to release two birds, a raven and a dove, to help him find land. The black and white birds are yet another way of visualizing the two opposed methods—predation and peacefulness, evil and goodness— which Noah uses evenhandedly to get information, but they also represent for Joyce the black and white of the inscribed page and of dirty clothes. When Noah sends his black and white birds from the Ark to "write" in the sky, God replies in color, with an arc of his own: the rainbow of seven colors, covenant of peace ("the reignbeau's heavenarches arronged orranged her" [FW 203.26–27]).

In the Bible, the Genesis story is a tale of re-creation, designed to show how God punished human violence, and why He decided never again to curse the ground because of human evil. In Finnegans Wake, Joyce weaves the story of Noah through the book to show how renewal follows destruc-tion, even naming Shem after one of Noah's sons. If we understand water as female, however, the story of Noah changes shape, becoming a comic tale about the erotic war between the sexes. Noah emerges as a male who tem-porarily triumphs over the waters, successfully riding and entering the woman they represent, as "with his runagate bowmpriss [renegade bow-sprit] he roade and borst her bar" (FW 197.34–35), or as he took the form of a salmon to return to her "home" waters to spawn: "they saw him shoot swift up her sheba sheath, like any gay lord salomon" (FW 198.3–4). He "erned" her, his little "Bunbath [Banba]," or Ireland, by "this wet of his prow [sweat of his brow]" (FW 198.5–6). After their war of the sexes, a covenant of peace is established between the mariner and the woman of the great wash. That sign of promise—the "rainbow"—is their daughter Issy, who is sometimes configured as Noah's two birds, a black raven and a white dove, and sometimes as the seven colors of the rainbow itself, the "maids . . . in Arc" (FW 202.17–18). In "Anna Livia Plurabelle," Joyce shows how white and black paradoxically combine to create or reveal color; he demonstrates how the black and white of the written or stained sheet becomes colorful and even hopeful in the memory and imagination of the active, responsive, and curious reader.

The difference between black and white, on the one hand, and color, on the other, is illustrated by the difference between God as a burden—"the load is with me" (*FW* 214.19) and God as joy, or "Gaud" (*FW* 207.23). That difference is also apparent in the different ways of viewing marks on clothes—as soil, or as a *stain* ("I know by heart the places he likes to saale, duddurty devil!" and "My wrists are wrusty rubbing the mouldaw stains" [*FW* 196.14–15, 17–18]. Clothes can regain whiteness through a scrubbing that turns the water black (*FW* 196.12), but when we say that something is stained, it means it has been colored, not necessarily blackened. To stain is to *paint* (Old Norse *steina*); to dye. And "dye" is a "color, hue, tinge," but it is also related to the idea of dirt via a second meaning of "secret, hidden, dark, obscure." Dye is colorful, but to die is dark (the spelling distinction between the two words didn't stabilize until the nineteenth century). The very stain that blackens clothes (or sheets, or writing) also gives them color, as Joyce underscores by identifying ALP as both a "judyqueen [beauty queen]" and a black "bushman woman" (*FW* 207.36, 34). Joyce registered his expanding understanding of textuality as colorful on the "sheets" of his drafts, which, beginning roughly with the draft for "Proteus," began to bear traces of different colors.[14] Joyce's drafts increasingly expressed not just the black and white of the Ark at sea, but the "promise" of the whole rainbow arc of imaginative possibilities that reflected and amplified it. He understood Noah's "Ark" as something God answered with a rainbow "arc," seeing the story as a "conversation" between a flooded earth and a colorful sky.

Moreover, this conversation symbolized a transition from an ethos of judgment and punishment of sin to an ethos of forgiveness, fuller comprehension (in the sense of inclusiveness), and acceptance. Examples of Joyce's celebrations of color in the ALP episode include the description of a pair of drawers as dirty, spotless, *and* colored: "bloodorange bockknickers, a two in one garment, showed natural nigger boggers [black], fancyfastened, free to undo" (*FW* 208.16–17). In the "grooming" scene, ALP colors herself by applying make-up, taking "the pick of the paintbox for her pommettes, from strawbirry reds to extra violates" (*FW* 207.9–11). The rainbow and its colors are also rendered as explicitly sexual when HCE (as the aptly named Reverend Michael *Ark*low) "enters" ALP, parting her waves: "the reignbeau's heavenarches arranged orranged her. Afrothdizzying galbs, her enameled eyes indergoading him on to the vierge violetian" (*FW* 203.27–29). In short, the "black pools of rainy" [lit. "Dublin of Erin"] are also a many-colored ark/ arc of promise.[15] The woman, the place, and the colors are organized to signify possibility, a possibility tied to vitality but also to the "dirty" soil.

In the unconscious, the sins of the world; the raven, dove, and rainbow; "the Oceans of Gaud [God; joy]" (*FW* 207.23)]; Noah's virtue and his drunken nakedness; his sons' voyeurism; and Lot's incest with his daughters are all one. "Continuarration!" (*FW* 205.14). This is a night bible. It all comes out in the wash. "All that and more [is] under one crinoline envelope if you dare to break the porkbarrel seal" (*FW* 212.20): food, sexuality, and letters generate blackness and secrecy, but also life and color.

At the fall of night, in the hands of these washing banshees, we are all reduced to the clothes and shadows we leave behind. As one of the washerwomen cries, "But all that's left to the last of the Meaghers in the loup of the years prefixed and between is one kneebuckle and two hooks in the front" (*FW* 214.3–6). The other answers, "Ussa, Ulla, we're umbas [umbras, shadows] all!" (*FW* 214.7). In the end, we are as great (or as small) as our "understandings" (Gerty McDowell's word for underwear in *Ulysses*). Mrs. Magrath's frilly monogrammed drawers show that "she has sinned" (*FW* 204.36), but the canon's underpants must also be scrubbed with ashes (*FW* 206.26–27). One of ALP's stranger talents is her readiness to teach young girls how to attract a man by showing them "how to bring to mind the gladdest garments out of sight" (*FW* 200.25–26). Joyce himself undertook to teach this to Nora in a letter dated December 6, 1909:

> I would like you to wear drawers with three or four frills one over the other at the knees and up the thighs and great crimson bows in them, I mean not schoolgirls' drawers with a thin shabby lace border, tight round the legs and so thin that the flesh shows between them but women's (or if you prefer the word) ladies' drawers with a full loose bottom and wide legs, all frills and lace and ribbons, and heavy with perfume so that whenever you show them, whether in pulling up your clothes hastily to do something or cuddling yourself up prettily to be blocked, I can see only a swelling mass of white stuff and frills and so that when I bend down over you to open them and give you a

burning lustful kiss on your naughty bare bum I can smell the perfume of your drawers as well as the warm odour of your cunt and the heavy smell of your behind. (*SL* 184)

The "letter to last a lifetime" (*FW* 211.22), one of ALP's gifts, is also hidden, transitory, and "dirty": like the secrets to be found in and on different kinds of "drawers," the letter, when found "down by the ashpit," reveals marks on a white sheet, signed with a stain. Compare the letter Joyce asks Nora to write to him on December 9, 1909, doubly stained with words and with the marks of her body:

> Write me a long long letter, full of that and other things, about yourself, darling. You know now how to give me a cockstand. Tell me the smallest things about yourself so long as they are obscene and secret and filthy. Write nothing else. Let every sentence be full of dirty immodest words and sounds. They are all lovely to hear and to see on paper even but the dirtiest are the most beautiful. . . . Write the dirty words big and underline them and kiss them and hold them for a moment to your sweet hot cunt, darling, and also pull up your dress a moment and hold them in under your dear little farting bum. (*SL* 186)

If we watch Joyce yet again translate the metaphor of how black and white contain and repel the entire spectrum of colors, respectively, we find the suggestion that life is quite literally a mixed bag. Both HCE and ALP carry something on their back: HCE has a hump or a hunch—"with a hump of grandeur on him like a walking wiesel rat" (*FW* 197.3–4)—and ALP has a sack that is at once a borrowed mailbag full of letters, a collection of litter, a bag of presents, ill-gotten plunder, a pipe full of tobacco (making her a candidate for the role of cad?), a bag of dirty laundry, and a womb full of children. Her "mixed baggyrhatty" (*FW* 209.10) is both divine and trivial, it is her godly burden ("the load is with me" [*FW* 214.19]) and a "Gaud" (*FW* 207.23), which is both a plaything and a joy (from the Latin *gaudere*). She is described as Santa Claus bringing every child a Christmas box apiece (*FW* 209.23, 27–28), alternately described as "the spoiled she fleetly laid at our door" (*FW* 209.28–29). By giving she spoils, but she is also a plunderer ("where in thunder did she plunder?" [*FW* 209.12]). She traffics in "maundy meerschaundize [merchandise, meerschaum pipe]" held in her "culdee sacco of wabbash [rubbish, Wabbash River]" (*FW* 210.2, 1). Next, her bag seems—like a magical pregnancy, half physical, half literary—to hold 1,001 children/tales/nights: "stinkers and heelers, laggards and primelads, her furzeborn sons and dribblederry daughters, a thousand a one of them, and wickerpotluck for each of them. For evil and ever. And kiks the buch [kiss the book]" (*FW* 210.3–6). This bag started out as a mailbag—a "mealiebag slang over her shulder" (*FW* 207.18–19, making it full of "slang"), a "zakbag, a shammy mailsack" that she'd borrowed from her son Shaun the Post (*FW* 206.9–10). Most importantly, however, ALP's bag, like HCE's hump, contains something hidden that can be variously interpreted. What both carry is a world of secrets.

It is secrets, in the end, that link the sexual, the textual, and the sacramental. Part of what allows Joyce's racy letters to Nora to move so fluidly between the "filthy" and the holy is that he understands the importance of privacy as that which connects the two. That is why he obsesses over the thought that Nora might have had contact with Cosgrave during the early stages of Joyce's own relationship with her; it is why he begs her to hide her drawers when they come back from the wash. The physical intimacy of Joyce and Nora partakes of the sacred in its honoring of their secret life together as well as in its refusal to shun any part of their shared reality. In his writing, Joyce is equally determined to see his subjects fully; as ALP writes in her letter about HCE, "He had to see life foully the plak and the smut, (schwrites)" (*FW* 113.13–14). Unexpectedly, perhaps, spirituality depends upon a similarly impartial willingness to accept the vastness of creation as something that can never be entirely known or mastered, whether we are contemplating a universe or simply a text designed to elude total control. Scripture is such an elusive text, and as such it resembles a human body, as we see when Issy collapses the two by referring to "our secret stripture" (*FW* 293n.2). Later, she swears by her own most cherished secrets and underwear, which reflect worlds of wonder: by "Sainte Andrée's Undershift, by all I hold secret from my world and in my underworld of nighties and naughties and all the other wonderwearlds!" (*FW* 147.26–28) Although *Finnegans Wake* may be, as Shaun suggests, "an openear secret" (*FW* 425.16), there is something both erotic and democratic in the obscurity of its satisfactions, which reminds all its unwatched and unwashed readers that there isn't one of us that couldn't use a cleansing, or an "outing" through publication: "Secret satieties and onanymous letters make the great unwatched as bad as their betters" (*FW* 435.31–32).

Above all, the "Anna Livia Plurabelle" episode urges readers to reevaluate their self-conceptions, accepting them as mottled, and doing so without shame or grandiosity. The good and the bad, the white and the black, the clean and the dirty inform one another, making the world more full of color and promise as well as threat.

3 ▸ ON SALMON

Joyce was always interested in odysseys. He might well have agreed with T. S. Eliot's lines in Four Quartets: *"And the end of all our exploring / Will be to arrive where we started / And know that place for the first time."[1] In* Ulysses, *a day was an epic-sized odyssey, but in* Finnegans Wake, *Joyce used a fish as his "Odysseus" figure. The salmon, which is born in fresh water but goes out to sea and then returns—somehow, arduously—to the freshwater place it was born to spawn and then usually dies, serves as a metaphor for the cycles of both reproductive sex (at least from a male point of view!) and death, if we see death as a "return." In Irish myth, the Salmon of Knowledge knows everything. As Joyce read it, the salmon's wisdom resembles that of a child.*

For over fifteen years, *Finnegans Wake* was known only by the provisional title *Work in Progress,* inspired by Ford Madox Ford when he published the first fragment in his *Transatlantic Review* in 1924 under the title "From Work in Progress."[2] Progress is a linear, temporal concept, one that suggests movement and development, but Joyce kept the title for many years. Either he had not yet decided on the overall structure of his evolving book, or else he kept his choice of title a secret. Textual evidence seems to favor the idea that the book's structure only coalesced in the last two years before it was published. Surprisingly, even grandly, this big, controversial book emerged as another odyssey, like the one that had shaped *Ulysses*, but it is important to ascertain what kind of an odyssey *Ulysses* was. Although the plot of *Ulysses* traces the course of a single day, it is also a portrait or perhaps "sculpture" of a man who both is and is not an artist, Leopold Bloom. Like Stephen Dedalus, Bloom has many flaws. Unlike many heroes, he is admirable not because he seems to approach perfection, but because his flaws, while compromising him, have not ruined him. Joyce subtly accents Bloom's shortcomings by calling the book devoted to him *Ulysses* instead of *Odysseus*, as it would have been titled if it referred only to Homer's *Odyssey*. *Ulysses* takes its name not from the *Odyssey*, but from Dante's *Inferno*. By using the Latin/Italian version of the name, Joyce points a shadowy finger at the fact that Dante placed Ulysses in hell as a trickster, a deceiver who was also a false leader who led his men to death. Joyce's hero, like most heroes, is also a villain, depending on where one's values lie. Via the title alone, Joyce subjects the idea of heroism to implicit scrutiny.[3]

Finnegans Wake, however, instead of being rooted in the Greek, Roman, and Italian epic traditions, was a specifically Irish Odyssey, which is why his "Odysseus" is a local fish. Joyce's night book, like its earlier counterpart of the day (*Ulysses*), depicts errancy, but the emphasis has changed. Instead of stressing a heroism shadowed by accusation, as in *Ulysses*, Joyce here makes transgression the main event. Not only is HCE himself culpable, undergoing a seemingly fatal fall at the outset of the book, but even the words used to record what happened to him seem "wrong." Errors in *Finnegans Wake* are not only portals of discovery, they are the precondition for wisdom, goodness, and grace, because as Joyce once wrote, there is no way to "the divine heart except across that sense of separation and loss that is called sin."[4] The book offers its readers an anti-morality: being good for the sake of goodness is not only *not* moral; it is nothing at all: neither thinking nor living. Transgression is the only avenue to greater understanding, and it is not a direct route. To quote Bob Dylan, "[T]here's no success like failure / And . . . failure's no success at all."

This is all to restate what Bloom thinks in *Ulysses*: "Longest way round is the shortest way home" (*U* 13.1110–1111). We only get anywhere by going away from it, by erring or straying, thereby spending the greatest percentage of our time feeling lost. As the narrator asks the reader in *Finnegans Wake*,

"You is feeling like you was lost in the bush, boy? You says: It is a puling sample jungle of woods" (*FW* 112.3–4). Reader, hero, dreamer must all lose their way even to have a hope of getting anywhere they might want to go.

The title of *Finnegans Wake* is most obviously rooted in the mid-nineteenth-century Irish American comic song, "Tim Finnegan's Wake," about an Irish mason who falls from a ladder, dies, and is resurrected at his wake when one of the mourners/celebrants spills whiskey in the coffin. The removal of the apostrophe from "Finnegan's" in Joyce's title pulls the reader away from identifying the book too closely with the song. Nonetheless, the book's major structural components all have some verbal stake in the name "Finnegan," and more precisely in the word "fin" (or "finn") with which it begins. Not only is *Finnegans Wake* about death (Fr. *fin*, or "end") and resurrection ("again"), but it is also *fun*, and about fish, designated by their fins. Jesus was represented by an *icthys*, or fish, but in this Irish epic Joyce lays particular emphasis on one kind of fish commonly found around Ireland: the salmon. The salmon works in several ways to structure the book: first, it is a fish with fins; second, it is a fish that undergoes an odyssey, since it journeys back to the place it was spawned to lay its own eggs (slowly dying while it does so, since it has become a saltwater ocean fish that goes back against the current to freshwater streams, although a small number survive to return to the ocean). Third, the salmon in Irish mythology is the joyous equivalent and alternative to the fruit of knowledge in Judeo-Christian lore, and it is connected with another Finn, Finn MacCool, the ancient Irish hero who mistakenly tasted it, thereby acquiring the knowledge of all things. Finally, the title is also haunted by the name of Mark Twain's Huckleberry Finn, the American boy who goes on an odyssey of his own at the age of fourteen with a runaway black slave, learning in the process something about the ethics of the white lie (or cunning fiction) of which Odysseus was the first recorded master.

Finnegans Wake urges "Finn" to come again and again (*FW* 628.14), but the Finns it calls to are multiple, and although they are primarily Irish and American, they are meaningfully related to the Greek Odysseus. I would like to go through each of these "finns" in turn, showing how they work in isolation and how they interconnect with one another to draw attention to different aspects and implications of the book's cyclical structure. But the main point I want to underscore at the outset is that by giving his book the title *Finnegans Wake* at the time of publication, Joyce took a work long associated with linear development, his "Work in Progress," and transformed it into a work that moves in cycles, and circles: it concerns circumlocution in space punctuated by the periodic cycles of time. Its structure emphasizes the interdependence of these spatial and temporal cycles. To fall and rise is also to experience exile and return, sleep and waking, darkness and light, ignorance and knowledge, death and rebirth.

Anyone with a sensitivity to homophones as marked as Joyce's will know that in English, the Christian narrative is closely linked to the fall and rise of the sun, since it begins with the Fall of Eve (evening) and climaxes with the rise of the Son (sun). This diurnal rhythm is important to both *Ulysses* and *Finnegans Wake,* in reverse order (*Ulysses,* Joyce's day book, begins with the rise of the sun; *Finnegans Wake,* his night book, with the fall of Eve and Adam). Both books also have a relation to Joyce's long connection with Nora Barnacle, who became his wife: *Ulysses* was set on the day he first walked out with her, June 16, 1904, and *Finnegans Wake* evokes the name of Finn's Hotel, where she was working as a chambermaid when Joyce first met her. But the main structural pattern I will address here is the master narrative: the odyssey—exile and return—of the salmon.

As he entered the final consolidating stages of composition in 1937–1938, Joyce seemed to be looking for complex matrices to draw together as many different motifs as possible. The salmon was one such matrix, partly because of its importance in early Celtic mythology, partly because it prepared a ground for the acceptance of Jesus as *icthys,* a wise fish that could be fed to the multitudes; partly because of its association with wisdom and imagination; and partly because actual salmon seem to do magical things as they return to the rivers where they were born in order to spawn: they can not only navigate back to their place of origin with astonishing accuracy, swimming upstream while fasting to do so, but they also overcome obstacles, leaping as high as twelve feet to surmount a waterfall cascading the other way (the word "salmon" comes from the Latin *salmo,* "to leap"). Salmon, then, are natural "homers" (or Odysseuses); they go home to spawn and die (90–95 percent of salmon die after spawning), and no one knows exactly how they find their way back. Some theories say they navigate by the stars; some say they pick up the merest traces of pheromones in the water.

The Salmon of Knowledge is a representation of the book itself— *Finnegans Wake*—as can be seen through two different lenses: the Christian and the Celtic. Remember Joyce's theological view of communion or communication: to take communion, or to communicate, is to incorporate the body—and thereby the being—of another into one's own with love. This action has inescapably erotic overtones, as we can hear in Jesus's words, commemorated in the language of the liturgy: "This is my body, which is given for you. Do this in remembrance of me"(Luke 22:19–20).[5] It is relatively easy to understand why the early Christian Church was pushed toward asceticism, given the ease with which the language of the Eucharist can be eroticized, thereby making Christianity even more socially threatening than it already was. The other dimension of communication that is important is that it isn't enough to *hear* a word (or Word); one must make it part of oneself, ingest and digest it. Through the act of eating, communicants perform an oral version of what Mary did when she became pregnant with the Word through listening: the Word is incorporated, so that it can be expressed not only through the lips, but also quite literally in the bodily lives of the communicants.

Communication, then, has an erotic dimension as well as nurturing and literary overtones: communication enables us to feed thousands with a relatively modest amount of verbal or literal "food" (bread or fish!). Furthermore, the listener/communicant, like a woman, takes another person's life—represented through his or her body—into her own. Now let us replace the liturgical lens with what in Ireland was an earlier mythical one by thinking about the salmon in relation to Finn MacCool (MacCumhaill). Mac Cumhaill is similar to Jesus in that he was believed to be a god due to "his ability to overcome death." Every time he dies, "he is somehow taken away to a hidden place where he 'sleeps' and will return to his people when he is needed" (MacKillop 7). Salmon are frequently found in Celtic folktales, where they are often associated with wisdom and prophecy. They were said to inhabit sacred wells, feeding on the hazelnuts that fell from the tree of life.

Of course, there are many different versions of the Finn legends, but I'm going to rely here on a few that Joyce would have had access to.[6] This first story is from Jeremiah Curtin's 1889 *Myths and Folk-Lore of Ireland*.[7] Finn's father, Cumhal MacArt, knew that he would be killed in the first battle he fought after he married, and so he delayed marriage for a long time. When he could no longer bear to put off marriage, he asked his mother to take care of the son that would be born after his death, because his wife's father (the king) would want to kill it. When the boy was born, the king had it

FIGURE 8. The Salmon of Knowledge eating hazelnuts. Illustration from *Irish Literature*, vol. 8, edited by Justin McCarthy. P. F. Collier and Son, 1904. Wikimedia Commons.

immediately thrown out the castle window into a loch to be drowned. The newborn sank, but after a while he rose again "and came to land holding a live salmon in his hand" (Curtin 205). Then Cumhal's mother knew that this was indeed her grandson, and she undertook to raise him in secret in a room of an old oak tree in the forest.

The best-known salmon story, though, is the one in which Finn tastes the Salmon of Knowledge. Joyce jotted down notes about this story in B.VI.30:30 from Cross and Slover's *Ancient Irish Tales*.[8] Here, the salmon's significance is primarily epistemological, and the knowledge it gives Finn is a good thing (unlike the fruit of the tree of life, which brings knowledge of good and evil but also sin and death in the Judeo-Christian tradition). Finn (then named Demni) went to learn poetry from Finneces, a druid who had searched all his life for the Salmon of Knowledge, which he finally caught. He instructed Finn to cook it, warning him not to eat any of it. As the fish cooked, Finn burned his thumb on it and put it in his mouth, whereupon he gained all the salmon's wisdom. He could thereafter recall this wisdom whenever he sucked his thumb. When the druid Finneces (see *FW* 377.16) saw that Finn had received the fish's knowledge, he renamed him: "Finn is thy name, my lad, and to thee was the salmon given to be eaten, and indeed thou art the Finn." This is how Finn got his name—from an encounter with a fish. And that name means "bright." (In other versions the name is more closely connected to the whiteness of Finn's hair.)

Interestingly, Curtin's version of this story is more closely related to Greek myth than the one in Cross and Slover. In Curtin's version, Finn and his dog Bran lie down to rest in a cave full of goats, and a little later the inhabitant of the cave returns, a one-eyed giant (like Polyphemus in the *Odyssey*) who has a salmon in his hands. He tells Finn to cook the fish and not to let it blister, so when it develops a blister Finn tries to push it down with his thumb and burns himself. He puts his thumb in his mouth "and gnawed the skin to the flesh, the flesh to the bone, the bone to the marrow; and when he had tasted the marrow, he received the knowledge of all things" (Curtin 211). He learns from his marrow that he (like Odysseus in the cave of the Cyclops) must put out the giant's eye, and when he does so the giant tells him he'll never get out alive. But Finn skins one of the giant's goats and puts it over him, and when the giant takes it by the horns, Finn slips away.

The story of the Salmon of Knowledge makes several things apparent: First, from an Irish point of view knowledge (or wisdom) is far from dangerous; on the contrary, it is constructive, desirable, and rare. Second, one can attain such knowledge by eating or incorporating a once-living body, as in the Christian Eucharist. Third, knowledge is associated not only with wisdom (heart-knowledge), but also with imagination and wonder, as we can tell by the fact that Finn can access it when he sucks his thumb (like a child; Joyce made a special note of this: "thumb in mouth," in Buffalo Notebook B.VI.41.[9] Salmon is rejuvenating, a distant cousin of the fountain of youth. Moreover, as something that lives beneath the surface of the water, the salmon (like Melville's white whale) can also function as an image of a being at home in the murky depths of the unconscious mind. We're getting closer to the nature of *Finnegans Wake*: to incorporate this book, a reader must recapture the wisdom and imaginative openness of a child, navigating by the stars or sensual memory rather than reason.

Even in the Finn cycle of tales, the salmon is associated with sexuality as well as knowledge. When Finn is pursuing Diarmuid and Finn's wife Grania after they ran off together, he follows a trail of uncooked salmon. As Joyce noted in the same Buffalo Notebook, "Know, O reader, that Diarmuid kept himself from Grainne, and that he left a spit of flesh uncooked [in Doire Da Both] as a token to Finn...that he had not sinned with Grainne, and... also that he left the second time seven salmon uncooked upon the bank of the Leaman."[10] Uncooked salmon is a symbol of chastity; by extension, once the salmon is cooked and eaten, that chastity is a thing of the past. Another of Joyce's notes reads "buncooked fish/Gr virgin" (B.VI.30 36 [44]), which Danis Rose and John O'Hanlon link to the following passage in *Finnegans Wake*: "Fisht! And it's not now saying how we are where who's softing what rushes. Merryvergin forbed!" (*FW* 376.33).[11] Here, merry virgins and the Virgin Mary are combined in their eagerness to go to bed, which is simultaneously a statement about what virginal Marys forbid.

The references to salmon in Celtic tales are even more pervasive and interconnected than I can do justice to here. To give just one additional example: when Finn comes to study poetry with the druid Finneces, Finneces is on the River Boyne, watching the salmon in Fec's Pool. But the Boyne was supposedly created when the goddess Boann attempted to draw water from the Salmon's well, which caused a flood. That well became the source of the River Boyne, which was named after Boann. Remarkably, Joyce synthesized the Christian, Celtic, and biological references to produce what amounts to a theory of salmon as one of several embodiments of communication, sexuality, and knowledge that would stand for the book itself.

To appreciate this synthesis, we should go back to some facts about the actual fish. Salmon tend to spawn from November to December in Great Britain and Ireland, which links their activity loosely to the time of the Christian nativity (and the setting of *Finnegans Wake* at the end/beginning of the year). Female salmon lay between 450 and 900 eggs per pound of body weight in depressions or "redds" they excavate in the riverbed where they themselves were born. The male salmon immediately fertilize the eggs, then the females cover them with gravel and 90–95 percent of the parents die. Depending on the water temperature, the eggs hatch and young fish called "alevins" remain in the redd, nourished by the yolk sac, for a few more weeks (94 percent of the eggs make it to the alevin stage).[12] They emerge from the gravel in April or May (around Easter), when they are one inch long. Only 8 percent of these "fry" will still be alive by the end of the first year. As they grow, they develop markings on their sides and are then known as "parr." They will stay in the river anywhere from one to five years, and then the fish, now known as "smolts," leave the river during the late spring to the deep-sea feeding areas, where they remain for one to three years. Most "grilse" (salmon that spend only one winter at sea before returning to spawn) feed in the Norwegian Sea, a fact that is important for *Finnegans Wake*'s Scandinavian and Viking motifs. Those who stay at sea longer tend to have the furthest migrations.

Amazingly, the age of a salmon can be told by concentric rings on its scales, not unlike the rings of a tree. During the warmer months, when the salmon grow and are feeding rapidly, the rings are more widely spaced, but in winter months salmon go for months without food and the rings, or "circuli," are closer together, forming a dark band called an "annulus." By counting the annuli or winter bands you can tell the age of a salmon. As far as the sex of the salmon is concerned, the males and females look very similar until they have been back from the sea for a little while, when the head of the males become elongated and they develop a protuberance called a "kype" from their lower jaw (kind of like a beard).[13]

The astonishing movement of salmon from the sea back to the freshwater rivers, where they swim upstream and jump waterfalls to return to the river from which they began, navigating "magically" with great accuracy, helps to illustrate the "odyssey" of *Finnegans Wake*, which also circles back on itself. They are most active after heavy rain (remember they don't eat anything once they enter fresh water, sometimes for many months). When they are jumping waterfalls, they must rest between jumps. Perhaps the best (and most famous) description of this phenomenon is by Robert Lowell, in the marvelous tetrameter lines of "Waking Early Sunday Morning":

O to break loose, like the Chinook
salmon jumping and falling back,
nosing up to the impossible
stone and bone-crushing waterfall—

raw-jawed, weak-fleshed there stopped by ten
steps of the roaring ladder, and then
to clear the top on the last try,
alive enough to spawn and die.[14]

Most salmon do die after spawning, but some—mainly females—survive to spawn two or three times (they return to sea in between spawnings).

Here are just a few of the multiple salmon references in *Finnegans Wake*, which illustrate how salmon serve to intertwine Christian, mythological, geographical, and artistic threads. In I.1, after Tim Finnegan ("good Mr. Finnemore") has been waked, the people at the funeral are trying to make him take it easy and lie back in his coffin, and they recall how he sat in a pub, here known as the Salmon House: "The menhere's always talking of you sitting around on the pig's cheeks under the sacred rooftree, over the bowls of memory where every hollow holds a hallow, with a pledge till the drengs, in the Salmon House" (*FW* 25.11–15). A little later, after exhorting him to "Repose you now! Finn [sin] no more," these same speakers swear by "that samesake sibsubstitute of a hooky salmon" (*FW* 28.33–35). In I.ii, the salmon is connected with the Boyne, with music, and with a tongue-in-cheek "salvation" for readers, identified as subjects of a Finn who is here both king and saint: the thrummings of a fiddle "caressed the ears of the subjects of King Saint Finnerty the Festive who, in brick homes of their own and in their flavory fraiseberry beds, heeding hardly cry of honeyman, soed lavender or foyneboyne salmon alive, with their priggish mouths all open for the larger appraisiation of this longawaited Messiagh of roaratorios" (*FW* 41.23–28). In I.iv, "Massa Ewacka" is compared to a salmon in fresh water who has stopped feeding: "like the salmon of his ladderleap all this time of totality secretly and by suckage feeding on his own misplaced fat" (*FW* 79.11–13). In the "Quiz" episode (I.6), the long description of HCE (identified by the answer "Finn MacCool") insists that "as for the salmon he was coming up in him all life long" (*FW* 132.35–36). In the same chapter, ALP swears by "Holy eel and Sainted Salmon" (*FW* 141.2–3). We know that Shem prefers "Gibsen's tea-time salmon tinned . . . to the . . . friskiest parr" (*FW* 170.26–28). Perhaps most importantly, in II.iii the salmon is identified as subliminal, an incarnation of unconscious awareness and sexual instinct, also associated with the wisdom of Solomon: "And be that semeliminal salmon solemonly angled ingate and outgate" (*FW* 337.9–10). Angling in and out, the wise and sexual salmon advises readers and characters to leave the letter to look for the "latter" (which is mortal life, but also the salmon ladder that helps aged travelers go back to where they began): "Leave the letter that never begins to go find the latter that ever comes to end, written in smoke and blurred by mist and signed of solitude, sealed at night" (FW 337.11–14).

Now we can return to the question of the eroticism of the salmon. The following conclusion is based on the synthesis of all that I have just sketched out, and it surprisingly confirms and expands Joyce's earlier interest in the Odyssey and helps to explain why he asked David Fleischman for a detailed synopsis of Huckleberry Finn in August 1937—an American Odyssey connected with another, younger Finn. Salmon, through their determination to get back to the place where they began, represent both the magic and the unlikelihood of human sexual reproduction. Specifically, they capture some of the strangeness of reproduction from the point of view of the male, as during heterosexual intercourse he reenters the birth canal from which he had emerged as an infant in order to fertilize eggs in the living "river" (or River Liffey) of the female. He undergoes un petit mort, a little death, in so doing. This process is not just sexual; for Joyce, it also describes the labors of artistic reproduction and helps to explain why Joyce returned with such specificity to the Ireland from which he was spawned for the settings of all his fiction. He made himself into the fish, icthys (an acronym for "Jesus Christ God Son Savior" in Greek), that which was designed to be eaten by millions for generations in an effort to facilitate communication that was corporeal as well as spiritual (the sign of the fish was used by Christians in Hellenistic and Roman Greece to indicate a secret meeting, and also to mark the location of a funeral). "Excruciated, in honour bound to the cross of [his] own cruelfiction" (FW 192.18–19), the salmon-writer dies in the effort to spawn, to continue the cycle of performing and facilitating future arduous and exciting homings. To eat the Salmon of Knowledge, or to read Finnegans Wake, is a difficult and strangely pleasurable "death sentence," but that it is not all. It is also a kind of rejuvenation, because as we travel back to where we came from; we grow younger at the same time. Like Finn MacCool, we not only learn many wondrous bits of knowledge, but we also put our thumbs in our mouths and remember, with childlike creativity, how to dream.

In 1937 and stretching into 1938, Joyce began to shape his massive work in progress for publication, after fourteen years of sedimenting and then expanding its layers (*Finnegans Wake* was published under its new title in 1939). Joyce had been slowly compiling it from notes and drafts, spending a total of seventeen years on its composition. As most people who have opened the book know, it incorporates sounds and spellings from more than forty languages, incorporating them into a structure that is "basically English" (*FW* 116.26). It is as much song as language; it makes "sense," but that sense should be understood not just in the usual way, as meaning (facilitated by convention and directed to the reason), but also as sensual perception. As Joyce put it, it is "nat language at any sinse of the world" (*FW* 83.12). It is directed first and foremost to the eyes and ears, a multilingual performance that unfolds in the darkness of the receptive mind. It is the only book in the history of the world to attempt to encompass the entire globe—not as an abstraction, but by reproducing verbal sounds from as many different countries as possible and allowing these sounds to be heard through English. It is as (comically) ambitious in its treatment of time as in its treatment of place: it attempts to incorporate sediment from multiple times and places, preserving moments from different epochs of world history into a moving river of sound and fragmented images. Finally, it attempts to replicate or enact the movements of the unconscious mind in sleep, to speak in the irrational "language" of dream. And it does this with an exquisite, almost unbearable particularity, fracturing the word in a way comparable to the "*abnihilisation of the etym*" (*FW* 353.22, "atom" here spelled as if it were the beginning of "etymology"). It is a verbal "echoland" (*FW* 13.5) that evokes the ghosts of half-forgotten phrases to resound beyond the text, in the tomb and womb of the reader's head. It is a book unlike any other: a raucous, irreverent, decomposed and embryonic, nonsensical and inspiring accumulation of letters, sounds, and images that goes on, theoretically, forever, since the book ends in the middle of a sentence that picks up again at the beginning.

The method that Joyce used to compose the book was one of decomposition combined with sedimentation: he broke down words, stories, songs, nursery rhymes, proper names of people and places in various languages and layered them, thereby producing a kitchen midden or an archaeological wasteheap-cum-treasure trove of linguistic artifacts. Joyce seemed to have no idea where this book was going, or even what form it would take, when he began taking notes for it in 1922–1923. He read prodigiously, widely, and opportunistically, not unlike a bird in search of worms, noting pieces of information or turns of phrase that struck him. As he began to draft episodes, he would go through his notebooks with a colored pencil and "harvest" phrases for incorporation into what was then a relatively straightforward draft. Different sweeps through the notebook are marked by different colored pencils, as layer upon layer of linguistic and literary references were superimposed upon the draft. By adding different layers of sound and signification, Joyce was putting the English language through a prism that allows readers to see and hear the obscured kinship of one word to many others in English and in other languages. He thereby exposed the hidden "colors" of language, showing how everyday speech is like light, composed of a spectrum of colors that are ordinarily invisible. These "colors" come from the similarity in spelling, sound, or etymology of one word to several others, a kinship that is typically only registered in the fleeting surrealist cinema of dream, or in the errors produced amid drunken revelry.

As the text evolved in time, subject to vision and re-vision, audition and fresh audition, enriched by more and more additions from Joyce's reading, Joyce referred to it only as *Work in Progress*. But as Europe grew increasingly dangerous and his material grew under his hands, he turned to the question of how to give his book a human shape and a name. He had solved that problem in *Ulysses* by giving the book the Latin name of a Greek hero of an ancient epic. Joyce's epic was about a man of Jewish descent, and he was delighted to discover Victor Bérard's theory that the *Odyssey* had a semitic origin, since it ratified his desire to make his work the textual embodiment of a "jewgreek" Irishman (*U* 15.2098). In searching for the title of *Finnegans Wake*, he found a similar unifying matrix in the American, Viking, and Irish character(s) of Finn, specifically the Irish American Tim Finnegan from the eponymous ballad; Finn MacCool (who was not only Irish, but according to Heinrich Zimmer, the "Victor Bérard" of *Finnegans Wake*, had a Scandinavian origin); and the American boy-hero, Huck Finn. (I am leaving out Finland, *fíonghort* (Irish for vineyard), *fíonghal* (Irish for fratricide), *finner* (a genus of whales with a dorsal fin), *fíon* (Irish for wine), and *finnoc*, a white trout that is a kind of salmon.)

The implicit comparison of *Finnegans Wake* with a drinking song ("Tim Finnegan lived in Walkin Street, / A gentle Irishman mighty odd") highlights the way the book aims to unify the spirit-ual (or spirit-filled) and the debauched, while drawing attention to language as music, collectively sung—what Joyce would call "storiella as she is syung" (*FW* 267.7–8). The ears are called "eyes of the darkness" (*FW* 14.29), and whiskey, like the River Liffey, is closely associated with the water of life through the meaning of *usquebaugh* in Irish and the proximity of the name Liffey to life.

The Finn MacCool material that Joyce drew upon, as I have tried to show, is rich and varied. According to Jacques Mercanton, who visited Joyce in the late 1930s with the idea of writing a book on *Finnegans Wake,* Joyce "expatiated on the character of Finn MacCool, the legendary Irish hero, the universal protagonist of his book."[15] The earliest gathering of Finn allusions dates from 1937.

Returning, like a salmon, to the place where one was spawned figures a return to the joy and knowledge of childhood. As Yeats wrote in the preface to *Gods and Fighting Men,* "The men who imagined the Fianna had the imagination of children," and the Fianna themselves are like children; everything they do "they do for the sake of joy"; "they live always as if they were playing a game."[16] And here is where (and how) Finn MacCool begins to overlap with Mark Twain's *Huckleberry Finn.*

HUCKLEBERRY FINN

In August 1937, Joyce wrote to David Fleischman, his son George's stepson, to ask him to read *Huckleberry Finn* for him (Joyce has just sent him a registered copy of what he calls a "cheap edition" that David could mark up and return to Joyce). He tells him he has never read it and has nobody to read it to him, and he asks David (now eighteen) to dictate to his mother "an account of the plot in general as if it were a new book the tale of which you had to narrate in a book review. After that I should like you to mark with blue pencil in the margin the most important passages of the plot itself and in red pencil here and there wherever the words or dialogue seem to call for the special attention of a European" (*SL* 387). In a subsequent letter to Helen Joyce, David's mother, dated September 11, 1937, Joyce registers his response: "Thanks for the precis of the book. It is what I wanted. The markings not so much. But I can find my way, I now see. I shall have to start back with *Tom Sawyer* so am reading that to Jolas. I like Twain's preface. It would suit *WiP.* And even a cursory glance at the text shows me that Pound, Hemingway, McAlmon and the others all came out of Samuel I. Clemens' work-basket."[17]

Luca Crispi has written that *Huckleberry Finn* has little genetic significance because it was a late addition to the text, and that is probably true for geneticists, who are primarily interested in the growth of the text through revision.[18] But Twain's book is of great significance conceptually if what Joyce was using it to do was to provide an American equivalent for Finn MacCool, and to understand the two figures together—in relation to the salmon—as human literary embodiments of the book he completed through its name.

Why was Joyce interested in *Huckleberry Finn*? Was it just the verbal coincidence of the name, reinforced by the felicity of the fact that it was penned by a man who had taken the name of Twain, meaning "in two pieces"? This book was important enough for Joyce to have inserted it into his schema in the final stages of the book's composition partly because he saw it as an American *Ulysses,* or *Odyssey,* set on the Mississippi (which Joyce parallels with the River Liffey when he refers to it as Missisliffi [*FW* 159.12–13]). Lionel Trilling compared *Ulysses* with *Huckleberry Finn* early on.[19] Whereas *Finnegans Wake* takes as its hero an older man with the kind of active curiosity more often found in children (HCE is described as an "overgrown babeling" [6.31]), *Huckleberry Finn* focuses on a fourteen-year-old boy whose rough-and-tumble experiences have made him prematurely old. In this respect Huck is comparable to Finn MacCool, a white-haired man who periodically sucks his thumb for guidance.

Even more strikingly, *Huckleberry Finn* may be said to have a compound protagonist, Huck and Jim, who epitomize the racial tensions that divide the United States as surely as the river they ride on divides its east from its west. The book's two heroes are younger and older, white and black, respectively. As they ride naked on a raft at night toward what they believe to be freedom, they emerge as not only opposite, but comparable in their wholeness. Both are depicted as a compound of white and black: Huck needs to "keep dark," and Jim is described as "white inside."[20]

Like HCE, Finn MacCool, and Huck's own father, Huck repeatedly dies and comes back to life. His father was believed drowned, but they eventually find out the drowned person was a woman. Then when they find a body in a floating house, neither the reader nor Huck knows who it is until the very last page, when Jim tells Huck that the dead man was Huck's father. Unlike his drunken father, however, Huck deliberately stages his own death—he creates evidence that he was murdered, which allows him to free himself from his father (203). Several times in the novel he is taken for a ghost, which resonates with Joyce's comparable appreciation of Finn MacCool as "a great shadow." Not only does Huck straddle the line between white and black, dead and alive, he also twice impersonates a girl, thereby linking himself with both sexes. First, he passes himself off as Sarah Williams, and at the end of the novel he again dresses up as a girl when Tom and Sid are freeing Jim.

However, the most important contribution that America makes to the naming of Finn and its importance as a context for *Finnegans Wake* is that it articulates what might be called a *morality of fiction*: a truthful or ethical mode of lying, not for profit but for freedom and survival. In this respect, Huck resembles Ulysses/Odysseus in his possession of *mêtis*, or cunning. Jim, Huck, and Tom form a kind of human spectrum that ranges from adherence to literal truth (Jim) to outlandish, even baroque lies (Tom); Huck occupies a middle position between the two. Jim wants people to say what they mean, whereas Tom colorfully tries to do everything in the most complicated way possible: the way they do it in books: "I've seen it in books; and so of course that's what we've got to do" (9). The pitfalls of Tom's method are demonstrated by what he puts Jim through in helping him "escape" at the end of the book, all of which was unnecessary because, unbeknownst to him, Jim was already free. Tom's insistence on designing what he considers a "romantic" escape, complete with rats, spiders, writing in blood, and digging a tunnel, emphasizes his commitment to stylish literary adventure that is exposed as irresponsible and even cruel. He objects that Huck's plan is "too blame simple" and says "I bet we can find a way that's twice as long" (211). In contrast to Jim's literalism and Tom's fanciful irresponsibility, Huck asserts that "sometimes the truth is better, safer than a lie" (169).

Finnegans Wake is like one of the stories told in *Huckleberry Finn* about a haunted barrel: it is a book with a dead and buried "baby" inside, a baby that babbles like the River Liffey. Its imprecations to Finn to wake, again, depend upon the instability between "finn" and "fun," a fun haunted by intimations of funeral (the wakean word for which is "funferall" [*FW* 13.15]). MacKillop argues that the Irish pronunciation of Fionn is "fewn," the first syllable of "funeral" (165). Like *Huckleberry Finn, Finnegans Wake* stresses the importance of understanding truth as something to be understood as double (Dublin, or Twain): it is not literal, practical, and plain, nor is it a romantic elaboration that causes unnecessary pain to oneself and others (Tom's devotion to romance gets him shot, but not fatally). Instead, truth emerges as a Houdini-style lie, designed not to cheat others but to keep the self alive and contradictory—white and black, old and young, male and female—always in the dark, as it flows down the Mississippi or Missisliffi rivers of life.

FIN, OR THE END

Of course, *Finnegans Wake* ends without ending, which is to say that the last sentence takes us back to the beginning, where that sentence is concluded: "A way a lone a last a loved a long the . . . riverrun, past Eve and Adam's, from swerve of shore to bed of bay, brings us by a commodius vicus of recirculation back to Howth Castle and Environs." We go back to where we started, like Odysseus or Huck, but the relief of return will be only a temporary respite before the next adventure or odyssey begins. Joyce takes us away from Dublin, via France and the United States, collapsed into "North Armorica" (*FW* 3.5). The book tells us it begins before "Sir Tristram" has returned from Brittany/North America by way of Cornwall to fight a "penisolate" war. I have focused not on the Brittany reference, which linguistically stresses the historical kinship between Brittany and Britain, but on the implicit association of Ireland and North America. *Finnegans Wake* prods us to recall that Ireland and the United States are both former colonies of England, and to ponder the significance of this connection. The next line draws our attention to Mark Twain's fiction— here *Tom Sawyer*—as an index of how Americanness might be seen as a double of Irishness: "nor had topsawyer's rocks by the stream Oconee exaggerated themselse to Laurence County's gorgios while they went doublin their mumper all the time" (*FW* 3.6–9). The clause is characteristically multilayered: it calls out for excavation via research, which has taught generations of scholars to learn that there is a Dublin in Laurens County Georgia with the motto "Doubling all the time" that was founded on the River Oconee. Moreover, Dublin, Georgia, has a formation called Topsawyer's Rock by a Dubliner named Sawyer.[21] At the outset of the novel, Joyce puts a growing America typified by *Tom Sawyer* (and his friend Finn) in dialogue with its smaller Irish cousin.

The odyssey that Joyce invites the reader to take brings us back to Dublin, at the beginning and end, via the rest of the world, but especially via North Armorica. We are brought back to the place from which we started in the hope that we may know that place for the first time. Such odysseys are compared to those of the salmon, for which dying and spawning (or rebirth) are simultaneous. ALP, as she flows moaning out to sea toward her death, her childhood, and her "cold, mad, feary father" commands, "Finn, again!" (*FW* 628.14) The book has put reason to sleep in the hope of awakening it. Like dreams and odysseys, it goes by contraries: the longest way round is the shortest way home. In our beginning is our end. Thus ends Joyce's long and difficult swan song. Finn, again!

4 ▸ ON WRITING BY HAND

Handwriting is a fast-disappearing art. Many schools no longer teach cursive, and few people believe that graphology reflects personality. Most of us now tap on keyboards rather than trace curves with a pen, and increasingly AI may enhance or even provide(!) the content. These changes may make Joyce's interest in writing, especially writing by hand, seem quaint. However, much of Finnegans Wake *is concerned with writing and penmanship (Shem is a Penman). Writing by hand obviously involves the body, as well as the bodies of birds and animals (the first pen was a quill, the primary wing feather of a large bird, and for centuries paper was skin, especially that of a young calf, such as the vellum of the Book of Kells). Joyce's writing always began by hand (manuscript) before more finished versions were given to a typist. In writing by hand, he was following a tradition: some of the most famous manuscripts in Irish history were recorded by scribes, and were handmade copies of important books, such as the Christian Gospels. Such copies left room for originality, though, as in the colorful illuminations that festoon the letters of the Book of Kells (see chapter 10, "On Letters").*

Joyce used the labor and skill of writing by hand to illustrate the double valence of literature more generally. Writing is an art, but it can also be seen as a

form of identity theft, if characters are drawn from actual people. In Finnegans
Wake, *Joyce's metaphor for such theft is forgery. Joyce was acutely aware that
realism (reproducing what is seen and heard) is a form of stealing life from others
for one's own ends. He uses the image of himself as a forger to offset his own
youthful tendency to idealize writers. Finally, Joyce extends the two sides of
writing—as creativity and theft—to what it means to be human. Outside of car-
toons, there are no heroes and villains. Every individual is both extraordinary
and deeply flawed.*

Joyce has a reputation for scurrilousness for his refusal to disavow the dirt
of being human. This refusal is best illustrated by his response when an
adoring fan came up to him in Zurich and asked, "May I kiss the hand that
wrote *Ulysses*?" Joyce answered, "No. It's done a lot of other things too."
Joyce always saw himself and his avocation of writing through a double
lens: whether he was decried as obscene and impenetrable or celebrated as
the greatest writer of the twentieth century, he maintained the careful discipline of representing himself as human, all too human: as someone whose
humanity spanned the full distance from divinity to excrement. An artist, in
his view, was not only someone who made art, but also a con artist (which
is—or was—the slang meaning of "artist" in Dublin). More specifically,
writing involves a talent for capturing other people's characteristics, which
is just a hair away from stealing other people's identities, manually "forging"
their unique signatures for profit and notoriety. Bloomsday, the day on
which *Ulysses* is set, could be crudely described as commemorating a hand
job in two very different senses of the term: it was the day Joyce walked out
with Nora Barnacle (and if we believe Brenda Maddox, Nora gave him a
hand job on that first outing[1]), and it's the day on which he set *Ulysses*,
painstakingly written and rewritten by hand over seven years.

Joyce represents not only his protagonists but also himself in his fiction
in ways that preserve this tension between exceptional talent and human
duplicity, a tension that is often enacted through manipulation (from the
medieval Latin *manipulare*, to lead by the hand). Not only are Bloom and
HCE based on figures with great strengths and criminal flaws (Odysseus
and Finn MacCool), but Joyce's semi-autobiographical characters, Stephen
Dedalus and Shem the Penman, are too. The Greek Daedalus was not only
an ingenious inventor and architect, whose creations included the maze he
built to contain the Minotaur, wings for humans, and the wooden cow that

allowed Pasiphae to mate with a bull. He was also a criminal who flung his twelve-year-old nephew "headlong down from Minerva's sacred citadel" and called it an accident. Daedalus was jealous of the inventiveness of his nephew, who had devised the saw and the compass when he was only a child.[2] After finishing *Ulysses*, Joyce chose a different model for his self-portrait, Jim the Penman (who is the basis for Shem the Penman in *Finnegans Wake*; he is even called Jim the Penman in the early drafts[3]), and once again he chose a criminal genius (with his own name) as a prototype for his semi-autobiographical double. Jim's crimes, however, were significantly different than those that haunted Daedalus. His sins sprang from love and a need for money. His crime, as well as his achievement, relied on manual dexterity, and a capacity to form mental images and capture characteristic rhythms to reproduce the unique traces (or "signatures") of others. His genius and his guilt are inextricably intertwined, and both are wrought by his own hand.

The greatest power of art is its capacity to accent the artificiality of *all* creation. Written expression is no more than a trace, a "crystallized gesture."[4] We learn to make these traces, these visible marks, by accepting a host of conventions that allow them to signify. Then two things happen—writing becomes habitual, and—simultaneously—it becomes more individual.[5] Like the world of material forms itself, the hand holding the pen is moving; it has a rhythm. Some traces last longer than others, but none are eternal, and none can do more than point at something in the flux of the real.

Writing is first and foremost a physical gesture, a bodily act that testifies to the fact *and* impermanence of embodiment. To write is to become a ghost and to create ghosts: to produce a transparent universe that may for an unpredictable length of time have a life of its own. To write is to balance presence and absence on the fulcrum of a moving, breaking line of graphite or ink: But why? Why do people make and respond to these tracings? And why was it important to Joyce not only to write, but to show himself writing, baring the device and accentuating the links between writing and the body even to the point of describing his ink as a product of his own feces and urine, and identifying his "paper" as his skin, "the only foolscap available"? What does it mean to be a penman, to hold a pen?

For Joyce, to write is to depersonalize oneself by multiplying the self—to forge other people's signatures, to appropriate their appearances,

manners of speaking, gestures, even their psychologies. It is to steal their
likeness, transferring it onto one's own page. In creating an imagined world,
the author simultaneously enhances and depletes the one that is external to
him or her. Writing is both an act of creation—a reproduction (in both
senses) of the self—and a crime—a theft from oneself (a loss of flesh, as
well as feces and urine) and the world. Joyce responds to the sense of
simultaneous transgression and transcendence by emphatically refusing to
endorse the myth of his own heroism or superiority, as we can see from his
partly excoriating portraits of himself as Stephen Dedalus and Shem the
Penman. He insists upon depicting himself as a protagonist who is also an
antagonist, a gifted yet fallible being who, while admirable in some respects,
is hard to like.

Shem the Penman is based not only on Joyce himself, but also on Jim the
Penman, an infamously successful forger. At the end of *Portrait,* Stephen
had vowed to "forge in the smithy of [his] soul the uncreated conscience of
[his] race" (*P* 213), but Stephen's intended meaning there was different: to
forge is to create something strong and unique out of metals heated to high
temperatures. (Joyce, however, is arguably aware of the other meaning of
forge as "to fake" even here, which allows him to accent the pretentiousness
of Stephen's goal). Increasingly, Joyce used it in its less glorious, more risky
sense to describe his writing. Forgery is clearly a form of impersonation, but
one that is performed, not through facial resemblances or imitated gestures,
but by copying the movement of someone's hand while writing *without hesitancy* (because any change in the rhythm will affect the pen stroke). Such an
understanding of the role of hesitancy in forgery could help to explain
Joyce's interest in the Piggott forgery that caused a scandal for Charles
Stewart Parnell. Piggott forged a letter that seemed to implicate Parnell in
the Phoenix Park murders of 1882. The forgery was exposed during the trial
by focusing on the word "hesitancy," which the forger misspelled. Parnell
spelled it correctly and was vindicated.

Forging a signature is a testamentary impersonation that is difficult to do
successfully, because handwriting, even more than character development,
involves reproducing a learned pattern that becomes increasingly individual
over time. Producing a signature requires a highly coordinated series of
movements by more than twenty muscles. Some are large and powerful,
others no thicker than a cat's whisker and capable of making the most subtle
and sensitive adjustments.[6] Forgery, then, is both an art and a craft devoted

to deception; the forger impersonates someone else's hand to steal money from him without his knowledge and consent, while gaining the authorization for doing so from the "hand" of the victim himself.

Joyce uses the allegations of forgery to counter the implicit self-approval that might otherwise be associated with the portraits of himself he included in his fiction, and that were sometimes reflected back to him by his admirers. Shem the Penman, with its allusion to the nineteenth-century Jim the Penman, becomes Joyce's ultimate satiric self-portrait, the counterpoint to the admiring early image of himself as Stephen Hero. We can see this not only through the relation between writing and forgery, but also through the way the forger was depicted in popular fiction, melodrama, and film: as a sympathetic villain, a misguided genius who commits a very human sin for understandable reasons. This sin of imposture, of plagiarism, is "piously" committed by someone who denies the existence of original sin and believes in the efficacy of good works, like the Irish heretic Pelagius: "Who can say how many pseudostylic shamiana, how few or how many of the most venerated public impostures, how very many piously forged palimpsests slipped in the first place by this morbid process from his pelagiarist pen?" (*FW* 181.36–182.3). The writer-forger labors mightily and his impostures are "venerated," but the traces that slip from his pen are also "shams," instances of plagiarism, "pseudo" styles. The process of writing is described as morbid, or literally "diseased."

THE PLAY

Jim the Penman was an actual man who became a popular legend. James Townsend Saward was a working barrister who also led a check forging ring in London in the 1850s.[7] Saward was tried at the Old Bailey on March 5, 1857, and sentenced to transportation. His criminal genius was further popularized by a play, *Jim the Penman: A Romance of Modern Society in Four Acts,* a Victorian melodrama by Sir Charles Lawrence Young, which was written in 1879 and opened in 1886.[8] After this "powerful melodrama of London society" premiered at the Haymarket Theatre in London, it opened a few months later in New York (on November 1, 1886), where it became "one of the greatest triumphs in the history of the New York stage," according to George Clinton Densmore Odell.[9] It was revived regularly for thirty years.

Joyce knew the play; he wrote to Sylvia Beach on July 17, 1924, "Could you please order for me from Samuel French a copy of an old play called *Jim the Penman*."[10]

The play enjoyed immense popularity. As a reviewer wrote in the *Los Angeles Times* for July 9, 1921, "You and I and John Smith, with our respective sweethearts, wives, mothers, and grandmothers, have seen 'Jim the Penman,' in its stage form, at least once, and probably more than twice." In *The Times* of London for June 19, 1913, a reviewer of one of the play's many revivals described the revived play's enthusiastic reception, and posited a reason for the play's continuing appeal: its "pathological ethics." The reviewer called it "right and proper" to combine forgery with heart disease, combining "poetic Justice with meticulous realism." The conclusion is that *Jim the Penman* is "a capital drawing-room melodrama," which he contrasted with the dullness of contemporary stage drawing rooms. It is "vastly amusing (in the grand sense of the term, as Mr. Henry James would say)—that is, thrilling, exciting, nerve-shaking—and it is acted with delightful gusto by all concerned . . . It is all an immense success" (p. 10). The play also gained the approval of religious authorities: it was identified as "good for Catholics to see in the theatres." (It was on the "white list" of the Catholic Theatre Movement that was sent to Catholics on April 10, 1914, a list of 135 approved plays produced over the last twenty-five years.[11])

What is most striking about the play is its movement toward the unmasking of an "invisible" agent known only as "Jim the Penman."[12] His identity is finally revealed on his daughter's wedding day, which falls on the anniversary of his own wedding, the day that he dies, significantly, of heart disease. The main theme of the play is that writing—forgery—is a crime of love. It begins as unconscious imitation, but it grows into a skill that can be used to make money and accrue power, at the cost of a constant fear of exposure. As James confides to Hartfeld, the man who has bound him to forgery for twenty years in return for not prosecuting him for his first offense, he longs "to live as other men live, to be happy with Nina and the children, to be without this horrible impression, this never ceasing dread, this feeling that the higher I climb the greater may be my fall. To be free from all this, oh God, what happiness!" (20). What destroys him is the necessity of living "with the knowledge [of what he has done] in his heart," combined with his dread of the day when his "wife and children know me for what I am!" (49). Act 3 climaxes in just such a moment, when Jim's wife tells him, "You won me for your wife by fraud. I am your wife no more!" (53) At the end of the play, when Jim has a heart attack and falls, Jim's old partner and enemy exclaims, "There is one enemy you cannot cheat—the heart!" (64). The play memorably dramatizes a view that despite the old adage, crime *does* pay, but it sickens the heart.

THE NOVEL

In 1901, a novel about Jim the Penman also appeared, by "Dick Donovan" (the pen name of Joyce Emerson Muddock[13]), which went through several printings, making it likely that Joyce either knew it or had heard of it. The author, in her prefatory note, described her subject as "a good linguist with cosmopolitan tendencies [who] chose the whole of Europe as his field of labour. . . . He changed his name as often as he changed his locality. . . . He was no ordinary, vulgar, commonplace criminal, but a Napoleon in the world of crime."[14] In the novel, "James"—like James Joyce—is an Irishman living in Paris. He turns to forgery as "an easy though dangerous method of living in ease and luxury" (3). His father had been ruined, and his son is in the stressful position of living beyond his means. His sin is extravagance— he was "the most hopeless of spendthrifts" (28)—which he redresses through his genius for forgery, and for escaping detection. Extravagance, or fiscal irresponsibility, is also one of Joyce's own flaws.[15]

This Jim's perspective is rather different from that of his theatrical coun- terpart: instead of being sick at heart and fearing exposure, he sees himself as skillfully and daringly subverting and profiting from an already preten- tious and materialistic social structure. As one of his associates points out, "Every one lives an artificial life more or less, and perhaps we are not many degrees worse than those who pose as saints" (52).[16] Jim decides to play "a great game" (51) when he discovers he has a genius for his particular con. He develops an ingeniously "scientific" method of forgery: he wets a docu- ment with water, then dips a camel-hair pencil into a tiny phial of white liquid and paints over the writing on, say, a letter of credit. He then dusts a fine violet-colored powder on the paper and moves it over the flame of a gas jet for a few seconds. He heats a small steel roller over the flame, polishes it with his handkerchief, and rolls the document to restore its original glaze and smoothness. Then he fills in the blanks he has created with an imitation of the original writing, substituting 20,000 pounds for 2,000 and claiming that "with a few strokes of my pen, wealth shall pour upon me" (58). Moreover, he defends his art by representing himself as an anti-hero "at war with society" (59).

For an understanding of Joyce's writing, the most important feature of "Dick Donovan's" Jim is not his scientific genius, but his facility for becoming so many different people, for playing such a variety of roles. We can see in him similarities to Shakespeare (as Stephen presents him in "Scylla and Charybdis"[17]), Bloom, and finally HCE, who goes by such a multitude of names in *Finnegans Wake*. Duplicity produces multiplicity, as one man becomes many. Jim the Penman's strategy is a version of that of the writer, to represent himself not as one but as many: Captain Bevan, Alfred Brookfield, James Henry Henderson, William Ackroyd, George Lingfield, Colonel Milnthorpe, Robert Ferdinand Walton. Jim's criminal talent might aptly be summarized in a phrase the young Joyce once used to characterize the artistic mastery of the sculptor Arnold Rubek in Ibsen's last play, *When We Dead Awaken*: "mastery of hand linked with limitation of thought." "There are great gulfs set between his art and his life."[18]

THE FILM

The popularity of the play was so great that there was even a racehorse named after Jim the Penman. Maurice Barrymore had played the original lover of Jim's wife, Louis Percival, in the London production of the play, and he played the part again in the United States. before his death (from syphilis) in 1905.[19] Then in 1915, a 3D film version was released, but there are no copies extant of this version.[20]

In April of 1921, a second silent film version appeared starring Lionel Barrymore (son of Maurice) in the role of Jim, who played opposite Doris Rankin, to whom he was married in private life.[21] Joyce may well have known the film, given his strong interest in cinema, which led him to establish (but not preserve) the Volta cinema in Dublin. There is a copy of the film extant at the Library of Congress, although the order of the scenes is scrambled. It is fairly faithful to the play, with a few exceptions, but, most importantly, unlike the playscript the film can give a more historically accurate feeling of what a contemporary production of the play must have been

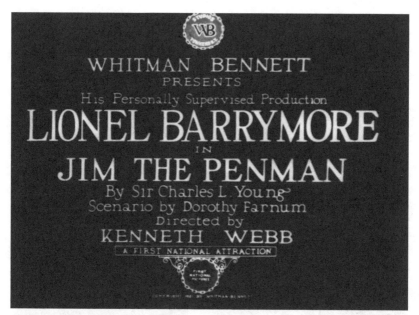

FIGURE 9. Title card from *Jim the Penman*. © 1921, Whitman Bennett Productions. Frame enlargements courtesy of the Motion Picture Research Center, Library of Congress.

like. Moreover, the change of medium from stage to silent film changes the visual texture of the piece in ways that are particularly meaningful in a story about writing and forgery. Silent film stresses not only the emotional expressions of the actors—through the camera's capacity to produce close-ups—it also emphasizes the textuality of the story through captions. Finally, silent film is arguably closer to the original meaning of "melodrama" as a "music drama," since the audience watches and reads images and words to the accompaniment of a musical score that underscores its dramatic moments and cues audience reaction.[22]

The 1921 film was described as "an Americanized version brought up to date."[23] Not only did the scenario writer, Dorothy Farnum, change the setting from London to New York, she also added a new and dramatic ending in which Jim, instead of dying of heart disease, meets his partners in crime on a boat, locks them into the cabin, pulls a gun, and sinks the boat by chopping a hole in the side with an axe, laughing crazily as the boat fills with water and his companions rage and struggle.[24] Like the novel, it portrays

FIGURE 10. At the opera in *Jim the Penman*. © 1921, Whitman Bennett Productions. Frame enlargements courtesy of the Motion Picture Research Center, Library of Congress.

Jim's concern for his daughter, a desire to protect her from the effects of his own crimes. He sinks the boat in order to avoid ruining his daughter's fiancé.[25]

In the film, like the play, Jim begins his life of crime out of love for a woman, Nina L'Estrange, whom he tricks into marrying him.[26] He writes his first forged check to save her father from financial ruin. His forgery is discovered, and he agrees to work for the man who found him out for twenty years in return for indemnity against prosecution. He also uses his talent against Nina, however. She is in love with Louis Percival, whom she has agreed to marry, but Jim forges letters between them breaking the engagement. She still cares for her lost love, however. (This becomes important later, in the discussion of forgery as a form of writing haunted by the "original" it aims to displace.) In one frame of the film, Jim's inability to "erase" his rival completely is captured in a view of Jim and Nina at the opera, accompanied by the ghost of her first fiancé.

FIGURE 11. Lionel Barrymore in *Jim the Penman*. © 1921, Whitman Bennett Productions. Frame enlargements courtesy of the Motion Picture Research Center, Library of Congress.

Eventually, all is revealed and Nina learns that her husband is the infamous forger; moreover, she discovers that he forged the letters that broke off her engagement.[27] The last frame of the film is a view of the water at night after the boat has sunk, followed by this caption: "And in the stars it is written: / There are other worlds—other lives—other chances for happiness."

Jim is depicted as an economically successful man who is not only hunted but haunted. He becomes "exceedingly powerful," described as "able to attain everything but—his wife's love."[28] He is haunted by all those he's injured; as Baron Hartfeld—Jim's "master"—explains in the film, "We all hate those we've injured, because we can't forget them!"[29] Impersonating other people keeps these people alive in Jim; like Shem the Penman, he lives in a "Haunted Inkbottle," the house of "O'Shea or O'Shame" (*FW* 182.30–31).

What is extraordinary about Lionel Barrymore's performance is his ability to stimulate both sympathy and revulsion in the viewer. This is apparent by viewing even one representative shot of his luminous eyes, which express not only his love for his wife and his pain over what he feels he has to do, but also his anger. This is perhaps the most important characteristic of Jim: his fallible humanity, combined with freak genius, a division encapsulated by his mixed motives. As the promotional material for the film stresses:

> The usual villain is drawn all bad. There is no conflict within himself. He is hard, ruthless, clear-cut in his villainy, while the usual screen hero is all good. He never stoops to an evil deed and apparently he is born with inherent goodness in him.
>
> That is why Jim the Penman, although the villain of the piece, appeals to every human being. He has terrible faults, but he has an underlying vein of fineness. The picture public can see in this man something of themselves, their own struggle to keep to the straight path, and they can also see their own weaknesses, their own temptations. [He] creates sympathy for himself, while at the same time causing disapproval of his acts.

This excerpt could almost have been used to advertise the publication of Joyce's *Ulysses* the next year, if instead of a "villain" *Ulysses* was said to feature a flawed man in pain over an act of infidelity he helped to facilitate. More-over, casting Lionel Barrymore as such a compromised hero was consid-ered a newsworthy event. An article in the July 10, 1921, *Atlanta Constitution* stressed that "Mr. Barrymore plays a character so entirely different from any in which he has hitherto been seen that it is a revelation as to the ability and versatility of this noted actor." Barrymore played two different versions of the "sympathetic villain"—a category that conflates the well-defined oppo-sites of hero and villain familiar from popular melodrama—at the same time: when *Jim the Penman* was playing at the Strand Theater in New York, Barrymore was also starring as *Macbeth* on Broadway, in what the promo-tional material referred to as the "Speakies." Barrymore's "sympathetic vil-lains" were all tragic in the sense that their stories end with their deaths. Joyce's contribution was to create a different kind of flawed protagonist for the comic novel: the imperfect, fallible man with many unusually admirable qualities, such as Stephen and Bloom in *Ulysses*, and HCE, Shem, and Shaun in *Finnegans Wake*.

Joyce, having been simultaneously reviled for writing a book banned for obscenity and worshipped for having initiated the revolution of the word, came to experience these two attitudes—contempt and adulation—as structurally identical, opposed only in their effects. And this perhaps intensified his understanding that writing, too, was both good and evil, gift and fraud, a bodily product comparable to eggs and semen, but also urine and feces. *Finnegans Wake* is designed as a testament to the instability and multiplicity of writing, to an understanding of legibility as intimately bound up with illegibility.

As a practice, *Finnegans Wake* anticipates Derrida's analysis of writing in "signature event context," and specifically his claim that the desire to anchor meaning to one living, present source (the author) and to bind that meaning to a legitimating context (intention) is impossible. It is only by convention, by general agreement, that we can see meaning as transparent, intentional, and authorized. That is not to say it is impossible to communicate meaning, only that the purity of meaning is an illusion, an illusion matched by the notion that meaning can be dirty. In Derrida's view, writing is both ghostly and duplicitous—it marks something that is both there and not there, something that seems singular or unique but which is actually capable of endless proliferation in the absence of its producer.[30] (That is why, in the film of *Jim the Penman,* when Jim uses writing to engineer the departure of Louis Percival, that absence can never be total; Percival remains as a ghostly presence, a "trace.") Writing litters: it is both generative and a waste product. There is something violent about writing: as Derrida describes it, "A written sign carries with it a force that breaks with its context, that is, with the collectivity of presences organizing the moment of its inscription. This breaking force is not an accidental predicate but the very structure of the written text" (9). Writing, then, is anarchic, resistant, we might even say criminal (because context-breaking) in its very structure. It takes a fragile whole (represented in *Finnegans Wake* by Humpty Dumpty) and shatters it into pieces that can never be reassembled, at least not by the state or the army ("all the king's horses and all the king's men"). The figure who concentrates in himself the creativity and duplicity of the writer is therefore the forger, someone who understands that because every individual contains multiple characters and is constantly changing, the concept of individual identity itself is a consoling and self-authorizing fiction. To imitate the "signatures of all things" (*U* 3.2) for glory, profit, or ignominy is to be divine *and* satanic, a genius *and* a criminal, a hand that has written *Ulysses* and done lots of other things as well.

The phrase "signatures of all things" is taken from Stephen's stream of consciousness at the beginning of the "Proteus" episode in *Ulysses*, which in turn echoes the title of Jacob Boehme's mystical book *Signatura Rerum; The Signature of All Things. Shewing the Sign and Signification of the Several Forms and Shapes in the Creation; and What the Beginning, Ruin, and Cure of Everything Is. It Proceeds Out of Eternity into Time, and Again Out of Time into Eternity, and Comprizes All Mysteries.*[31] I will not try to characterize Boehme's thought as a whole, only his presupposition that the universe is comprised of all God's signatures, and these "signatures of form" are merely receptacles, containers, or cabinets for the spirit, that can be good *and* evil; the spirit moves through these containers like wind through an instrument (10). An appeal to Boehme helps us recall that the only reason God is not a forger is that He (or She) has signed *everything*. Duplicity is only evil if one believes that all things are separate.

Joyce's representation of the author as a mere forger, the fallen "shadow" of a divine being who has learned to imitate and duplicate the uniqueness of all things, is rooted in Stephen's theory of Shakespeare in "Scylla and Charybdis." Stephen suggests that what made Shakespeare generative, able to play so many different parts, to become so many different characters, was his experience of being unmanned, mastered, by a woman. His capacity to split and multiply the self began as an experience of helplessness, incapacity, being in someone else's control—specifically, in Shakespeare's case, letting Anne have her way with him. What happened to Shakespeare is a version of what happens to Finnegan when he falls, what a forger does when he studies how to sign someone else's name, and what a reader must do to tolerate *Finnegans Wake*: one must consent to being unmade, erased, usurped, re-created as other. Understanding, or connection, is dependent upon one's willingness to dissolve, undo, or erase oneself, and to consent to the feeling of immolation. Good writers and readers work hard at such self-unmaking. To submit to one's undoing is to confront, in a way that is both brave and cowardly, the (partial) fiction of one's own autonomy, uniqueness, and permanence.

The signature, then, need not denote a powerful or rich or knowledgeable individual. Instead of a fetish, a magical miniature representation of a person's identity and worth in society, it can be seen merely as a mark created by bodily movement.[32] Writing is demystified; it appears as ordinary, physical, involving effort and coordination among brain, eye, and hand.

Practice at the manual labor of writing becomes more important than the degree of prestige it confers or represents: writing, like childbirth, becomes a product of labor.

The hand can be seen as generative, then, like the genitals but with greater dexterity and with an almost hermaphroditic power to penetrate and/or encompass or hold. We know that Joyce toyed with the relation between the penis and a finger, because in *Finnegans Wake* a condom is referred to as a "glove": "Never divorce in the bedding the glove that will give you away" (*FW* 586.5–6), and the child Issy sees her father's penis as a finger: "That's a funny place to have a fingey." But the hand can also enclose, make contact (think of the "handtouch" and "lonechill" of the parting of Stephen and Bloom in *Ulysses* [17.1249]). It begins to make more sense that Shem conceives of ink, too, as an extension of his physical body: a mixture of urine and feces.

The hand is not only hermaphroditic (metaphorically speaking); it is also double. There are *two* hands: we might call them Shem and Shaun. It isn't enough to write the letter; someone must also deliver it, and the deliverer, as the overtones of the word suggest, may well be the more heroic role. The author (or scribe, or forger) needs a publisher, an agent, a patron: Sylvia Beach, Harriet Shaw Weaver, to name just a few of Joyce's "deliverers," who, as has often been noted, were usually female.

In *Finnegans Wake*, we learn that "Jem is joky for Jacob" (*FW* 169.1). In fact, the name James (or Jim) is cognate with the name Jacob. Joyce associates Shem (and himself) with Jacob because Jacob is, in a sense, the first forger, the original "sympathetic villain," who tricks his father into giving him his blessing and uses his duplicity to wrestle with angels. He can be seen as a forger in that he disguises his hand(s), covering them with the skins of kids so that, when they are touched by his blind father, he will think he is feeling Esau's hairy ones. Jacob pretends to be another man—here his brother—in order to steal his assets. His blind old father Isaac, when he is about to give this son his blessing, ruminates, "The voice is Jacob's voice, but the hands are the hands of Esau" (Gen. 27:22).[33]

Another Jacob, Jacob Boehme, ends *The Signature of All Things* with Jacob and Esau, arguing that "in Jacob the hand of Christ got the upper hand . . . ; [whereas] Esau [represents] the fall of Adam": "The blessing belonged to Esau, that is, to Adam, but he fooled it away in the Fall, and so the blessing fell upon Jacob, that is upon Christ" (217). Boehme argues that the original sin was Esau's, who (like Adam) "would live in his self-hood" (218). Joyce seems to have extrapolated this to suggest that duplicity is both a crime and the means of redemption, because it releases the forger from the constraints of selfhood, blessing him with a dis-united kingdom in which everyone is a revised version of everybody else. Signatures are all related, as the self ruptures and multiplies to form a world. As Nick Groom writes in *The Forger's Shadow: How Forgery Changed the Course of Literature,* to forge is to "imagine a whole new world in minute detail."[34]

Joyce seems to be alluding to such a dissolution and/or multiplication of self when, in the letter chapter of *Finnegans Wake* (I.v), the narrator asks, "So why, pray, sign anything as long as every word, letter, penstroke, paperspace is a perfect signature of its own?" (*FW* 115.6–8).

In Boehme's words, the writer is he who contemplates and reproduces the signatures of all things for the benefit of the reader, so "He may behold *himself* in this looking-glass both within and without, and find what and who he is" (220). The writer leads the reader home, which in Shem's chapter is meaningfully respelled "howme" (*FW* 173.29) or "how me."

When Shem, then, is described as someone who subverts the art of writing in *Finnegans Wake,* he is at the same time doing something less reprehensible and more self-wasting: "Instead of chuthoring [tutoring] those model households plain wholesome pothooks . . . [he studied] how cutely to copy all their various styles of signature so as to one day to utter an epical forged cheque on the public for his own private profit" (181.12–17). Shem's cheating may be fueled by self-interest ("for his own private profit"), but it also has the potential to benefit his descendants, at the cost of reducing himself, who is "excruciated, in honour bound to the cross of [his] own cru-elfiction!" (*FW* 192.18–19). To imitate the signatures of all things, Joyce must erase his own.

Writing, then, is a learned, wavelike motion made as the fingers move up and down across the page.[35] A good forger learns to approximate this wave-like motion without interrupting its rhythm to *look* at what he's copying.[36] Instead, he memorizes the image of a signature and practices it until he can reproduce it without hesitancy. As a bodily movement, writing can be seen as a *gesture* designed to express emotion. The word "gesture" stems from the same Latin root as "jest" and "gestation," a root meaning "to carry." A writer is a carrier, haunted by the traces of other people's lives. With any luck, the ges-ture of the writer's hand can also engender a gestation in an unknown reader. As Stephen once proposed to Cranly as early as *Stephen Hero*, "There should be an art of gesture.... Of course I don't mean art of gesture in the sense that the elocution professor understands the word. For him a gesture is an emphasis. I mean a rhythm."[37] Later, in "Circe," a drunken Stephen shatters light over the world, proclaiming all saved "so that gesture, not music not odour, would be a universal language, the gift of tongues rendering visible not the lay sense but the first entelechy, the structural rhythm" (*U* 15.105–107) For Stephen, the writer—like the forger—has mastered the rhythms of other people's self-representation. The instrument used by the gesturing hand is a pen. That pen is both a wand and a baton, and it can have two very different effects, like the opposed gestures of Justius and Mercius at the end of "Shem the Penman" in *Finnegans Wake*. Like a hand, writing can destroy—"He points the deathbone and the quick are still" (*FW* 193.29)—but it can also perform small miracles: "He lifts the lifewand and the dumb speak" (*FW* 195.5).

Joyce's writing—we might call it scripture—was designed, like a good signature, to be both legible and illegible. Like a signature, it is aimed at the sweet spot between a set of socially conditioned traces that can easily be decoded and a highly individual mark that is unique and (in theory) resistant to imitation. Similarly, for writing to challenge the fiction of individual self-sufficiency, the writer (or penman) must be both a hero and a villain, someone who simultaneously epitomizes and challenges the consensual standards of the day. *Finnegans Wake*, especially, is presented as a collection of signatures that are forged, which makes them valuable imitations, not unlike the writings of scribes who recorded the word of God. The book's status as a forgery means that its traces are duplicitous and ephemeral—they are fraudulent copies of living "originals"—but they are also, paradoxically, as strong as steel. Joyce's work may be described as "forged" in both senses of the word: his novels are unauthorized, fraudulent transcriptions of the signatures of all things, but they were also, as Stephen vowed they would be, forged in the smithy of his soul.[38] Joyce's words, like Siegfried's sword, might be named "Nothung"—which is both Nothing and inexorable Necessity itself.[39]

5 ▸ ON FAT

One of the many surprises of reading Joyce comes from his reminder that historically, fat meant power, for both men and women. In highly developed consumerist countries of the twenty-first century, where food is abundant, leanness has replaced fat as a sign of health and wealth, which sometimes causes high-achieving young people—especially women—to go to extremes in their pursuit of the desirability they associate with thinness. Joyce—slender in build himself—offers a more balanced view of how values associated with fat operate in relation to society and history. As an Irishman born in the late nineteenth century, he was acutely aware of the danger and effects of famine, and the value of fat as "insurance" against food shortages. He also knew that biologically, one of the signs of female sexual maturity is an increase of fat, especially in the breasts and buttocks. His works serve as a reminder that fat is closely associated with female sexuality, that a woman's physical difference from a man—the trigger of desirability—is signified through the soft curves created by fat deposits.

In Finnegans Wake, Joyce performs an astute analysis of how young men and women differ in their access to power by embodying them as various fatty foods (the men as butter and cheese, women as margarine), and then dramatizing the resulting power dynamics in relation to Shakespeare's Julius Caesar *and the history of margarine. One significant implication of Joyce's comic analysis of "our social stomach" (FW 163.34) is the suggestion that female desirability is socially "manufactured" to meet a particular male need, which he implicitly compares to the invention of margarine. Society is structured to allow women access only to an artificial or imitative kind of power. On the other hand, the desire for fat is unveiled as the urge of someone looking to consume the other rather than nurture it; fat awakens erotic, appetitive, and sometimes violent desires.*

Looking at the "Burrus-Caseous-Marge" episode of Finnegans Wake *(in I.vi) through the double lens of Roman history and food illuminates how closely insignificance and meaning inhere in each other. On one hand, fat is that which imparts flavor to a diet. The word "diet" is another word for everyday life; it stems the Greek* diaita, *or "way of life." An individual's diet reveals the principles of selection that govern her daily existence (and subsistence); it helps to show how well she is able to balance the opposing desires for abundance and moderation. On the other hand, however, the composition of diets is influenced by culture as well as by individual taste: the Latin word* diaeta *refers to a "prescribed way of life." Insofar as the prescriptions governing competitive, patriarchal societies mark successful, mature men and desirably plump young women as "food" for hungry young men, fat embodies something more dangerous—a resource to be killed and "cannibalistically" ingested.*

Joyce begins his exploration of food in *Ulysses,* in which Molly Bloom's plump breast and buttocks are presented as the "hemispheres" of Bloom's world, his promised land, on which all his conflicting sentiments and reflections eventually converge. When he climbs into bed at the end of the day, he feels "satisfaction at the ubiquity in eastern and western terrestrial hemispheres . . . of adipose anterior and posterior female hemispheres, redolent of milk and honey and of excretory sanguine and seminal warmth, reminiscent of secular families of curves of amplitude, insusceptible of moods of impression or of contrarieties of expression, expressive of mute immutable mature animality" (17.2227–2236). When Bloom thinks of Molly's fat as "redolent of milk and honey" he is unconsciously repeating one of the root meanings of "fat," the Proto-Indo-European *poid,* "to abound in water, milk, fat, etc." He responds physically with "An approximate erection," and then he kisses "the plump mellow yellow smellow melons of her rump, on each plump melonous hemisphere, in their mellow yellow furrow" (*U* 17.2238–2243). Joyce's wife Nora, when asked if she was a model for

Molly, would answer "No." "She was much fatter."[1] To be precise, Molly weighed eleven stone nine, or 163 pounds. For Bloom her mass only increased her gravitational attraction. Molly's body, for Bloom, is a round, sweet homeland: maternal, delicious: "melonous."

In *Finnegans Wake,* Joyce develops the relation between women and fat more fully, connecting it not only with men's hunger for women, but also with their hunger for the power and position of other men. He respells Oedipus Rex as "adipose rex," or king of body fat (*FW* 499.16), which stresses the tragedy of Oedipus's great appetite for power and sex, which consumed his father and mother, respectively. The "Burrus-Caseous-Marge" episode of *Finnegans Wake* (I.6, 161.8–168.12), in particular, focuses on the younger generation: ALP and HCE's twin sons, Shem and Shaun, and their sister Issy. Joyce plots the sexual attraction (licensed by physical difference) between the males and females, connecting it to the tension between sons and father caused by differences of power. He structures these dynamics in relation to two half-buried contexts: the plot of Brutus and Cassius to kill Caesar in Shakespeare's *Julius Caesar* and the similarities and differences between butter and cheese, on the one hand, and margarine, on the other.

Joyce, then, gives resonance to his episode by playing off *Julius Caesar* and food, Shaun's favorite subject—especially fats and salads. What we discover, by looking at the nexus of connections that unite the different stories, is how the young girl Issy unexpectedly resembles the powerful father through the desire of the sons to possess or steal the richness of both; how attempts to seduce her are versions of the threats against his life. In the terms of Henrik Ibsen's *The Master Builder,* the young girl knocking on the door is not only the object of the powerful man's desire, experienced simultaneously as antagonist and successor, but also his counterpart insofar as both will be hunted by young, ambitious, and desirous men.

Joyce presents girls as *man*-ufactured: they are made by men. As Jacques Lacan would contend years later, *la femme n'existe pas* (the woman does not exist).[2] She is simply a role, and her function is to stimulate (and simulate) hunger and desire in men. Her fat, the secondary sexual characteristic that signifies her maturity and marks her desirability, makes her the edible version of the threatening Oedipal father that the boys plot to kill. Joyce summarizes this complex relation of men and women, parents and children, as the "eatupus complex" (*FW* 128.32). Freud's Oedipus complex, according to which the male child unconsciously desires to supplant the father—both killing him and replacing him in the mother's bed—is rewritten as a situation in which the children want to "eat up" both parents, but the father must be killed (knifed or shattered) before he can be eaten, and the mother is devoured at one remove, in the person of the daughter who has supplanted *her*.

Let us begin by examining the name of the daughter in *Finnegans Wake*—Isolde (also known as Issy)—in relation to the flesh she embodies and represents. If we sink a line through the various verbal constructions of her name, it immediately suggests "I sold" (as Issy notes in II.ii, "One must sell it to some one, the sacred name of love," *FW* 268n.1). The allusion to selling oneself draws attention to a woman's power to barter with her body, but an anagram of Isolde is "soiled," which can be contracted into "solid." The connection between these two words recalls Hamlet's desire "that this too too solid flesh would melt / Thaw, and resolve itself into a dew!" (1.2). The famous textual crux—whether Shakespeare wrote "solid" or "sullied"—that has puzzled editors of these lines also changes Hamlet's meaning, depending upon whether we think he reviles the flesh as too solid (which renders his desire ethereal or ghostly) or sees it as too sullied or soiled, which makes his wish for transformation seem guilt-ridden and self-punishing. When we think of Isolde in *Finnegans Wake* in relation to these anagrams of her name, the evocation of something solid contrasts with Joyce's presentation of her elsewhere as a little (nebulous) cloud, and the suggestion that she is sullied, or dirty, would seem to contradict her close association with clouds (as Nuvoletta) and cleansing rain. Joyce directs us to apprehend the ways in which this young girl may be seen as both solid and sullied, real and adulterated, by referring to her here as "Margareen," or margarine, which is made by making a liquid (oil) solidify. If we construe the name "Isolde" another way, by splitting it, the phrase that results makes a similarly paradoxical suggestion: that the young girl "is old." And if we are careful to remember that she literally remains young, it is also possible to see that she is also, in a figurative sense, old: a version of the father, the principle of desirable abundance, whom the sons try to possess or consume.

When Joyce calls Issy "Margareen," he is also connecting her with the Maggies of "The Mime of Nick, Mick and the Maggies" (*FW* II.1). The word "margarine" shares a root with "Margaret," the Greek *márgaron*, or "pearl" (a reference to its luster). Maggy (either singular or plural, as the 7 days of the week/colors of the rainbow or the 28 and sometimes

29 days in February) is a diminutive of Margaret that also brings "Magdalene" to mind, especially Mary Magdalene, the woman once possessed by seven demons who was cured by, and became a follower of, Jesus. Mary Magdalene was long believed to be a prostitute or "loose woman," which is why the Magdalene laundries for fallen women were given that name. Magdalene is the root of "maudlin," meaning tearful or weeping, which helps to contextualize Issy (as Nuvoletta) crying over the "bannistars" before she falls.

Both margarine and butter melt, which makes it easier for them to resemble tears. Buck Mulligan in *Ulysses* cries tears of molten butter onto his scone when talking about Stephen's mother's death (*U* 15.4179). Stephen, echoing the Upanishads, thinks of Hiesos Kristos as "the sacrificial butter" (*U* 9.64). That which melts is ripe for sacrifice. In *Finnegans Wake*, not only is Issy/Margareen/Nuvoletta margarine, her virginity ready to be sacrificed, but the father is too, if we hear the "fat" in the word "father." Issy/Margareen is a female version of the father, only young and poor (margarine was invented to supply affordable fat to the poor). As a food, she is both the object of his hunger and the target of his desire (he in turn has the power to fatten or impregnate her). However, in her role as a cheaper imitation food, she is not as satisfying as the butter she imitates. In the "Burrus-Caseous-Marge" episode, real butter is represented by her brother "Burrus"/Shaun (a name derived from the French *beurre* ["butter"], in combination with Brutus) who by implication is ultimately more valuable than the synthetic margarine that was invented to substitute for it.

Butter, as incarnated by Burrus, represents richness and traditionally has been categorized as one of the best and purest of foodstuffs. As Margaret Visser writes, butter is not only delectable but "comes haloed with all the complexities and perversities of status. . . . Butter has always seemed magical because of the mystery of its solidification out of milk."[3] Its name is indebted to a centuries-old belief that cows who ate buttercups made yellow butter (85). (Issy has a cat or pussy named Buttercup; see *FW* 145.9–14 and 561.11–12). Rich people once coated their hair in butter to discourage vermin and add shine (Visser 92). Finally, Visser argues that in mythologies all over the world, butter symbolizes semen, with churning as the sexual agitation that conceives a child (93). Ireland has a special relation to butter; supposedly the Irish "may still eat more butter than any population on earth," and some of the most common bog finds in Ireland are barrels of ancient butter. The Irish St. Brigit fed strangers on butter, which was then magically restored (96–97, 101).

If we see the story of Burrus-Caseous-Marge through the lens of *Julius Caesar*, it becomes apparent that Isolde/Marge (like Caesar) is sacrificed as a result of the same hunger that renders her desirable. She is related to Caesar through the way that similar sounds express (hidden) connection: when the men *see her*, they want to *seize her* (Caesar). Moreover, in their desire for *fame* (or in their *faim*, Fr. "hunger"), as consumers, they wish to consume her. There is nothing "natural" about a solid/soiled young woman in "our social stomach" (*FW* 163.34). Instead, Issy is man-made like the margarine whose name she bears. She represents a "product," manufactured, a substitute food. In the homosocial economy of male competition and power, she doesn't exist in her own right, serving instead as a nonthreatening substitute for the father. Finally, like Jesus in a Christian framework, she represents not only the power of the Father but his Word as well. The father whose word she embodies, however, is a mortal father, and his word—which in honor is not supposed to change—will inevitably be broken.

The "Burrus-Caseous-Marge" episode follows the "Mookse-Gripes-Nuvoletta" passage, in which Issy (as Nuvoletta) is a cloud overseeing the contest between the Mookse and the Gripes (who replay Aesop's Fox and the Grapes, with significant additions). When depicted as vapor, not only does she anticipate the name of Caseous/Cassius (by being gaseous), but she also advertises her status as a dream, dramatizes the loneliness of her elevation, and (in her incipient wetness) offers the promise of female sexual arousal. As a cloud, she represents the quintessence of virginal girlhood in that she is bodiless, idealized, and pure. When she jumps over the "bannistars" [banisters, stars] into the river as a tear (*FW* 159. 6–18), this constitutes a fall: she literally undergoes condensation and displacement, which Freud, speaking more metaphorically, identified as the primary characteristics of a dream.[4] As a tear, she is expressing the sorrow of her numinous existence, and as a falling woman she is experiencing the gravity of sexual maturity, insofar as she becomes liquid and adulterated ("her muddied [married] name was Missisliffi" [Mrs. Liffey/Mississippi [*FW* 159.12–13]). This propensity to liquefy is a defining feature of female sexuality throughout the *Finnegans Wake*, whether Issy is a cloud who turns to dew ("A dew! A dew!" [Adieu, adieu]), a flower who starts to flow, a micturating girl, a juicy peach, or margarine, which melts at warmer temperatures. Male sexuality, in contrast, is more typically represented as solidification, a hardening, and a rising, which Joyce associates with defecation as opposed to urination.

In the context of an episode dominated by fats, is useful to remember that Joyce always loved Greece (the country), its name a homonym for "grease." His love of fat (unexpected in one so thin) is apparent not only in his decision to define *Ulysses* as an epic of Greece/grease, but also in his linkage of *Ulysses* to *Hamlet*, a name that includes ham that had been ascribed in an unkosher but equally piggish way to a man named Bacon (see the allusion to Francis Bacon as the author of Shakespeare's plays in "Scylla and Charybdis," when Stephen thinks of Shakespeare as "Bacon's wild oats" [*U* 9.410]). Molly, too, is lusciously fat, and it is her fattest part, the rump or "two lumps" of lard, that Bloom is fondest of kissing.

In *Finnegans Wake*, however, men are also depicted as fat and it is *male* asses (or arses) that get most of the narrative attention, partly because of the association of male sexuality with solids. In their incarnation as Butt and Taff, the brothers both have names suggesting fat and buttocks—not only does "butt" suggest "butter," but "Taff" contains "fat," spelled backward. In the "Museyroom" episode (I.i, 8.9–10.23), which is concerned with the conflict between Wellington and Napoleon at the battle of Waterloo, Joyce presents Napoleon as the son figure, divided into two or three separate people and renamed "lipoleum boyne." The word "boyne," in addition to evoking "boys," recalls another battle—the decisive Battle of the Boyne that established William of Orange's hegemony over Ireland—and "lipoleum" derives from the Greek *lipos*, or fat. (In this incident, as in the episode where Buckley shoots the Russian general in III.ii, the "lipoleum boyne" eventually shoot Wellington in his big white arse, or butt, which here appears as the tail of his big white horse). In the "Burrus-Caseous-Marge" episode, Joyce turns Shem and Shaun (at war against each other and against the father whom they will become) into Brutus and Cassius of *Julius Caesar*, suggesting their opposition to one another through the faint suggestion that one is an animal (a *burro*, or ass) suggestive of a male butt and the other merely gaseous (a ghost or pure spirit). Finally, the twins are also identified through their names with butter (Burrus/*beurre*, Fr. "butter") and cheese (Caseous/*Käse*, Ger. "cheese"), perhaps (in part) to emphasize the sons' status as both confusing and confused, since to make butter and cheese of someone is to confound or bamboozle them (*OED*). Butter and cheese are also related etymologically, if we understand the root of butter as "*bou-tyron*," or "cow cheese" (*Online Etymology Dictionary*).

A brief digression is necessary to answer the question of why Joyce may have used Shakespeare's *Julius Caesar* as a background for the "Burrus-Caseous-Marge" episode. A few reasons are readily apparent: *Julius Caesar* is about two "brothers" (Cassius is married to Brutus's sister) who kill Caesar because they believe him to be a tyrant. In this respect, *Julius Caesar* is a version of the father-son conflict dramatized throughout *Finnegans Wake*. Joyce seems to have associated Caesar not only with a Caesar salad (which was invented in Mexico in 1924), perhaps because the dressing is made with the fatty yolk of an egg, but also with cheese, since "tyrant" resembles the Greek word for cheese: "*tyros.*" But most importantly, Joyce heard Brutus and Cassius's desire for fame as the French *faim*, or hunger (*FW* 163), a connection that is reinforced not only by the fact that Brutus and Cassius kill Caesar with a knife, or tableware (think of Stephen's drunken comment about a table knife in "Eumaeus": "Oblige me by taking away that knife. I can't look at the point of it. It reminds me of Roman history" [*U* 16.815–816]), but also by the famous passage in which Caesar deplores Cassius as *too lean*, too hungry. He cries,

> Let me have men about me that are fat,
> Sleek-headed men and such as sleep a-nights.
> Yond Cassius has a lean and hungry look,
> He thinks too much; such men are dangerous. (1.2)

Caesar is clearly afraid of being eaten; he knows that he himself is rich or "fat" (like cheese or a Caesar salad), and that fat is a symbol of power *and* age. He therefore repeats his comment about Cassius, "Would he were fatter!" When Joyce recasts Cassius as Caseous, he underscores both his difference from and similarity to Caesar by making him cheese, "the brutherscutch of puir tyron [the butterscotch/brother of pure, powerful, boylike—from Latin *puer*, boy—tyrant, which is also the Greek for cheese (*FW* 163.8–9)]. Joyce also puns on the French word for cheese, *fromage*, as "from age," remarking that "the older sisars [Caesars] . . . become unbeurrable [unbearable, unbutterable] from age" (*FW* 162.1–2). Powerful men become cheese—and tyrants—with age, as Joyce shows by presenting Caesar as a big cheese (or, as Bloom once put it, "mity cheese" [*U* 8.755]) who has become unbeurrable—he can't be buttered up—and Cassius as a tyrant/cheese in the making. Such cheeses are different from Burrus/Brutus/*beurre* in that they are incapable of melting or changing, and for that reason are unbearable.

Burrus is not only Issy's brother Shaun, but also Marcus Junius Brutus (85–42 B.C.), whom Marc Antony famously eulogizes in *Julius Caesar* as "the noblest Roman" of them all, and whom Joyce also calls the "betterman [better man, man of butter] of the two" (*FW* 161.19). Burrus is introduced as good, pure, and natural food, the food which, along with honey in the prophecy of Isaiah 7:15, teaches consumers to "refuse the evil and choose the good" (Joyce refers to the prophecy in Latin at *FW* 163.3-4). "Burrus . . . is . . . full of natural greace, the mildest of milkstoffs yet unbeaten as a risicide [regicide; killer of the Latin *risus*, meaning "laugh"]"; he is "obsoletely unadulterous" (*FW* 161.15–17). As the irony that shadows these praises might suggest, Burrus is being introduced not only as pure (like "pure" butter as opposed to adulterated margarine), but also as a Puritan (the Puritans were regicides for their role in the beheading of Charles I). Moreover, he is, appropriately, a roundhead—"Burrus has the reachly roundered head that goes best with thoftthinking defensive fideism"; he is a defender of the faith (*FW* 162.22–23). Finally, Burrus is an ass, a *burro*; the language suggests that people who define themselves as pure—purest butter or milky whiteness— are also asking us to eat their stinking shit (see chapter 6, "On Adultery and Virginity").[5] When Burrus and Caseous kill Caesar, the family dynamic is represented as a salad, with Issy serving as the lettuce (referred to there as Lettucia in her greensleeves [*FW* 161.30]), "and you too and me three, twinsome bibs but handsome ates, like shakespill and eggs!" (*FW* 161.30–31). As a salad, she is again linked to Caesar. The salad bowl of the family is also a *bowel*—a "Slatbowel [salad bowl/bowel]" (*FW* 161.27) from which Caesar has been "sort-of-nineknived and chewly removed" (*FW* 162.5). Or as the narrator explains to his students, "To understand this as well as you can . . . I have completed the following arrangement for the coarse use of stools [course use of schools, the use of stools]" (*FW* 161.33–35).

Another conceivable reason for setting the "Burrus-Caseous-Marge" story in relation to Shakespeare's *Julius Caesar* is suggested by a different pun. In *Finnegans Wake*, Joyce is attempting to map out relations between different genders and generations, and he does this via Roman history, which he rewrites as "home and his try" (*FW* 161.22). Burrus, Caseous, and

Marge are domestic versions of characters from Roman history, which is being retold as the attempts of men to govern their homes.[6] Joyce depicts the wife's perspective on husband and home by punning on the Hungarian (or hungry) word for house, *haz*. A husband (from the woman's perspective) is a has-been and a house bane, whom the wife dislikes (as the French say, she has him in her nose): "Every hazzy hates to having a hazbane [husband, house bane, has-been] in her noze" (*FW* 162.20). For the wife, then, as for Brutus and Cassius, a tyrant/husband is also a has-been. Interestingly, the Hungarian word *hus* (the beginning of the English word "husband," pronounced "hoosh") means "in flesh" or "fat."

Joyce's decision to make his two young men (and Issy) into food may also be indebted to how Dante depicts them in *Inferno*. In the last canto, Canto 34, the Dante pilgrim sees Satan in all his gigantic ugliness, with bat wings and three faces on his head. "In each mouth he champed a sinner with his teeth." Virgil tells Dante that the one most tortured is Judas Iscariot, but the other two are Brutus and Cassius: "The one that hangs from the black muzzle is Brutus: see how he writes and utters not a word; the other is Cassius, who seems so stark of limb."[7] Satan is literally chewing them for eternity.

But the "Burrus-Caseous-Marge" episode is primarily about men and women before marriage, when they are still boys and girls and on the market. Joyce refers to the marketability of young people by rewriting a line from "Love's Old Sweet Song" not as the dear dead days beyond recall but as "the dairy days of buy and buy" (*FW* 161.14). By referring to the economics of the dairy industry, Joyce not only highlights the reading of Isolde's name as "I sold," but he also underscores the idea that boys and girls, however natural or artificial they may seem, are all packaged *products* in the cash system.[8] Or, in the language of the Mookse and the Gripes, all the characters are *fables*. A fable, as the word suggests, is both able and feeble. As the narrator explains, "And from the poignt of fun [fun point of view] where I am crying to arrive you at they are on allfore as foibleminded [foible, feeble, fable] as you can feel they are fablebodied" (*FW* 160.32–34).

The Caesar "Slatbowel [salad bowl/bowel]" brings us to Margareen, who may resemble butter, but who is made of oil (like the Caesar of salad fame). Margareen (sometimes referred to as Margareena) is a version of HCE/ Caesar, the man for whom Burrus and Caseous think they hunger but on whom they covertly make war. Joyce rearranges the word "males" as "meals"; Margareen is what the males turn to for satisfaction between meals: "Positing . . . too males pooles . . . and looking wantingly around our undistributed middle between males [meals] we feel we must waistfully woent a female to focus on [she is a waste who is good for the waistline, since the males are the real meals; she is also "the appetising entry . . . on a full stomach"] (*FW* 164.4–164.16). The narrator hails Margareen as a lump of gold, perhaps referring to the way people had to add color to margarine when laws protecting the dairy industry prevented manufacturers from selling something that looked too much like butter: "*O Margareena! Still in the bowl is left a lump of gold!*" (*FW* 164.20) The narrator also reminds us that she too is waste, offering to explain "how and why this particular streak of yellow silver first appeared on (not in) the bowel [bowl]" (*FW* 164.25–27). Issy, we can see from a passage on the next page (*FW* 165.22), doesn't really exist in her own right; she is merely the means to an end, a ladder for the men to climb. Like Caesar, Issy is actually a "rhomba," a trapezoid, a ladder or climax (*klimax* is the Greek word for "ladder") up which Burrus and Caseous climb in their desire for meals/males: "Rhomba, lady Trabezond (Marge in her *excelsis*), also comprised the climactogram up which B and C may fondly be imagined ascending" (*FW* 165.22–24). She is described as secretly male, using HIM (His Infant Majesty) "to conceal her own more mascular personality by flaunting frivolish finery over men's inside clothes" (*FW* 166.24–25). She "complicates the position . . . by implicating herself [as Cleopatra) with an elusive Antonius [Antony]," the "good" version of Caesar, who later replaces him (*FW* 166.35–167.1).

If Antonius-Caesar is inside Issy, Issy is also—like Burrus, her young male counterpart—the underside of the father's power, as we can see through her association with margarine, "the poor man's butter." Margarine is younger than butter, less costly than butter, and more strategically assembled than butter, as we can see from the strange history of margarine. Margarine was invented in 1869 by Hippolyte Mège-Mouriès.[9] In response to the shortage of butter during and after the Napoleonic wars due to a cattle plague, Napoleon III offered a prize to anyone who could come up with an economic alternative to butter. Mège-Mouriès won by using margaric acid and oleo, beef fat, or beef tallow churned with milk. (Margarine was first called butterine and then oleomargarine, although the beef fat in the formula was dropped.) The production and sale of margarine was almost immediately restricted in several countries for a variety of reasons: it was often sold in big tubs and people were afraid that it was being adulterated by vendors, a fear that fueled the establishment of regulative and punitive laws against it. In America, the first great agricultural depression occurred in 1873, which gave rise to a militant dairy lobby. In the United Kingdom, the Margarine Acts of 1887 and 1899 were relatively mild, aimed at differentiating margarine from butter. Margarine and butter were rationed during both world wars, when there was a ban on coloring margarine (which helped to differentiate it from butter), a ban that meant consumers had to mix the color themselves. Moreover, margarine was taxed, which almost defeated its purpose as a low-cost alternative to butter. In Italy, in an attempt to protect the butter industry, the agricultural and bakers' association banned the production of margarine for household use in 1934 and banned margarine entirely in 1937. In France, the coloring of margarine by manufacturers was outlawed as early as 1897.[10]

Why would Joyce have been interested in the governmental efforts to restrict the sale of margarine? First of all, the diet of many people in the late nineteenth century was quite poor—high in carbohydrates but low in fats and protein. Margarine was developed for nutritional reasons, and it would have been an important invention for a famine-stricken land fed largely on potatoes, such as Ireland. Yet governments artificially increased the price and decreased the attractiveness of margarine.[11] Second, margarine is a representation of a harmonious and nutritious combination of incompatible extremes, oil and water, since the trick of making it is to introduce water or milk into an oil emulsion.[12] Third, Joyce presents margarine as a representation of the daughter's position as it has been treated by the legal system: the daughter, like margarine, has been devalued for being artificial and easily adulterated, a cheap and unsatisfying imitation of "pure" butter, which serves as the (male) standard. And margarine was discriminated against for almost a century despite its value for the population as a whole (it is almost unique as an industry that survived such restrictions to be widely successful). Finally, the fact that margarine is made of oil allows it to underscore the way in which the power of the daughter is akin to and at the same time is the obverse of the power of the father or Caesar in *Finnegans Wake.*

So, is Isolde old? One answer to this is no, insofar as she is margarine, which is only about twenty years older than Joyce, and insofar as she represents the daughter. But there is also a sense in which she *is* constructed as old: as Joyce suggests at the end of I.6, Isolde represents not only a food but also the Word itself. According to Roman Law, whatever bond someone makes with his tongue is binding, and men like Burrus and Caseous declare, "My unchanging Word is sacred. The word is my Wife, to exponse and expound, to vend and to velnerate. . . . Till Breath us depart! Wamen [Amen; women]" (FW 167.28–31).[13] Men would construct women—like the Word—as unchanging, a product to be venerated and sold. To the extent that she accepts such an assignment, Isolde is a product, or icon of sorts, to be sold again and again; as such, she must appear forever young and unchanging. As the narrator warns her, "Beware would you change with my years. Be as young as your grandmother! [this is old!] . . . the rite words by the rote order" (FW 167.31–33). Isolde is under pressure to be old, soft, faithful, pure, and fat—to be "better," and, impossibly, to be butter.

Joyce's "raiding" of language reminds us that fat signifies a reserve; it offers a backup power supply of energy, stored in the body, and it therefore easily represents comparable reserves of wealth or power. It is a sign of luxury. When, in Shakespeare's The Merchant of Venice, Antonio cannot pay Shylock the money he owes him, Shylock demands payment in flesh. The question is whether or not one has a pound of flesh to spare: the only "extra" flesh that could be spared is fat. Fat in females traditionally signified sexual power; in men, it indicated social, political, or economic power.

When Joyce associates the "father" with a Caesar salad dressing, he is implicitly linking him to the fat of the egg, simultaneously noting his fullness and his fragility, his susceptibility to a fall (like that of Humpty Dumpty, with whom the father is linked throughout Finnegans Wake). But all the characters in this family romance are "fat" and golden: if the father resembles an egg, the sons emerge as butter and cheese, and the daughter as margarine. Joyce uses different varieties of fat to show that all the family members have power and limitations, but of different kinds. Cheese is solid but can have holes; butter and margarine are prone to melt. There is a kind of tyranny in sons and daughters that is comparable to, yet different from, the tyranny of fathers, and the tyranny of girls is different from that of boys. A feminist lens becomes helpful here, because girls are not presented as the only victims of the social stomach in Finnegans Wake; men are eaten, too. But the tyranny of girls over men is largely unconscious and operates through identification with the powerful father, whereas the rebellion of the sons is subversive and violent: they are armed with knives, plotting to kill and possibly ingest that which engendered them.

Joyce's method of storytelling (or "stolentelling" [*FW* 424.35]; see chapter 4, "On Writing by Hand") intensified over time. He simultaneously tells the story of Roman history—specifically a regicide that is also—metaphorically speaking—a parricide—as an everyday story about hunger and fat, the consumption of a daily meal in the home. Joyce also associates another sacrificed leader with cheese: He spells "Jesus" as "Cheesugh" (*FW* 164.10). Jesus, too, has become food for millions through the celebration of the Eucharist. The method of reading these stories, of connecting the famous and the ordinary, is a method adapted from Freud and employed with joy, using generative techniques that make the reader—like HCE himself—"king of the yeast" (*FW* 578.4).

In a land that had been decimated by famine in the nineteenth century, fat was a particularly vital resource. In *Ulysses,* Bloom carries a shriveled potato that his mother had given him years earlier, presumably to protect him against hunger ("Potato preservative against Plague and Pestilence" [*U* 15.1952]). Many Irish writers have alluded to the superstition that carrying a potato serves as protection against the "famine grass," which grows out of the grave of a famine victim and causes the person who walks on it to feel starved. It is the subject of a poem by Donagh MacDonagh, to take just one example. In "The Hungry Grass," MacDonagh writes:

> Crossing the shallow holdings high above sea
> Where few birds nest, the luckless foot may pass
> From the bright safety of experience
> Into the terror of the hungry grass.[14]

Grass can instill hunger, but it also serves a more complex function in countries wracked by famine. In famine after famine—in Ireland, but also North Korea, Malawi, Ethiopia, Sudan—we read of starving people eating grass, dying people with green-stained mouths, corpses found with grass in their stomachs. Grass provides a temporary feeling of satisfaction, but it has no nutrients (and no fat!), so it will not prevent starvation, and any relief it offers will be brief. In "Song of Myself," Walt Whitman calls grass "the beautiful uncut hair of graves": graves of young men, old people, offspring, aged mothers, coming from "under the faint red roofs of mouths." (Joyce alludes to "lush grass, the hair of graves" in *Giacomo Joyce*).[15] Grass is the seasonal bloom that grows like hair out of death.

Hunger for food is just one kind of hunger. Hunger for power (as in *Julius Caesar*) and hunger for sex are important parallels. To eat is to ingest bits of one's environment, which helps to explain why refusing food can be a form of protest, as in hunger strikes.[16] The environment in a broader sense is being rejected as unacceptable. The environment can also be unable to provide sufficient sustenance, which turns hunger into a disease rather than a conscientious choice. What people hunger *for* is not grass or the graves that underlie it, but the feeling of temporary satiety provided by fat, wealth, or postcoital satisfaction.

The reflections inspired by the "Burrus-Caseous-Marge" episode of *Finnegans Wake* are social as well as individual. They concern the intimate interrelation of love and hate, insemination and murder associated with the various nether "mouths" of men and women. In men, as we have seen, fat serves as a metaphor for wealth and power (as in "fat cat"), and hunger signifies need that in some cases can morph into a threat. Ireland is a nation of starving people, both literally (in the nineteenth century) and figuratively (in their long history of colonization and consequent impoverishment). In women, "opulent curves" indicate abundant female sexuality, a promised land of milk and honey. This older view contrasts sharply with the dominant images of female desirability today, which depend on a thinness so marked that prepubescence has come to seem the epitome of sexuality. These current cultural ideals predict, even help to create, conditions favoring child pornography and childhood sexual abuse. They leave men as well as women starved.

Sexuality itself is fraught as an appetite necessary to life (for pleasurable flesh marbled with fat) that can tip over into murder and a desire to consume the other. Hungry young men (like Brutus) lust to "score" with attractive women (see the "Tristan and Isolde" episode, I.4) and also to see their father naked (like Shem with Noah, and Buckley with the Russian general). Their desire for the father is a mixture of lust and rage, as we see when Buckley feels tender about the enemy general when he has pulled his trousers down to defecate. What enrages him is the general's action of wiping himself with a piece of turf (literally sod-omy), and his feeling of tenderness changes to hate as he shoots him in the ass, much as the lipoleum boyne [Napoleon as three fat—*lipos*—boys] shot Wellington (and/or his horse) in the "Museyroom" episode.[17] The different holes for men and women are both sites of desirability and vulnerability, upon which are visited thrusts of life or death.

Such a view makes sexual assault, for example, less surprising if no less horrific: it is an act of hate that may have sprung from earlier frustrated desire, as well as from a social system that stokes violent hunger. It helps to explain why so many soldiers have described the terrors of war as eerily sexual. Sex and appetite both teeter on a fulcrum between life and death, and only an acute self-awareness and concern for the other can help to regulate them. Hunger, whether for food or sex, is not only necessary to life, it is also intimately interlaced with death.

6 ▸ ON ADULTERY AND VIRGINITY

At first glance, (female) adultery and virginity might seem to be strange bedfellows, despite the fact that Joyce links Molly Bloom with both (her association with virginity comes from the fact that she shares a name and birthdate with the Virgin Mary). Adultery here refers specifically to female adultery, which is regarded very differently than its male equivalent. In Joyce's Flaubertian view, what adultery and virginity have in common is that both are concerned with regaining or retaining idealism and even purity of being.

My focus here is not on the effects of adultery, which can be devastating, but on what lies behind the rigid prohibitions against it. Thinking about adultery and virginity makes it possible to imagine a different blueprint for conceptualizing the female self, one that embraces development and change. In addition, our longer life expectancy seems to warrant a redefinition of fidelity as something that must be reconceptualized again and again as the individuals involved grow more multifaceted over time.

If a woman's adultery can be a symbolic or enacted response to self-multiplication and change, the idealization of virginity denies and even defies such *change. As seen by others, unchanging innocence makes the virgin an idol or a commodity. From the perspective of the virgin herself, virginity depends upon a lack of self-understanding and self-acceptance. That "blindness" pairs neatly—if somewhat pornographically—with male voyeurism, as is especially apparent in the "Nausicaa" episode of* Ulysses. *Both the prohibition against adultery and the idealization of virginity are offshoots of the historical sexism of the Judeo-Christian tradition, a sexism which Jesus tried (apparently unsuccessfully) to disrupt.*

ADULTERY

How are we to understand the tension between Joyce's personal terror of being cuckolded and his decision to make adultery the central event of *Ulysses,* an event that Bloom must struggle with and at least partially over-come to return home? The fear of sexual betrayal not only affected Joyce's life (he reacted with outrage to the attractions of friends such as Vincent Cosgrave and Roberto Prezioso to Nora), it also haunts his writing: the tale of Michael Furey's love for Gretta spoils Gabriel's romantic plans for their night at the Gresham hotel in "The Dead," and the anxiety stemming from possible betrayal erupts into a climax of uncertainty in Joyce's play *Exiles.* The agony of feeling cuckolded can be dangerous, since as Shakespeare's horned image that mirrors Stephen and Bloom points out in "Circe," his crown of horns refers to "how my Oldfellow chokit his Thursdaymornun [how my Othello choked his Desdemona]" (*U* 15.3828–3829).[1] But Joyce, far from telling a story of Molly-murder, shows Bloom climbing back into a bed that still holds "the imprint of a human form, male, not his" (*U* 17.2124) and doing so "with circumspection, . . . with solicitude,. . . . prudently,. . . . lightly, . . . reverently" (*U* 17.2115–2120). The antagonistic sentiments of "envy, jealousy, abnegation, [and] equanimity" affect his subsequent reflections (*U* 17.2155). Bloom contemplates retribution, but his imagined methods are darkly comic. Only assassination and duel by combat are off the table. Still under consideration are "exposure by mechanical artifice (automatic bed) or individual testimony (concealed ocular witnesses)," and a suit for damages, hush money by moral influence (*U* 17.2201–2205).

What Joyce ultimately does in *Ulysses* took at least fifteen years for him to accomplish: without minimizing the depth of Bloom's pain, he shifts the main focus from the individual's devastating but also mixed feelings about betrayal to an implicit interrogation of fidelity. To whom or what does a person pledge to be faithful? Is it to a particular point in time (such as the memory on the Hill of Howth in *Ulysses*), to a vision of the beloved as he or she was at the beginning of the relationship, or is it simply a pledge of forbearance, a refusal to cultivate any kind of intimacy with anyone else? And what happens when the loved one changes, given that change is inevitable?

Another way to ask these questions is to examine the intersection between adultery and ordinariness that Joyce used to define June 16, 1904. Is Molly's adultery an extraordinary event, or is Joyce presenting it as simply one aspect of a typical day? Is adultery shocking or, as Barbara Leckie argues, "the most bourgeois of transgressions"?[2] My own view is that adultery is both shocking *and* banal, a transgression and an enacted confession of loneliness, need, and perhaps even greed. But as I hope the brief history that follows illustrates, adultery is closely akin to adulteration, and it is conceivably a metaphor for what happens when adults—especially female adults—can no longer lay claim to innocence and purity. When two individuals in relationship have multiplied themselves, their connection mutating in response to the march of time and the vagaries of circumstance, it becomes impossible for all the complex versions of one person to remain faithful to all the differing versions of the other. Growth is itself a kind of adultery; or, to put it another way, adulteration is a pejorative way of designating the increasing complexity that can come with maturity.

I propose to retrace Joyce's reading on adultery as it is represented in his notes on *Exiles*. His most important touchstones were three French writers in the seventeenth and nineteenth centuries: Molière, Paul de Kock, and Gustave Flaubert. It is significant that France, like Ireland, was a Catholic country, because Catholicism ramps up the cultural prohibition against adultery (English-language Protestantism, in contrast, is arguably based on it, via Henry VIII's desire for Anne Boleyn). I will begin by making a few overarching claims: for most French writers on female adultery that influenced Joyce, adultery constituted a titillating, fantasy-laced, and dangerous *alternative* to the routine of everyday life. The question of *what* gets adulterated or shamefully transformed by betrayal varies significantly, however. In Molière's plays, the husband fears that *he* will be changed; he will metamorphose from man to beast as he is altered or "decorated" with animal horns. About one and a half centuries later, in Paul de Kock's novel *The Cuckold* (1831), the protagonist's main concern is less for himself than for the authenticity of his bloodline.[3] Later in the nineteenth century, Flaubert will refocus the source of the problem; he portrays adulteration (and the betrayal that attends on it) as paradoxically generated by the religious and social insistence on female purity. Religion, morality, and romantic novels shockingly create the very sinful transformations they prohibit.

In his wildly popular Sganarelle comedies (especially *The School for Husbands* (1660) and *The Imaginary Cuckold* (1661), Molière dramatizes the husband's fear that his wife's adultery will transform his image, turning him (through the addition of imagined horns) into a risible admixture of man and beast. The purity of a wife, according to Sganarelle, is essential if a man is to sustain his humanity and his honor; anxiety about seeing his honor publicly besmirched is the occasion of much comic misunderstanding. For Paul de Kock, in the early nineteenth century, a wife's adultery (imagined or real) can still be the occasion for comedy, but in the case of the protagonist of *The Cuckold,* it also produces great conflict and ultimately pathos. The novel's wrenching conclusion exposes a highly problematic inconsistency in social mores: a guilty wife must be severely punished to avoid adulterating the man's bloodline. The problem, though, is that the social directives are inconsistent. Blémont's wife strays because of her jealousy over *his* infidelities, which are considered unimportant to everyone else. It is dashing for men to engage in adulterous liaisons, but disastrous for women to protest men's infidelity by behaving similarly because they must never conceive and give birth to another man's child. De Kock clearly appreciates the injustice of this disparity, which he portrays as tragic, but, according to the novel, there is no solution to it.

Flaubert changes the French formulation of the problem yet again, most controversially in *Madame Bovary* (1857). Paradoxically, he depicts the problem of female adultery as an unexpected *consequence* of the social imperative for women to be pure. Moreover, he identifies the source of Emma Bovary's passionate purity—her desire to transcend the lackluster ordinary—as generated by the conjunction of two different influences: romantic novels and, more controversially, the Catholic Church. Adultery here is no longer comic at all, although the cuckold, Emma's husband Charles, is presented as both pathetic and strangely admirable in his continuing adoration.

This brings us to Joyce, who wrestled with the tradition he saw evolving through Molière, de Kock, and Flaubert. Joyce, in the tradition of Flaubert, viewed the ideal of purity as fatally flawed in that it idealizes arrested development. In *Ulysses,* Joyce presents adulteration as inevitable, connecting it with the process of becoming an adult. Adulteration is what happens to adults who continue to grow, or Bloom. It is not an alternative to the humdrum quotidian, but a part of it. The challenge for adults is how to bear the continuing and inevitable adulteration (sometimes expressed through adultery) of someone they love, or how to negotiate their changing desires and needs with their loved one through communication.

Adultery has not been a hot topic for literary criticism since the early 1980s. The landmark study is Tony Tanner's *Adultery in the Novel* (1979), in which he argued that the violation of the marriage contract served as a vehicle for larger concerns about the overly restrictive social contract.[4] In nineteenth-century literature, the adulterous violator of this contract—when she is female and a protagonist—draws attention to the strictness of the law constraining women while eliciting sympathy and understanding for its transgression. It is crucial that it be the *wife* who transgresses because men enjoyed much more freedom (including sexual freedom)—the faithful wife served as the lynchpin for the larger social contract. Tanner argues that in the nineteenth century, the depiction of a woman's adultery served as a "frontal assault" on the entire social structure (17). The most famous examples of how this works in the continental novel are *Anna Karenina* and *Madame Bovary.*

Joyce's treatment of adultery in *Ulysses* builds on the pattern that Tanner so clearly analyzed in *Madame Bovary,* but Joyce is also doing something different with it.[5] The larger question of what exactly Joyce learned from Flaubert about adultery and everyday life has not yet been fully addressed. Is Joyce's change of tack significant, and if so, how? Because it is abundantly clear that Molly Bloom is no Emma Bovary. In the notes for his first exploration of adultery, *Exiles,* Joyce is pondering its important popular treatments in French literature, and we see him puzzling about the changes that have taken place as Molière is displaced by de Kock and then Flaubert. Joyce singles out *The Cuckold,* a book that Joyce owned in Trieste, commenting that de Kock is "a descendant surely of Rabelais and Molière."[6] The fact that de Kock is in conversation with Molière is made explicit in his novel through the introduction of a minor character, Monsieur Roquencourt. Roquencourt is an amateur actor who talks all the time about parts he has played, and one of his most successful parts was that of Sganarelle in Molière's *The*

Imaginary Cuckold—he played it in both Bordeaux and Paris. In the twentieth chapter, he goes on at length about his impersonation of Molière's famous character (played by Molière himself, dressed all in red, in his lifetime). De Kock is clearly mapping his own serious treatment of cuckoldry as an ironic, even tragic, bind against the comic fears of Sganarelle, a complex buffoon.

Molière makes an interesting starting point for literary treatments of adultery because of what his plays reveal about the absurdities of the social structure. It is important to recall that *The Imaginary Cuckold* and *The School for Husbands* were among his most popular plays in Molière's lifetime. Both sport with the extreme restrictions upon women and their permanent position in society as nonadults who are never allowed autonomy. *The School for Husbands,* in particular, stresses the helpless dependence of women by making the two female protagonists both the child-wards and the intended wives of their guardians (two brothers, one of whom is Sganarelle).[7] In both plays, Sganarelle is ludicrously afraid of being cuckolded, not understanding that he is already a figure of fun because of his pomposity, cowardice, and rigidity. For Sganarelle, being a cuckold is the epitome of sexual humiliation for men—his fear of growing horns accents his obliviousness to his other (nonsexual) limitations and inadequacies.

In thinking about French depictions of adultery, Joyce notes that there is an important difference between de Kock and his comic, ribald precursors. He writes about *The Cuckold,* "Salacity, humor, indecency, liveliness were certainly not wanting in the writer [de Kock] yet he produces a long, hesitating, painful story—written also in the first person. Evidently that spring is broken somewhere" (*E* 127). De Kock's novel begins the process of shifting sympathy to the cuckold by transforming the narrator, Blémont, from someone who once seduced married women into a married man who is himself cuckolded. When a young man, he was proud of his prowess as a seducer of neglected wives and contemptuous of the husbands he supplanted. Once cuckolded, Blémont suffers, but he cannot forgive the adulterous wife he still loves, who is relentlessly punished (to the death). The novel accents the tension between the sexual freedoms of men (that enhance their desirability) and the sexual restrictions on women (that diminish theirs, due to their role as mothers, potential or actual). Blémont solicits the reader's sympathy not only because he is the narrator, but because he becomes so painfully conscious of the potentially tragic implications of the double standard.

In another note to *Exiles,* Joyce focuses on Flaubert's treatment of adultery, opining that it was the publication of the lost pages of *Madame Bovary* (in the 1910 Louis Conard edition) that caused sympathy to shift from the lover to the cuckold (*E* 115). Whether or not this is true, it seems that, for Joyce, reading a fuller version of the novel gave him deeper insight into the complexity of the character of Charles Bovary, who would ultimately become one of the precursors of Leopold Bloom.

As a heuristic exercise, I propose to reconstruct Joyce's understanding of what Flaubert accomplished in *Madame Bovary.* Flaubert's social criticism goes far beyond that of de Kock in that it implicitly attacks not the double standard, but the widespread idealization or romanticization of marriage. He does this by portraying the mutually exclusive directives for women (to idealize consummation while remaining pure) as tragic on the personal level and disastrous on the social one. Adultery comes from the Latin *adultare,* "to corrupt" (through admixture). It is crucial to note that the opposite of adultery in etymological terms is not fidelity but purity (in Middle English, adultery also designated "sex between husband and wife for recreational purposes," according to the *Online Etymology Dictionary,* "adultery"). One of the most ingenious aspects of *Madame Bovary* is that it constitutes an indictment of purity on several levels, but the two that I will focus on briefly here are stylistic and what I call intrapsychic. The stylistic "impurity" of Flaubert is a consequence of his narrator's impartiality, his interest in many conflicting points of view. His intrapsychic critique extends his knowledge about the reader's expectations of Emma and Charles—that they should be faithful and angry, respectively—to the reader. As Joyce will do after him, Flaubert holds a mirror up to the reader's self-conception, exposing it as unrealistic. That distorted image of the self is what fuels judgmental reactions to the mistakes of others. The social standard is not only a double one; it perpetuates a lie, and that lie is that everyone is—or should be—a romantic hero.

Critics have commented on Emma's discovery that marriage and adultery are the same thing once the thrill is gone, but it is sometimes difficult to go one step further by appreciating that what marriage and adultery have in common is the adulteration of different kinds of purity.[8] If adultery is defined as the loss of purity, then isn't marriage itself a kind of adulteration, at least for women, in that it involves a loss of innocence, however socially sanctioned? Female purity, then, unbeknownst to most young women, solicits its own adulteration. Joyce plays with this idea in *Finnegans Wake* when HCE declares himself "incalpable . . . of unlifting upfallen girls wherein dangered from them in thereopen out of unadulteratous bowery, with those hintering influences from an angelsexonism" (*FW* 363.32–35). "Bowery" here can be read as a play on "Bovary." Idolatrous becomes "unadulteratous," a love not of idols but of unadulterated purity in nonadults. In *Madame Bovary*, Emma's downfall paradoxically results from the idealistic *purity* of her romanticism, which makes her heedless of costs (whether monetary or human). And her "pure" romanticism was absorbed from not one but two external influences: novels and religion. Like the boy in "Araby," she is turned into a "creature" (in the sense of "created being") by the confluence of romantic literature and Catholicism, which means that the Church is partly responsible for the purity that can only be fully realized through repeated sullying: by Charles, Rodolphe, and Léon. It is fitting that Emma's liaison with Léon begins in a church, which Flaubert likens to a "vast boudoir" (213). And earlier, Flaubert writes that when Emma "knelt at her Gothic prie-dieu, she would address the Lord with the same sweet words she used to murmur to her lover in the ecstatic transports of her adultery" (188).

Emma, with her capacious, vivid imagination, does not live in the world as it is. She disdains the ordinary, feeding on the unworldly sublimity promised by both religion and novels. After she has consummated her affair with Rodolphe, the narrator recounts, "*Ordinary life appeared only in the distance, far below, in shadow*" (142, my emphasis). "Then she recalled the heroines of the books she had read" (142). It isn't until the end of the novel that the ink of those novels is unveiled as arsenic, a kind of poison, when Emma greedily crams the white powder into her mouth that begins to taste like ink (280) and a stream of black liquid ran out of her mouth like vomit" (295). She is poisoned by glorious lies: the lies of pure, sustainable bliss promulgated through different forms of fiction. Romantic novels promise never-ending love coupled with an erotic fire that never diminishes, whereas the Church postpones the ecstatic consummation from marriage to death, represented as the door to eternal life.

How does the tragic ending of *Madame Bovary* compare to the treatment of adultery in *Ulysses*? Although the adultery in Joyce's novel is not comic in the usual sense, the ending insists upon an ethos of acceptance and sustains a desire for reconciliation, for beginning again. Emma and Molly are alike in one way, in that their purity is so thoroughly intertwined with their "corruption" that readers can only disentangle the two through a kind of interpretive violence (Molly is associated with both the Virgin Mary and Moll Flanders, Daniel Defoe's fictional whore, through her name—Marion—and her nickname, Molly).

Flaubert mounted a similar critique of purity at the level of style, or more specifically point of view, when he disciplined himself to resist providing narrative commentary or judgments. Multiple points of view—a truly adulterated narrative—are more stimulating, sensually and imaginatively. A vivid illustration of that point can be found in one of Lydia Davis's stories from *Can't and Won't*. Davis is of course the gifted translator of the (relatively) new English version of *Madame Bovary* from which I have been quoting. She illustrates what she calls "Flaubert's lesson concerning the singular point of view" by describing two pug dogs amid the varied scene of a Blessing of the Hounds. They represent—rather comically—purity of vision "as they strain at their leashes to reach one particular spot on the ground, intent not on the horses, the riders, the speech of the Master of the Hounds, the hunting dogs, or the squawking duck or goose, but only on the yellowish-white dollops of foam that have dropped from the mouth of a high-spirited horse nearby onto the dark pavement and that are so strange to them and so fragrant."[9] Davis succinctly captures Flaubert's satire of the self-interested single-mindedness of the traditional narrator through her portrayal of him as a pug dog pursuing only one scent in defiance of the richness and complexity of the scene around him. The alternative is to present multiple points of view without commentary, which is what Flaubert did, but it gave rise, ultimately, to Joyce's more radical assault on point of view. In *Ulysses*, point of view changes with the time of day, and it can be private (stream of consciousness), narrated by someone in a bar (Noman in the "Cyclops" episode), or a riff on different stylistic forms of discourse. The novel itself has been adulterated.

When we turn from stylistic purity to psychological purity (or a "pure" self-image), it becomes apparent that women are far more vulnerable to injunctions to remain pure than men. Both Flaubert and Joyce are intensely aware of the fact that to remain pure is to remain *young*: the prohibition against adultery has as its correlate the prohibition against education for women, because education *develops* women, thereby corrupting their youthful innocence and tarnishing their desire for a consummation devoutly to be wished. Women's desirability, then, is linked to a youth that can only be sustained through artificial means: by insulating them against experience itself. Development makes them not only autonomous but also "ugly" or "sinful." In contrast, for both Flaubert and Joyce adulteration is part of becoming an adult; it is the alternative to preserving the purity and limited frame of reference associated with children. Flaubert accents this when he describes Emma's feelings after she has yielded to Rodolphe (her first adultery) as a transfiguring experience; it was as if "she had come into a second puberty" (142). In *Finnegans Wake*, Joyce uses the word "Adultereux" to mean adults (*FW* 250.12). To mature, to age, is to multiply and mix perspectives, which has been socially proscribed—*especially* for women—as a form of corruption. Flaubert's character Homais, as Tanner brilliantly argues, epitomizes the kind of pharmaceutical activity society asks us to perform: he is someone who labels and classifies pure ingredients, mixing them only in a prescribed way (280). In return, he gets everything he wants, including the cross of the Legion of Honor. In a rare instance of narrative commentary, Flaubert writes, "he sold himself, he prostituted himself" (308). Significantly, it is from Homais's pharmacy that Emma procures the poison that kills her.

Can we know, then, how Joyce understood *Madame Bovary*? Can we extract an implicit interpretation from what he wrote in Flaubert's wake? I think we can, but the conclusion I have come to surprises me. Emma is not the prototype for Molly Bloom; she is an important precursor of Stephen Dedalus (as well as the boy in "Araby"). Flaubert, who famously proclaimed, "Emma Bovary, c'est moi," produced in *Madame Bovary* a portrait of the artist (or reader) as a young woman, and Joyce recognized his own brand of religiously and literarily inspired romanticism in her. She never appreciated Charles as a possible antidote to the poison that corrupted and killed her because he was such a *common* hero, and she "detest[ed] common heroes and moderate feelings" (72–73). Like Emma, Stephen is a highly intelligent, romantic victim of a culture that poisons him with impossible and escapist fantasies. Emma's last word, "L'aveugle" ("The blind man") (290), draws attention to her own blindness, but instead of burning in anguish and anger like those of the boy in Joyce's "Araby," her eyes close in death. Joyce's achievement was to turn this blindness—ultimately—from a tragedy into a comic invitation to achieve a more accurate understanding of the self and of the culture that shapes it.

Emma's similarity to Stephen is especially apparent in the following passage. After she allows herself to be seduced by the calculating Rodolphe, the narrator writes,

> She was entering something marvelous in which all was passion, ecstasy, delirium; a blue-tinged immensity surrounded her, heights of feeling sparkled under her thoughts, and ordinary life appeared only in the distance, far below, in shadow, in the spaces between those peaks.
>
> Then she recalled the heroines of the books she had read, and this lyrical host of adulterous women began to sing in her memory with sisterly voices that enchanted her. She herself was in some way becoming an actual part of those imaginings and was fulfilling the long daydream of her youth, by seeing herself as this type of amorous woman she had so envied. (142)

In *A Portrait of the Artist as a Young Man*, Stephen has similar fantasies of exaltation associated with romantic love. As an adolescent, dreaming of the figure of Mercedes in *The Count of Monte Cristo*, he longs "to meet in the real world the unsubstantial image which his soul so constantly beheld" (*P* 84). He is certain this image will encounter him, and he anticipates that they will meet quietly in some secret place "surrounded by darkness and silence: and in that moment of supreme tenderness he would be transfigured. He would fade into something impalpable under her eyes and then in a moment, he would be transfigured. Weakness and timidity and inexperience would fall from him in that magic moment" (*P* 84). The woman he encounters at the end of this chapter is akin to Emma Bovary's host of adulterous women, the heroines of books. Stephen's real-world "Mercedes" is a prostitute, and "in her arms he felt that he had suddenly become strong and fearless and sure of himself" (*P* 85).

After Rodolphe's rejection, Emma turns to religion as the highest kind of love (Flaubert 187–190). There existed "a love above all other loves, without interruption and without end, one that would continue to increase through all eternity! She could glimpse, among the illusions born of her hopes, a state of purity floating above the earth, merging with heaven, and this is where she aspired to be. She wanted to become a saint" (187). As she writes love letters to her other lover, Léon, "she saw a different man, a phantom created out of her most ardent memories, the most beautiful things she had read, her strongest desires; and in the end he became so real, and so accessible, that she would tremble, marveling" (257). Something similar had happened to Léon earlier, when he hopelessly loved Emma and "she was divested, in his eyes, of the fleshly attributes from which he had nothing to hope for" (93).

Similarly, when Stephen is dreaming of *his* Emma, he codes romantic, erotic desire as spiritual. When he awakens at dawn, something is "dewy wet"; he calls it his soul. In fantasy, his imagination becomes the virgin womb of Mary where the Word is made flesh. A "rose and ardent light" begins to glow in his spirit: "That rose and ardent light was her strange and wilful heart, strange that no man had known or would know, wilful from before the beginning of the world: and lured by that ardent roselike glow the choirs of the seraphim were falling from heaven" (P 182–183). Then he begins his poem about her, in which she is Eve, "lure of the fallen seraphim."

Like Flaubert, Joyce indicted romantic fiction (such as Scott's *The Bride of Lammermoor,* in whom Emma recognizes herself when watching the operatic version), as "lying drivel about pure men and pure women and spiritual love and love for ever: blatant lying in the face of the truth" (SL 129). Joyce's comic antidote to this poison, Leopold Bloom, is a sympathetic cuckold based at least in part on Charles Bovary. Charles felt more agony than Emma when she was dying, although unlike Molly, Emma never saw the irony that her husband loved her more completely than her lovers. What makes her husband's love so extraordinary is its realism: he gradually discovers all her shortcomings and loves her in spite of them, even (in part) because of them. Charles dies holding a lock of Emma's hair even after he has learned the truth of her adulteries, read all her love letters, and faced financial ruin from her extravagance. Like Bloom's, his is a love that does not despise the ordinary, the everyday. Although there is a stodginess to him, although he is compared to a "mill horse" and his name (cognate with "bovine") designates him as an ox, this ordinary man gives evidence of an extraordinary love that can love what is real.

What Joyce seems to have seen in Flaubert's treatment of adultery, then, is that for women it is often a blinkered attempt to obtain at last what they were promised in the form of a wedding night. It is like eating Turkish delight in secret (see "A Mother" in *Dubliners*). Why, then, would Joyce make his Emma a young man, and remake Charles as the cuckold of a different kind of woman; not a romantic, but another realist who seems to understand and even mirror him in certain ways?

It may be because Joyce was using adultery to search for a model of adult love, one that recognizes the complexities created by the adulteration and proliferation of people who *grow* instead of being poisoned or stagnating in a kind of psychic paralysis. How may adulterated adults "bloom"? Can literature give us an example of two married people who recognize and support the autonomy of the other, and who can endure the suffering such autonomy causes? When people commit to a relationship, to what are they committing? Is it to the fiction that the other will never change—never grow? Or is it to the hope that growth for all involved will be compatible, or at best inspirational?

We know that the Blooms both idealized their first sexual encounter on the Hill of Howth and both mourn its unrepeatability. But both also understand, perhaps intuitively, that (to quote Wilde) "it is only in voluntary associations that man [or woman] is fine" ("The Soul of Man under Socialism").[10] At the end of the day, Bloom feels more abnegation than jealousy, less envy than equanimity because "from outrage (matrimony) to outrage (adultery) there arose nought but outrage (copulation)" (*U* 17.2195–2197). Or, as Flaubert puts it in *Madame Bovary*, the "disillusionment of adultery" is *produced* by "the defilement of marriage" (196). Flaubert's characters could not survive it, but the Blooms will live to see another day.

The questions Joyce raises about social objections to adulteration also affect his treatment of the everyday. It is the struggle to accept adulteration—the multitudinous and contradictory nature of raw experience—that transforms a single day into an epic journey. The sustained effort he makes to accept the inevitability of adulteration and even its many pleasures is what makes Bloom heroic—his heroism is intimately bound up with his experience of humiliation. Joyce presents readers with the possibility of accessing the humility offered by humiliation. In Lydia Davis's terms, he offers us the whole bustling scene of the Blessing of the Hounds in place of the pug dogs' blinkered pursuit of fragrant puddles of horse spittle.

VIRGINITY

In the "Nausicaa" episode of *Ulysses*, Gerty MacDowell is the virgin on the beach who leans back and kicks her legs so that Bloom can see her "understandings." His hand discreetly hidden in his pocket, he explodes in synch with the fireworks of the Mirus bazaar. Part of the unexpected humor of this episode is that at the same time that Gerty is displaying herself to Bloom, the priests in the nearby church are elevating the host for all to see at a temperance retreat for men. Both activities, Bloom's and the men's at the retreat, involve watching "a projected mirage" (which Joyce listed in his schema as the "meaning" of the episode). "Mirage" is derived from the Latin *mirare*, "to look at" and also "to mirror," and *mirus*, meaning "wonderful." Significantly, the wonderful but unreal image the men all worship is virginity.[11]

The humor created by this juxtaposition of different kinds of visual "worship" has the potential to open up a space for self-reflection and even self-recognition in the voyeur—here the reader. The potential for self-awareness arises because the person observing (or reading) may react strongly, perhaps physically, to the person being watched (or read about). They are peeping through a window at something that affects them, but humor can turn that window into a mirror offering insight into the observer's own reactions. The very observant faculty that fuels voyeurism can be turned back upon the self, so that what started as a pornographic impulse becomes a means of self-awareness and even self-reappraisal.

Humor, especially black humor—which is more significant and ironic than funny—opens up a space between watcher and watched, the person laughing and the person being laughed at, a space enabled by the distance between them and also charged by imagined connection. Black humor has a self-consciousness to it that may potentially turn the observer into a critic, perhaps even a self-reflexive one. The difference between voyeurism and self-reappraisal, then, is shorter than we might think, because objectification contains within it the seeds of objectivity that may in some cases be turned back upon the observing subject.

In *Ulysses*, Gerty is young, desirable, and in some ways pitiable. In several respects she resembles what Angela Carter once called "the beautiful clown," epitomized by the Marquis de Sade's Justine, and more recently by Marilyn Monroe.[12] To some extent readers of "Nausicaa" laugh *at* Gerty, especially at the way she disguises her feelings and sexual desires through a sickly-sweet narrative of romantic and novelistic clichés. Ultimately, however, the very thing we laugh at—Gerty's naivete—comes to seem frightening. Gerty's lack of self-awareness, her narrative alienation from her own body and its most intimate workings, is a little terrifying. In the end, the humor sparked by the beautiful clown isn't very funny at all.

Gerty's self-alienated desire is a kind of inadvertent hypocrisy, as Joyce suggests when he lists hypocrisy as one of the symbols of the episode. It's a refusal to accept a bodily reality, a denial of the pent-up power of her desire. Writing over fifty years later, Angela Carter in *The Sadeian Woman* helps to illuminate what is going on in "Nausicaa" not by analyzing it, but by looking at the pornographic writings of the Marquis de Sade. "Nausicaa" is a particularly rich example of what Carter calls "moral pornography" because it reveals social norms as in some ways obscene. The reader of "Nausicaa" comes to occupy a position very similar to Bloom's: he or she is gazing at a book that for one chapter becomes the equivalent of Gerty's drawers, exposing something that is typically hidden from view, in this case masturbation.

Could the encounter between Bloom and Gerty be called pornographic or is it "moral pornography"? Following Carter, did they "meet" (or agree to look and be looked at, respectively) in order "to assuage desire in a reciprocal pact of tenderness"? (8). If so, that mutual tenderness constitutes a "moral contradiction" (19): there is something we might call *loving* about the reciprocity of their exchange, even though each party has arguably abstracted (or differently idealized) the other and therefore used him or her for purposes of self-gratification and relief. Part of what makes "Nausicaa" an example of *moral* pornography is that it contains no cruelty, no violence. Despite Bloom's fear that he has on some level deflowered Gerty, taking her virginity in a physical or literal sense, when he thinks he sees her in Nighttown as a whore (U 15.372–376), the depiction of sex without violence or physical violation; without coercion, masochism, or sadism; without knowledge of or responsibility for the other suggests that this mutual using affords both Gerty and Bloom a respite from their lives, a respite that is not abusive. It is an example of what Carter calls "pornography in the service of women" (3). On the other hand, insofar as *both* Gerty and Bloom reduce one another to a fictional archetype or an object, respectively, their encounter is more pornographic and (surprisingly) more "religious" than it is loving. It is startling to see a kinship emerging between pornography, love, and religion in the context of "Nausicaa" (see Carter 7), a kinship that Joyce acknowledges and even accepts with humor.

In view of this mutual contradiction I've just outlined—that Bloom and Gerty use but do not abuse one another by tacit mutual consent—one can posit that reading, love, and even religion are pornographic when the person engaging in them does not receptively *change* in response to the encounter, when he or she fails to expand imaginatively and to recontextualize the importance of selfhood in relation to that enlarged perspective. Such resistance to change makes Sade's Justine obscene, at least from Carter's perspective: "Things happen to her but do not change her . . . [even] rape is unable to modify her intransigent singularity in any way" (5). Pornography, then, while fueled by fantasies of extraordinary encounters, may be defined as an experience of sexual release *without* transformation. The desirable transformation (which a pornographic encounter fails to produce) is not a reduction or diminution of the self but an expansion of vision: a movement toward greater elasticity and comprehensiveness.

To define pornography—and therefore to understand how religion and love as well as reading can be pornographic—it is useful to begin with Carter's view of pornography as a *reductive* mode of representation. She argues that pornography is a mode of *abstraction*—"an abstraction of human intercourse in which the self is reduced to its formal elements, . . . the probe and the fringed hole, [which produce] a universal pictorial language of lust" (4). She sees graffiti, the "*reductio ad absurdum* of the bodily differences between men and women," as illustrations of such abstraction (4). She makes a crucial move that helps to explain the religious accompaniment to the voyeurism in "Nausicaa": she argues that when we enlarge some aspect of the human, simplifying it and presenting it as the single most important aspect of humanity, we are doing pornographically what we do when we mythologize or idealize sexual difference: denying the complexity of our existence as social and historical beings. In short, then, both pornography and religion *abstract* the human; in particular, both rely on false universals to reduce women to their sexual and reproductive functions (virginity, motherhood, whorishness—Nausicaa, Oxen, Circe), thereby savagely denying "the complexity of human relations" (6). According to Carter, "All the mythic versions of women, from the myth of the redeeming purity of the virgin to that of the healing, reconciling mother, are consolatory nonsenses" (5).

However, there is an advantage to schematizing or simplifying the relations between the sexes as pornography does: it allows us to see the social and economic structures at work in society much more clearly: "The sexual act in pornography exists as a metaphor for what people do to one another" (17). Carter argues that what we can see so clearly in Sade (and sadism) is that it reinforces the status quo, in which the actors (usually men, but sometimes women as well in Sade) are monsters with an insatiable appetite—not for flesh, but for bloody meat (see Carter's last chapter, "Speculative Finale"), and that those who are acted upon are as resistant to change as their abusers. Although beautiful women are raped, many of them (like Sade's Justine) remain mentally inviolate—retaining the innocence of children—and therefore retain a moral superiority. Despite this moral superiority, though, abused women are "good" only in the way children are good—they do what they're told and do no evil—but they are incapable of doing good actively in the world because they remain unaware or "innocent" of the larger social contexts in which they *could* act. In other words, such victims are simply deluded and amoral—they, too, are as incapable of change as their tormentors.

Carter suggests that in Sade's fiction we can see not only the horror of the relations between the sexes, but also of those between the upper and lower classes, the fuel of the French Revolution. The libertines of Sade's fictions are not only in the privileged position of the male, they are also in the privileged position of the aristocrat, and the stubborn ignorance or "purity" of their sacrificial victims is that of women *and the poor,* who end up suffering degradation because their conception of "goodness" precludes autonomy, or "free" thought. Freedom is for libertines, who are "in exile from the world in their abominable privilege, at the same time as they control the world" (25). Pornography can become moral "when it begins to comment on real relations in the real world," to confront "the moral contradictions inherent in real sexual encounters" (19). When we describe "the real conditions of the world in terms of sexual encounters," the "real nature of these encounters illuminates the world itself," and we discover that "the area of our lives where we believed we possessed most freedom is seen as the most ritually circumscribed" (21).

The moral pornographer, then, is an artist who might use pornography as a critique of current relations between the sexes. His business would be the total demystification of the flesh and the subsequent revelation, through the infinite modulations of the sexual act, of the *real* relations of man and his kind. Such a pornographer would not be the enemy of women, perhaps because he might begin to penetrate to the heart of the contempt for women that distorts our culture even as he entered the realms of true obscenity as he describes it. "Sexual relations between men and women always render explicit the nature of *social* relations in the society in which they take place, and if described explicitly, will form a critique of those relations, even if that is not and never has been the intention of the pornographer" (20). It was not Sade's intention (presumably) to produce a social critique, but Carter argues that he gives readers to the opportunity to do so. It *was* Joyce's intention—but his critique is, importantly, also comic. Humor is crucial because it can free the perpetrators of the very guilt or shame that prevents change or development.

"Nausicaa," then, can be described as a softly pornographic narrative, enhanced for Gerty by love stories from women's magazines, which Carter calls "the softest of all forms of pornography" (22). The account of Gerty's perspective of her encounter with Bloom is presented in the third person to accent the fact that she has distanced herself from her actions and feelings, like Sade's Justine. Joyce, however, has subverted the usual pornographic tale. According to Carter, "A male-dominated society produces a pornography of universal female acquiescence. Or, most delicious titillation, of compensatory but spurious female dominance" (of the sort Bloom enjoys in "Circe," 20). Joyce does not present Bloom as the main actor—the action is simultaneously initiated (if also disavowed) by Gerty. It would be tempting to use this fact to rewrite the hagiographic account of the Virgin Mary. The mythic (and official) version of the story presents her as an acquiescent, obedient vessel, but a real version would see her as an unmarried young woman who had found herself pregnant. (The word translated as "virgin" in the Christian Scriptures actually means "unmarried" in Aramaic.)[13]

Gerty is much more active than the usual pornographic heroine—her body is freer than her mind. Her body longs for the pleasure of revealing its hidden secrets, but her imagination is in thrall to social and religious ideals of female "innocence." Instead of offering her whole self as an idol to be worshipped by Bloom, Gerty offers him a glimpse of one hidden thing: her underwear, her bloomers, her drawers, what the narrator refers to in euphemistic Gerty language as her "understandings." What gets mystified and (metaphorically) desecrated is not her body but her (as well as Bloom's) clothing, an implicit commentary on the way the host being consumed in the chapel nearby both is and is not the body of Jesus. However unusually free her body may be, though, Gerty's mind is and remains virginal—and to the extent that we define the pornographic as that which is resistant to change, it is pornographic as well. She is mentally and imaginatively a virgin, but there is also a sense in which she is a whore, because she is "selling" not herself but her cosmetically enhanced image, and this is what Bloom enjoys without feeling any threat from (or commitment to) her sexual being. Here, too, she resembles Sade's Justine, the "beautiful clown."

Sade's Justine is a lovely young woman who is repeatedly used and raped without ever feeling an instant of pleasure or enjoyment: this is what in her mind allows her to remain "good." Carter argues that for her, virtue is frigidity (49); She describes her as "a selfless heroine of Rousseau in the egocentric and cruel world of Hobbes" (47). She is a Christ figure whose martyrdom is "absolutely useless," "the heroine of a black, inverted fairytale" (39). "Upon her lovely and innocent head fall an endless stream of the ghastliest misfortunes and her virtue, the passive virtue of a good woman, insures she can never escape them because the essence of her virtue is doing what she is told" (46). "Repression is Justine's whole being—repression of sex, of anger, and of her own violence; the repressions demanded of Christian virtue, in fact" (48). "The price she has to pay for resolutely, indeed heroically, maintaining her role of bourgeois virgin against all odds is a solitary confinement in the prison of her own femininity" (50). She is especially like Gerty in that "her freedom is involuntary"—in fact, it is her punishment because it is at odds with the idealization of femininity she stands for (51).

Carter controversially contends that "a lovely woman is always a comic figure" (68). When students—especially female ones—discover with Bloom that Gerty is lame, they tend to get angry with him for having "used" her. Although we would no longer reduce physical disability to a metaphor, Joyce is still arguably using it as an external sign of her crippled consciousness, a consciousness disabled by the way she has been interpolated into a male-dominated society. She is a comic figure—like all beautiful young women—because she cannot allow herself to know *why* she is pretty, because, as Carter argues, sex is a source of sin (67). She is a "boob" in the sense of a stupid awkward person, a product of the "moral irreconcilability of physical attractiveness and sexuality" (60). The source of her beauty—her sexuality—is perceived by her as immoral and so she cannot "know" it. The tension between her beauty and the need to deny her sexuality alienates her from her own image—like Issy in *Finnegans Wake*, she is "more like her image in the mirror than she is like herself," as Carter puts it (63). She experiences her appearance as extraneous to her, which Joyce underscores by having her think of herself in the third person (70). She markets her image to men—which makes her an imaginary prostitute (67), but, as Carter explains, "Since she is not in control of her own marketing, her hypothetical allure and not her actual body is the commodity. She sells a perpetually unfulfilled promise" (67). Paradoxically, the unfulfillment *is* the consolation, as well as the disappointment.

The pathos of this comic figure comes from the "dreadful innocence" that arises out of her "lack of self-knowledge" (64). It is "not stupidity but a naivety so perfect it is functionally no different from stupidity" (66). Her lack of self-awareness is self-defeating, if not deadly: "She is not in control of the laughter and contempt she arouses. They are in control of her, modifying her opinion of herself, indignifying her" (Carter 70). What is most frightening about the beautiful clown is that "in herself, this lovely ghost, this zombie, or woman who has never been completely born as a woman, only as a debased cultural idea of a woman, is appreciated only for her decorative value. . . . She is most arousing as a memory or as a masturbatory fantasy" (70). She cannot get married because she does not exist—it is the illusion of her existence that will disappear with marriage. As Carter asserts, "She is obscene to the extent to which she is beautiful. Her beauty, her submissiveness and the false expectations that these qualities will do her some good are what make her obscene" (57).

What is the function of this desirable, comic, ephemeral phantasm who believes herself to be a good girl—a virgin—but whose "final humiliation is to realize that her value has never resided in herself but in the values of the open market," so that she, "like a common criminal, has a price on her head" (74)? Her function is to arouse men without ever allowing her sexuality to make them feel inadequate (67). That is why she sells her *image,* not herself—her image is the least threatening part, and she sells it so that a man can preserve his self-image, so that he can experience self-gratification with no fear of impotence. If a man can read "Nausicaa" without feeling a desire to change—to move on to "Oxen" and "Circe"—that reading is pornographic. The challenge for the female reader is to see the Gerty in herself and change, using this knowledge to unshackle the mind and cleanse the body of shame.

7 ▸ ON LOVE

Joyce is cautious about the meaning of love, carefully differentiating it from desire or erotic love, which Søren Kierkegaard once called "the beautiful giddiness of eternity."[1] Dubliners ends with Gabriel Conroy's startled realization that he has never experienced love: when picturing a sick young man's determination to see Gretta before she leaves, even if it put his poor health at risk through exposure to cold and rain, he thinks, "He had never felt like that himself towards any woman but he knew that such a feeling must be love" (D 223). In his only play, Exiles, Joyce returns to the subject, positioning his semi-autobiographical protagonist, Richard Rowan, between two women he has "loved" in different ways: his muse, aptly named Beatrice (after Dante), who has inspired him from afar and for whose eyes he writes, and his domestic partner, Bertha, who has borne his son. (Richard is also drawn in relation to two men he loves: his friend Robert, and his son Archie.) Richard slowly comes to understand that love is not possession, despite the erotic attraction and later the security of such a view. Indeed, love is the opposite of possession, which demotes the beloved to an object to be owned and used: instead, it inheres in the difficult, even self-wounding promotion of the freedom of the beloved, especially the freedom of choice. The tricky part of allowing freedom to the beloved is that such freedom cannot be given, as Richard *tries to do by giving Bertha the freedom to have an assignation with Robert. To give freedom is not only to reify it, to make it a thing that one has the power to give to another. It is also an attempt to control the other by telling (ordering?) him or her to be free. The play suggests that love depends upon the disciplined recollection that the lover does not know or understand the beloved. The recognition of one's ignorance of the other (which is often obscured by the familiarity of long habit) need not be a cause of despair, however, but a spur to renewed receptivity. Love is the willingness to be and remain open to the changing conditions of another's (unknowable) being. This is as true of reading as it is for loving: an author cannot give freedom to the reader any more than a lover can give freedom to a partner. The only thing one can do is to write in a way that rewards an open-minded willingness to see familiar things with a new eye, while respecting any disinclination or unreadiness to do so.*

As Richard says to Robert, to love someone over time is to accept the responsibility of being a person through whom the beloved experiences him or herself. The way a person develops (or fails to develop) is in part a function of the part he or she plays in an ongoing dialogue with intimate other(s). As they talk about Bertha, Richard asks Robert whether he has the "luminous certitude that yours is the brain in contact with which she must think and understand and that yours is the body in contact with which her body must feel" (E 63).

Like Richard Ellmann in his preface to the Gabler edition of *Ulysses,* I would say that *Ulysses* is indeed about love, but (unlike Ellmann) I would specify that love, like darkness, needs to be carefully redefined because Joyce means something very different by it than do most casual users of the word.[2] As Joyce demonstrates in "Cyclops," love as it is most commonly used is childishly narcissistic and sentimental; it is self-satisfied optimism at its most ludicrous, the product of romantic and religious brainwashing aimed at the kindergarten set, and its function is to make everyone feel connected:

Love loves to love love. Nurse loves the new chemist. Constable 14 A loves Mary Kelly. Gerty MacDowell loves the boy that has the bicycle. M.B. loves a fair gentleman. Li Chi Han lovey up kissy Cha Pu Chow. Jumbo, the elephant, loves Alice, the elephant. Old Mr Verschoyle with the ear trumpet loves old Mrs Verschoyle with the turnedin eye. The man in the brown macintosh loves a lady who is dead. His Majesty the King loves her Majesty the Queen. Mrs Norman W. Tupper loves officer Taylor. You love a certain person. And this person loves that other person because everybody loves somebody but God loves everybody. (*U* 12.1493–1501)

As Joyce redefines the term, love offers a more complex challenge. Joyce subjects love in *Ulysses* to a treatment comparable to the one he gave passion in "The Dead": he took the popular idea of passion as white-hot desire (which the lover assumes to be reciprocated) and had his protagonist, Gabriel Conroy, act it out. Joyce then pitted Gabriel's model of passion as a frenzy to possess the aestheticized object of desire against an older model of passion that captures the original meaning of the word: to suffer. Michael Furey's willingness to suffer in order to see Gretta before she left Galway stands in such sharp contrast to Gabriel's self-satisfied assurance of his own desirability that he is pricked to see himself as a fatuous, self-important clown who has experienced lust but has never known love: "He had never felt like that himself towards any woman but he knew that such a feeling must be love" (*D* 223).

The problem with the Michael Furey model of love, like that of Christ's Passion on which it is based, is that in the act of giving everything for the beloved, the self is destroyed: Furey's gift to Gretta is a ghostly or pyrrhic victory.[3] The question then becomes: Is it possible to give love without relinquishing one's life? (As Stephen thinks when he imagines trying to save a drowning man, "I want his life still to be his, mine to be mine" [*U* 3.327–328]). Joyce first addresses this question in his only play, *Exiles*: How can love be *given*? Is it something that *can* be given, or *possessed*? To understand Joyce's treatment of love in *Ulysses*, a reader must first come to terms with what Joyce learned in *Exiles*, which he finished as he was beginning the composition of *Ulysses*.

Exiles is a play about homecoming in which Joyce imagines what it might be like for him to return from Italy to Dublin with his lover and their son. The play centers on the interactions of four main characters and two minor ones: Richard Rowan, loosely based on Joyce; Bertha, his partner; Archie, their son; and Brigid, their servant, form one group. The other two characters are cousins who have remained in Dublin while the Rowans were abroad in Italy: Beatrice Justice, who has been an inspiration for Richard's writing and with whom he corresponded while he was away, and Robert Hand, a journalist and friend of Richard's who is trying to help Richard get a professorship at the university. The play consists primarily of conversations between shifting pairs of characters. The dialogue ranges from cliché to melodrama as the audience learns more and more of each character's secrets. Beatrice is a despairing, chilly woman who ventriloquizes her hidden pride and scorn through Richard's writing. Richard is feeling guilty because he has inadvertently fostered Bertha's increasing dependence on him. He had hoped that their evasion of marriage would give them both more freedom, but the shame and uncertainty of their relation, her greater isolation, and the responsibilities of motherhood have curtailed her freedom and awakened in her a wistful, romantic nostalgia for the beginning of their relationship. Robert wants to steal Bertha from Richard, and is secretly courting her in Richard's own home, but Bertha keeps Richard informed of every move Robert makes. Richard wants everyone to be free to choose his or her own course of action, but he doesn't want anyone to act secretly, "in the dark" (E 69). Therefore, when Robert is expecting a visit from Bertha, Richard shows up ahead of her and tells Robert that he knows everything. Robert is quite naturally embarrassed, but Richard rather unexpectedly tells him to carry on, that he isn't going to try to stop Robert from seducing Bertha. He just didn't want Robert to think he was putting anything over on him. Richard leaves, Bertha shows up, and Robert is annoyed at her for not having told him that Richard knew. She explains that she is an honest and straightforward person and tells him she would have been honest with him too if he had ever asked her what Richard thought. Act 2 ends while Robert and Bertha are still together in Robert's cottage, and the audience never learns what happened there, or whether anything happened.

Act 3 opens early the next morning. We see Richard suffering, Bertha sleepless but concerned about Richard. She offers to tell him what happened, but he responds that even if she tells him, he will never know. Beatrice comes in to show them the morning paper, which contains a leading article that Robert has written about Richard called "A Distinguished Irishman." She tells them Robert is leaving town, and Bertha sends for him immediately. Bertha chides Robert for planning to leave without talking to Richard, reminding him that such an act would leave Richard with the wrong impression. Robert and Richard speak, and the play ends with Bertha and Richard expressing their feelings of isolation and doubt, respectively.

As this summary might suggest, Exiles was not likely to be a box-office success. It's the kind of play that would have driven Artaud wild; if the life of theater is gesture—physical contact and conflict of the sort represented by a Balinese cockfight—*Exiles* has no life. The only way it could possibly succeed as theater is if it were staged as anti-theater: an ultra-conventional "ghost story" set in the stifling atmosphere of two enclosed rooms, where the only relief comes from opening a window or a door. The unreality of the characters could be emphasized by unchanging, larger-than-life masks—Richard's set in a habitual scowl, Robert's in a knowing smile. Beatrice's mask would give her a thin, pale, bitter expression, and Bertha would have no mask until the beginning of Act 3. This is still to visualize what Joyce demanded that we hear—the tinny insincerity of four voices jockeying for advantage under the guise of mutual regard.

Like Gabriel in "The Dead," the four characters in *Exiles* have tried to love, but their efforts seem wasted. More specifically, the characters are unable to reconcile love with either freedom or responsibility. *Exiles*, then, might best be described as a thought experiment in dramatic form. The problem it explores is this: Is it possible to *give* freedom? Is freedom a *thing* to be given or awarded (to a lover, a child, or a reader)? What is the relation between generosity (giving) and forgiveness? What does it feel like for an author, lover, or parent to give this gift? Finally, does the recipient of this gift experience the blended joy and responsibility of genuine freedom, or does he become irresponsible and immoral, lacking any remorse of conscience? (This last change seems to describe what happens to Robert and perhaps even Archie.)

I want to address each of these questions in turn, but first I'd like to draw closer attention to my parenthetical suggestion that freedom may be offered to a lover, a child, or a reader. Part of what differentiates *Exiles* from "The Dead" and ties it to *Ulysses* is that, for the first time, Joyce sets out to explore the connections between generosity, responsibility, and freedom on *three* levels, or in three different kinds of relationships. Most critics focus on the (non)sexual relation in *Exiles*, understandably, because it is most central. What I want to emphasize, though, is that Joyce is treating all three forms of relation—sexual, textual (or artistic), and parental—as analogous, and that these three kinds of relationship again overlap in significant ways in *Ulysses*.

Let me start with the parent-child relationship, which is explored in the play through three different sets of parent-child relations: Richard's relation to his parents, Beatrice's relation to *her* parents, and Archie's relation to Richard and Bertha. In Act 1, Richard introduces the dilemma of how love is related to generosity by contrasting the generosity of his (dead) father with the hard-heartedness of his (dead) mother. Richard's last memory of his father is of an act of generosity: when Richard was fourteen, his father called him to his bedside to give him permission and the money to do something he knew Richard wanted to do: hear *Carmen*. He died while Richard was gone. Richard calls the memory "sweet and noble," referring to his father as "the smiler," whereas his mother he remembers as hard, cold, and begrudging. He claims to "pity her cold blighted love" for him, but he confesses that he is still inwardly battling her spirit. Her miserly spirit is apparent in two ways—in her obdurate refusal to forgive him, even on her deathbed (forgiveness, as the word suggests, being associated with giving), and in her effect on his life. He says that "on account of her I lived years in exile and poverty too, or near it" (*E* 23). Richard clearly prefers the gift of pleasure and music granted him by his dying father to the grim letter of warning sent by his dying mother, but he prays twice not for his father's warmth but for *her* hardness of heart (*E* 22, 25). Love is not reducible to mere generosity, then, as much as Richard would like for it to be. And it is not generosity but principle that Richard needs, as we can see in his indulgent relation to his own son, Archie.

Beatrice's parental influences mirror Richard's with the genders reversed. It is her father who epitomizes gloom, seriousness, and righteousness and Robert's mother (Beatrice's aunt) who gives the gift of music. Joyce adds this information to clarify the point that an affinity for generosity or principle is not linked to gender: men as well as women can be severe, and women as well as men can be joyous and musical. Richard is generous, like his own father, leaving the discipline to Bertha. Bertha perceptively understands that he is repeating the pattern of his own family of origin, projecting onto her the role of "cruel mother" because he never loved his own mother. She also intuitively understands the destructiveness of a generosity that lacks restraint, as she denies the implication that her discipline is loveless. (Her solicitude for Archie is particularly apparent in Act 3, when she cleans his mouth with her handkerchief, which she has moistened with her tongue [*E* 92]). Bertha diagnoses the problem with Richard's generosity: he is helpless to be anything other than generous; he cannot say no—to Archie, to Robert, or to her (*E* 52, 56). Beatrice, according to Bertha, is Richard's exact opposite—she cannot give; she is not generous. In fact, Beatrice needs Richard *because* she is unable to give; he expresses the generous senti-

ments that she has choked off. If love is not reducible to generosity, Beatrice
shows that neither is love possible in the *absence* of generosity.

To give a quick recap, then: Robert is greedy, trying to steal (or rob)
Bertha from Richard, whom he sees as both generous and—as his name
suggests—rich in love. Beatrice is *not* generous, but neither is she acquisitive; she lives vicariously through the expressions of others—Richard's writing, Archie's piano playing. Richard is compulsively generous, and Bertha is
simply bewildered by Richard's desire to give her and Robert's desire to take
her. What she wants is to keep things as they were when she and Richard
first met. The question is, do any of these positions represent a truly loving
attitude? At first, it may be tempting to equate Joyce's position with Richard's, because he is the autobiographical character and because he claims to
have outgrown Robert's romantic and demonic philosophy of self-assertion.
Moreover, Richard tries to justify his compulsive generosity by reframing it
as sacrifice. When he asks Archie if he understands what it means to give a
thing (*E* 46), he is outlining the ethos of sacrifice. He explains that giving is
the only guarantee of eternal possession. This is clearly a theological idea—
he is giving in order to receive, sacrificing in the literal sense of "making
sacred" the object of his desire. What is odd—maybe even unique—about
this ploy is that Richard is applying it to not to food, as the ancients did, but
to the realm of sexuality: he is giving away his "wife" in order to forestall los-
ing her, while at the same time sacralizing (or resacralizing) their union.
This is such an unconventional idea that it can easily be confused with a
radical, even a feminist position: instead of having his Nora walk out on
him, as Ibsen's heroine so controversially walked out on her husband and
children in *A Doll's House,* Joyce imagines himself *giving* her freely to another
man for whom she feels desire.

But Richard's attitude toward love is not that of the mature Joyce. The
questions Richard never asks are first, whether Bertha is his to give, and second, whether she is a *thing* ("Do you understand what it is to give a thing?" he
asks Archie [*E* 46]). It should be obvious that the answer is "no" to both questions. Despite his predilection for masochistic sacrifice, Richard's motives are
as possessive as Robert's. He tries to possess not only by giving, but also by
remembering; as Richard boasts, he never forgets anything. Yet another indirect way Richard tries to possess those he loves is by insisting on telling them
everything he knows (to tell one's secrets is also to number or count them, to
render them "real" by putting them into words). He tells Bertha about his

infidelities, and he tells Robert everything he knows about Robert's attempts to seduce Bertha. Then (and only then) he offers to give them their freedom as a gift from him; he must first possess or master this freedom to give it to them—their freedom must pass through his mind and hands.

Robert is just as acquisitive as Richard, although his rationalization is that of a hedonist rather than a saint. Not only does he want to steal Bertha and win over Archie, he also wants to *give* Richard a reputation for distinction by composing and publishing his importance, literally authorizing Richard's talent. He recognizes and resents Richard's position as the prodigal son when he tells him that the fatted calf will be eaten in his honor at the vice chancellor's dinner. What Robert resents is the indirectness of Richard's acquisitiveness, its pretensions to being spiritual (and therefore higher) than Robert's carnal appetite. In their youth, they shared a pride of possession, symbolized by the two keys they had to the cottage where they enjoyed a succession of women. Richard boasts that he has given up his key, but Robert senses he did so as an attempt to own one woman more totally. Robert's attitude, however, is not an ethical alternative—he gets not by remembering but by forgetting, by denying the burdens of consciousness and conscience (he says, "I have no remorse of conscience" [E 41]). He frames his defense in the language not of God but of Lucifer, arguing that he (like Richard when he was young, and like Stephen Dedalus) will not serve: "I am sure that no law made by man is sacred before the impulse of passion. There is no law before impulse. Laws are for slaves" (E 87).[4] He tells Richard with Nietzschean fervor, "All life is a conquest, the victory of human passion over the commandments of cowardice. . . . The blinding instant of passion alone–passion, free unashamed, irresistible–that is the only gate by which we can escape from the misery of what slaves call life. Is not this the language of your own youth?" (E 71).

What Robert calls freedom is simply revolt; what Richard calls freedom is dishonest philanthropy; Beatrice feels free by ventriloquizing through Richard's writing; and Bertha experiences what the others call freedom as simple loneliness. Although the play is set in Ireland two months after John Redmond had succeeded in getting an Irish Home Rule bill on the docket in Parliament, it is ironically clear that none of the characters (with the possible exception of Archie) has a clue what freedom is. Freedom is neither a thing to be given (as England is considering giving it to Ireland) nor a refusal of law (the Irish rebel position). What, then, does Joyce suggest it might be?

Can freedom be a love-offering, something made available to a child, a lover, or a reader without covert implications of coercion and the anxiety attendant upon it?

The answer is important politically, ethically, and textually—because freedom is also something Joyce badly wanted to give to those he loved, including his readers. But if he had to discover, like Richard, that freedom is not a thing to be given, and it is not his to give, how then could he encourage freedom of response? Not by doing what Robert does—writing for the common person, using the language of people whose opinions he doesn't share. Although Robert claims to be a patriot, Richard reads Robert's style as lacking independence. In one of the excised fragments of the play, Richard accuses Robert of having "taken the smooth path, accepting ironically everything in which you disbelieved and building for your body and for that function of it which I suppose you call your soul a peace of prudence, irony, and pleasure." Richard boasts that he, in contrast, has "lived without prudence, risking everything, destroying everything in order to create again."[5] Richard's claim rings false, although romantically so, but Robert has sold out too; he is simply more pragmatic about it.

At some point in the composition of *Exiles,* Joyce realized the romantic hypocrisy of Richard's position, seeing that it matched Robert's while seeming to oppose it. What Richard discovers while trying to *give* freedom is that it can't be given, that it is not always a welcome gift, and that freedom without principle produces nothing more than hedonism or crass materialism, on the one hand, or loneliness, on the other. All the characters glimpse, painfully, restlessly, with brief moments of joy and clarity, how difficult it is to resist (but not defy) temptation, to listen to what is in their hearts, to balance generosity and justice, freedom and principle, in their interactions with others. This is the definition of love that Joyce would take with him when he turned to *Ulysses*: love is the care-ful creation and preservation of an artful, precarious balance between freedom and limits, generosity and principle, engagement and detachment, open-handedness and justice. Richard is struggling with the difficulty of achieving this balance, however melodramatically, at the end—he refuses to despair, but does not wish to be deceived either. Richard does, however, catch a glimpse of a love so finely calibrated that it rivals great art, but he can only apprehend this idea by first acknowledging a basic limitation of his own: he cannot read the hearts of those he loves.

The most important moment in *Exiles* is Richard's acceptance of the fact that he cannot read Robert's heart, or Bertha's either. When Bertha accuses him of abandoning her when he refuses to tell her what he wants her to do, and he answers, "Your own heart will tell you" (*E* 75), he experiences a wild delight. She has become the text and he a reader who sharply registers and attentively enjoys but cannot control that text. He has learned—briefly—to forget his own desires to control her, either by giving her or by interpreting her; instead, he asks, "Who am I that I should call myself master of your heart or of any woman's?" (*E* 75) Richard ultimately directs Robert, Bertha, and Beatrice to "free themselves" (*E* 71)—*he* cannot free them. But he can try to model the process of self-emancipation, and he does this by acknowledging the difficulty of understanding them without relinquishing his curiosity and wonder at their ability to elude reductive categorization.

The problem with this vision of love, so perfectly poised between self and other, is that it is fiendishly difficult, perhaps even impossible, to sustain. *Exiles*, like *Ulysses*, is haunted by the possibility that the experience of freedom, like the gift of virginity, may be unique and unrepeatable. This is Bertha's position. She tells Brigid, anticipating a view that Molly Bloom will express later, "that time comes only once in a lifetime. The rest of life is good for nothing except to remember that time" (*E* 91), and she tells Richard, "Not a day passes that I do not see ourselves, you and me, as we were when we met first. Every day of my life I see that" (*E* 111). She begs Richard to turn back the clock to that irretrievable moment: "Forget me, Dick. Forget me and love me again as you did the first time" (*E* 112). But if freedom of choice is only possible once, the play offers the tenuous possibility that it can live again in children, who signify a temporary renewal of lost innocence. As Robert tells Richard, pointing to Archie, "Perhaps there, Richard, is the freedom we seek—you in one way, I in another. In him and not in us" (*E* 109). For those who decline the presumption of knowing or understanding the hearts of those they love, children, too, may sometimes relieve loneliness. For the most part, however, *Exiles* is peopled by characters who seem helpless to palliate their exile, even when they are most at home.

This insight—that love requires a recognition of but not a resignation to exile—infuses *Ulysses* at every level. It shapes Stephen's understanding of the soul as a dark shape born of sin, which makes him in turn value obscurity over transparency of language (he distrusted "aquacities of thought and language" [*U* 17.240]), riddles over journalism, and dark men over their sunnier, more successful counterparts. Parental love in *Ulysses* is haunted by the same insistence on uncertainty: the Blooms had two children, one dead and one living, which leaves them forever pulled between love and grief. The two Bloom children function like the two thieves that Beckett's tramps puzzle over in *Waiting for Godot* as they half remember St. Augustine's dictum, "Do not despair, one of the thieves was saved. Do not presume; one of the thieves was damned."[6] Erotic love, too, is shadowed by betrayal: Leopold and Molly are united by multiple bonds, but Molly's adultery is a sign of Bloom's abandonment of Molly as well as a counter-abandonment of Bloom by Molly herself. Both Bloom and Molly need a renewed awareness of the bleakness in each other's lives. And Molly echoes Bertha's fear that a free and joyous mutual exchange may be a unique and unrepeatable event in the plot of a relationship. As she thinks in "Penelope," "with all the talk of the world about it people make its only the first time after that its just the ordinary do it and think no more about it" (*U* 18.100–102).

What does love have to do with reading? As it turns out, the two are intimately related in the world of *Ulysses*. Reading a text with mastery and ease is like claiming to be able to read the heart of a lover: it may be reassuring, but it is hardly enriching and seldom inspiring. Frustration with reading that resists easy appropriation is a sign of the expectation that most things are easy to penetrate, to assimilate, to conquer. This is what most readers think they want—to *possess* knowledge, as Gabriel desired to *possess* Gretta in "The Dead," but paradoxically, when a text or a lover is less accessible, it may kindle the reader's sense of wonder. In *Exiles*, Richard says that "to take care for the future is to destroy hope and love in the world" (*E* 34). One could paraphrase and extend Richard's comment by saying that to understand a book on a first reading is to destroy all curiosity and wonder in the world. To make understanding difficult but not impossible *is* a gift, but it is not philanthropy. It is a gift of labor that allows the reader the freedom to free herself from self-limiting assumptions. As the narrator cheers in *Finnegans Wake*'s "The Ballad of Pierce O'Reilly," "*Hirp! Hirp! for their Missed Understandings!*" chirps the *Ballat of Perce-Oreille*" (*FW* 175.27–28).

Love and reading work in tandem, then; and for Joyce, as for Yeats, the main gift that a writer can give a reader in a written work, or love letter, is a renewed appreciation for what Yeats called "heart mysteries." The recognition that love depends upon an awareness of the final unknowability of the beloved, although future insight remains both possible and desirable, is to say that love demands an acknowledgment of bleakness, but not a surrender to it. It is Joyce's way of saying what Crazy Jane says so memorably in Yeats's late poem: "Love has pitched his mansion in / The place of excrement, / And nothing can be sole or whole / That has not been rent" ("Crazy Jane Talks with the Bishop"). The darkness that Deasy would project outward onto women or Jews, and that a frustrated reader would erase from the pages of *Ulysses,* is actually within us. "Darkness is in our souls, do you not think?" Meaning is an arrangement of that darkness against its pale, bleak background: "signs on a white field" (*U* 3.421, 414–415).

8 ▸ ON RELIGION (AS REREADING)

In *Finnegans Wake*, Joyce rewrites "pray for us" as "Prayfulness" (twice repeated), which is just a click away from "playfulness" (FW 601.29). I propose that we take that equivalence between prayer and play seriously by examining more closely the relation of religion and playful humor.[1] How can we understand their connection in the work of Joyce, when even to align religion and humor is such a controversial and even a dangerous proposition? For many people, including those of different faiths, religion is almost by definition no laughing matter. The question of the relation between religion and humor is also intertwined with another issue, one that has to do with the kinship between religion (here religions of the book) and the Word and story, or sacred Scripture. Christianity and Judaism, for example, are both invested in the importance of listening and reading as part of a spiritual practice, but what kinds of listening and reading are being endorsed? And how did Joyce come to understand that vocation to listen, and to read, and to reread? Did it inform his increasingly comic writing, and if so, how?

Critics seem to agree that Joyce decisively discarded religious belief and became either an unbeliever, a heretic, or an apostate.[2] Strictly speaking, that is true. As a young man, Joyce left the Catholic Church and refused to follow its dictates. It is more difficult to explain why Joyce's (as well as Stephen Dedalus's) "mind [remained] supersaturated with the religion in which [he said he] disbelieve[d]" (P 202). Beryl Schlossman went so far as to claim that "the sacred is at the heart of Joyce's writing experience."[3] But the question remains: What exactly was sacred to him as a writer, and how was that able to accommodate playfulness, humor, and reinterpretation? I would argue that Joyce believed in the beauty and truth of *stories,* including the Jewish and Christian stories (so often taken to be at odds with one another). Most people assume that the only alternative to truth (meaning factual truth) is a lie, but writers know that there can be truth in fiction, as well. Fiction can be emotionally and spiritually true in ways that real life is not. To adapt the words of Jesus, the kingdom of fiction "is not of this world." Both religious writing and certain kinds of fiction or poetry can be understood as what Yeats called "heart mysteries" ("The Circus Animals' Desertion"). If religions can be regarded as emotionally true and exceptionally powerful, long-lasting stories, then they can and in fact must be revised to retain their immediacy and power. Jesus was a Jewish rabbi who reinterpreted and even claimed to fulfill the promise of the Hebrew Scriptures.

I am not really interested in the question of belief, which for most people means uncritical acceptance.[4] If that is what it means, Joyce indeed does not believe—in anything. The question here is also crucial to comedy: How can we come to accept all of reality while remaining *skeptical* and *analytical*? The challenge is not to "believe or not believe"; that is *not* the question. Instead, it is how to accept the real without being turned to stone by it, much as Perseus used his shield to be able to see the Medusa without dying. It is accepting reality without denying or being imaginatively paralyzed by its many disappointments, its inevitable losses. Such clearsighted adaptability requires a flexibility of perspective more closely akin to humor than to institutionalized religion.

Drawing upon one of the few essays on the subject of "Humor and Faith" by the American protestant theologian Reinhold Niebuhr, I propose that religion and humor share an emphasis on incongruity.[5] Joyce, of course, is a writer who specializes in incongruity. Incongruity is—perhaps more than any other feature—the problem that he is always addressing on multiple levels, and it is also something he celebrates through the polyphonic voices he increasingly incorporates into his work. It informs his work microscopically as well, in his style and later in his orthography. That is what makes it so intriguing to think of Joyce in relation to the incongruities addressed by both religion and humor: he is the apostle of incongruity: from *Dubliners*, which is primarily concerned with narrative, psychological, and sociopolitical incongruities, to *Finnegans Wake*, in which incongruity has infiltrated the word until it reaches out to characterize the globe, while also connecting the rational mind with its subconscious substratum of linguistic and experiential "waste." *Finnegans Wake* is incongruity on steroids: the disruption of convention at the levels of orthography, grammar, and narrative threatens received understandings of meaning itself, driving away potential readers in droves, but it inspires a few to reconceive the relationship of the book to legibility as we usually understand it. Joyce's last midden of letters issues a formidable challenge to our usual presuppositions about the human individual's capacity to master (or even engage) a much larger and more dynamic world of people and letters.

Once again, I am not speaking of religion in its institutional form, or as an orthodoxy. Instead, I am stressing the Latin etymology of the word, at least as it was explained by Cicero, as coming from *relegere*, "to read again" (Online Etymology Dictionary). Religion in this sense always involves a juggling of two incongruous "readings," separated in time. The most obvious example of religion as rereading is the way in which the Christian Gospels work typologically as a rereading of the Hebrew Scriptures. Most people, when they think of religion, think of it not as rereading, but as an institutionalized practice of echoing and thereby affirming prescribed words and phrases, and there is an etymological basis for this sense of the term, too: popular etymology derives the word from *religare*, "to bind fast," "to place an obligation on," which makes it akin to the word "rely." When it is institutionalized, religion turns into obligation, but the word is also said to derive from *religionem*, "respect for what is sacred," and there is even an alternate derivation from *religiens*, "careful" (the opposite of *negligens*, "negligent"), which is compatible with the idea of religion of rereading: it is a rereading of what is sacred with care. I am treating religion, then, not primarily as a system of constraints, but as a spiritual perspective designed to bring the reader or listener more fully alive to the self, the other, and the greater environment. It is the name given to the encounter between an individual human being and the great Unknown, or what Lacanians might prefer to call the big Other. Religion in this sense derives from openness of mind, care, and self-awareness, combined with a determination to *relegere*, or to reread "the signatures of all things" over and over with discipline, care, and awe (see chapter 4, "On Writing by Hand").

The incongruity that lies at the root of humor is best illustrated by irony. Irony, like both religion and humor, can be understood in two very different ways. Most of the time, when people speak of irony, they use it to mean something like sarcasm: the *OED* defines irony as "a figure of speech in which the intended meaning is the opposite of that expressed by the words used; usually taking the form of sarcasm or ridicule in which laudatory expressions are used to imply condemnation or contempt." In other words, irony in this sense works tonally to undermine the literal meaning of an utterance; it is derisory, in much the same way that humor, in the form of ridicule, can be derisory. But the *OED*'s second and third definitions of irony move in another direction: they emphasize irony as "a condition of affairs or events of a character opposite to what was, or might naturally be, expected; a contradictory outcome of events," and as the "dissimulation and ignorance practiced by Socrates as a means of confuting an adversary." These other definitions are edging toward a definition of irony as double-voicedness or paradox, in which two incompatible truths are being simultaneously affirmed with equal emphasis. In Oscar Wilde's taut phrase, "A Truth in art is that whose contradictory is also true" ("The Truth of Masks").[6] In *Finnegans Wake,* the fact that the diametrically opposite Shem and Shaun are twins is ironic, as is the coincidence of contraries advocated by Giordano Bruno of Nola (whom Joyce also portrays as the "bookshop" twins Brown and Nolan), or—one might say—the opposing orientations (horizontal and vertical) of a cross. Such irony, if we hark back to Cleanth Brooks, "does not leave out what is apparently hostile to its dominant tone, . . . [it] is able to fuse the irrelevant and discordant, [it] has come to terms with itself."[7]

This understanding of irony balances two incompatible perspectives so perfectly that any writing that achieves it becomes "invulnerable to irony." As Brooks explains, "Invulnerability to irony is the stability of a context in which the internal pressures balance and mutually support each other. The stability is like that of the arch: the very forces which are calculated to drag the stones to the ground actually provide the principle of support—a principle in which thrust and counterthrust become the means of stability" (4). This is the kind of irony I am interested in exploring: as a definition of humor, as an understanding of Christianity, and as Joyce's great achievement. It is even a way of understanding Ireland—if we pun on Eire not as "air," as Yeats did in his early poetry, but as "eir"; the root of irony in Greek is *eironeia,* which means "assumed ignorance," but it may derive from *eirein,* "to speak." Ireland, according to such a reading, is a country that speaks division, a division so finely balanced that one cannot win by choosing a side. It is perhaps the constitutive division within Ireland, its seemingly irreconcilable double-voicedness combined with the emphasis on religion that is part of that division, that makes Ireland so productive of what I would call an implicitly philosophical comic literature.

In "Humor and Faith," Niebuhr helps to suggest how Joyce could have used humor and religion to create a comic scripture in which the created world is seen as a "book" to be (re)read. Niebuhr contends that, despite the paucity of laughter that can be found in the Bible, "humour is, in fact, a prelude to faith; and laughter is the beginning of prayer. Laughter must be heard in the outer courts of religion; and the echoes of it should resound in the sanctuary; but there is no laughter in the holy of Holies. There laughter is swallowed up in prayer and humor is fulfilled by faith" (111–112). If we look at the entire arc of Joyce's oeuvre, it seems that the opposite is true for Joyce: religion is the prelude to delighted laughter, rather than vice versa. In *Dubliners,* he begins writing with the scrupulously accurate observation of a Jesuit priest, but when he gets to what Niebuhr calls the sanctuary, or the heart of the vision his writing affirms, his propensity to judge is swallowed up in a laughter that affirms life comprehensively, its ignominy as well as its glory. Joyce begins his career by registering a balance between compassion and judgment that is far from humorous—it is in fact acutely painful—and he ends his career with a celebration of "religion" understood not as *one* religion, but as the collage of many different systems of belief, with their various ways of registering the great incongruities between life and death, the known and the unknown. The spirit in which Joyce celebrates this crux is comic, but that does not mean he makes light of the great incongruities of human mortal existence. It simply means that he strives to realize logically (or even experientially) incompatible opposite truths to the full, and to embrace that incompatibility rather than denying or attempting to resolve the discomfort it causes. As he writes in *Finnegans Wake,* "God has jest"

(*FW* 486.10), which is simultaneously (through the phrase it echoes) "God is just" and "God has a joke." Justice and humor are one with compassion and imagination, and the result is a joy associated with the divine. Divinity, from such a point of view, is a vast capacity for en-joyment, an enjoyment that Joyce tries to foster in his readers. This view of divinity is akin to the one that Nietzsche's Zarathustra preaches: "Learning better to feel joy, we best unlearn how to do harm to others and to contrive harm."[8]

Religion and laughter come together in a puzzling way in the first story of *Dubliners*, "The Sisters," at the end of which two sisters remember their brother, a priest who has died. After they have coffined him, they tell the narrator and his aunt (come to pay their respects) how their brother was once found in a confession box in the middle of the night, wide awake and laughing to himself. What did that laughter mean? Right after Eliza tells the story about how the other priests found her brother laughing, she stops to listen, and the boy narrator listens too, as if to see whether they could hear any laughter now. As they listen, the boy says he "knew that the old priest was lying still in his coffin as [they] had seen him, . . . an idle chalice on his breast," and then Eliza resumes, repeating the description of the priest as "wide-awake and laughing to himself," which is what made "them"—the two priests and the clerk—think "there was something gone wrong with him" (*D* 10).

It isn't clear why the priest was relieved of his duties to his parish after this incident. Niebuhr's theory that humor is a path to faith helps to clarify what has gone wrong. The priest's laughter was not humorous, but hopeless—even faithless. He is deriding his own insignificance without the counterbalance of respect for a larger, perhaps divine, perspective. For Niebuhr, humor, instead of being irreconcilable with a religious sensibility, is closely akin to it in two ways. First, both humor and religion depend upon an acceptance or even an embrace of incongruity *as* incongruity; in both cases, two incompatible truths must be paradoxically and equally affirmed, despite the fact that they pull the listener in opposite directions. Second, Niebuhr asserts that both humor and religion require what he calls a degree of self-transcendence. As he explains, "Both humour and faith are expressions of the freedom of the human spirit, of its capacity to stand outside of life, and itself, and view the whole scene" (112). When someone has a sense of humor, he or she is demonstrating an ability to see the self from a more detached perspective. Someone who can laugh at herself is able to see that, to quote Niebuhr, "we are rather insignificant little bundles of energy and vitality in a vast organization of life. But we pretend that we are the very center of this organization. This pretension is ludicrous; and its absurdity increases with our lack of awareness of it" (120). Niebuhr would have us see that "the sense of humour is the beginning, but not the end, of a proper humility" (122) because we should only laugh at the smallness or insignificance of the self, but not at its capacity to do harm. Because individuals have the power to destroy or hurt, we need a paradoxical religious sensibility to help us come to terms with the human capacity for evil. This is why he relegates humor to a subordinate position in relation to religion, because "humour is concerned with the immediate incongruities of life and faith with the ultimate ones" (112). The priest is expressing his sense of the absurdity of the immediate incongruities of life, having seemingly forgotten the ultimate ones.

Humor is the product of the self's capacity to split in two as a way of accommodating incompatible perspectives. The incompatible perspectives that such a split allows us to balance are, according to Niebuhr, mercy and justice, both of which "are provisionally contained in laughter" (119). Laughter allows us to judge *and* simultaneously to let something go as minor. That is why, for him, humor is ineffective and even appalling when what we are judging is not simply annoying, but seriously threatening. How do we balance justice and mercy when confronting a massive evil, such as the Holocaust? Niebuhr argues that this can only be done when the person making the judgment himself suffers under the judgments that are enacted (117). The obvious example of this is Christ on the cross, but a more practical and ordinary example is one Niebuhr draws from parenting, when he says that a parent can best creatively temper rigorous judgment with mercy when the parent himself suffers through the punishments he or she devises.

When analyzing humor, Niebuhr is careful to say that "humour manages to resolve incongruities by the discovery of another level of incongruity" (113). In other words, there needs to be some meaning or "poetic justice" about a misfortune if we are to be able to laugh at it. The example he gives is of a proud man slipping on the ice; we laugh not only because of the contrast between his dignity and the undignified nature of his plight, but because we feel that his situation constitutes "a just rebuke of his dignity" (113). Another example of how this operates can be seen in a piece of anti-commercial propaganda from the internet: a photograph of a crucified Santa in suburbia that was published in a newspaper in Washington state.

FIGURE 12. Crucified Santa. Artist's rendering by Dennis Haugh. Used by permission.

This is obviously a Santa Claus hanging on a cross, and the original seemed to be a rather effective mode of protesting against the commercialization of Christmas. The cruelty of crucifying a jolly old man in a red suit known for generosity to children is resolved by the higher level of incongruity: this is meaningful because it is about a social incongruity between the humility of which Christmas is meant to be a reminder and the feeding frenzy of shopping that has displaced it.[9]

The image of Santa Claus on the cross at Christmas isn't exactly funny; we can feel some bitterness or derision in the man who erected it toward the shoppers he was addressing. Niebuhr might argue that the offense that this man objected to is insufficiently trivial, which causes the element of forbearance in laughter to be eliminated. As Niebuhr contends, "Laughter against real evil is bitter" (116). I don't want to exaggerate the evils of commercialism here, because I don't think the evil of Christmas commercialism is comparable to the evil of Hitler, but this image does give a good way of illustrating an incongruity that is too serious to be comfortably funny. The man who put Santa on a cross in front of his house could be described as angered by the incongruity between the two meanings of Christmas. In the photograph, judgment outweighed sympathy. In Dennis Haugh's artistic version, the balance between sympathy and judgment has been restored.

What seems to have happened to Father Flynn in "The Sisters" is that he lost the ability to balance judgment with sympathy. He developed his scrupulousness to the point that he forgot empathy, wonder, and gratitude, and that forgetfulness rendered the "chalice" of his faith both empty and "idle." His laughter is the laughter of impotence, a laughter that cannot be productively confessed or absolved because he does not even understand what has happened to him. Only the title of the story, pointing to the sisters who cared from him with a care that seems unreciprocated (he certainly doesn't seem to have even helped them with their grammar), points to the part of his faith that he has lost: the imaginative curiosity about the experiences of others that produces empathy (one of Bloom's signature capacities in *Ulysses*).

Father Flynn's laughter, then, signifies not humor but what Niebuhr calls a "'no-man's land' between faith and despair" (115); it expresses a perception of life as meaningless. What Father Flynn is "confessing" to the void in the empty confession box is that the chalice of his faith is both empty and broken, and that his life and vocation as a priest amount to a private joke. He can laugh, but he cannot achieve what I am calling a "religious" or even a truly humorous perspective, the ability to maintain self-respect (and respect for others) while retaining an awareness of the ultimate insignificance and impermanence of individual existence. (Stephen Dedalus arguably shares this problem; he, too, lacks a sense of humor and the attendant perspective it requires.) In a sense, Father Flynn has learned to read, but not to *reread*, or re*legere*. He read the book of human insignificance, but he could not then re-learn the value of human life, to be cherished and protected all the more because of its brevity. The sisters represent the other half of the crucial incongruity of human existence that the priest has forgotten: that care for the well-being of ourselves and others, taking responsibility for that well-being, helps to make the insignificance of existence more bearable. The story, then, knows what the priest and the boy do not: it has encompassed the whole profound contradiction at the heart of both religion and humor, a contradiction that has made life seem absurd to the priest.[10]

When we look at the confessional laughter of this "father" named James, this embodied "gnomon," this man with a rotting mouth who has lost his capacity to move and yet whose teachings have had such a strong impact on an impressionable young boy (the narrator) to the point that he may have reproduced himself in the boy, we might well recall another, earlier confession in the story. This confession also happens in the middle of the night, in the boy's dream that the priest is confessing to him in some far-off place, perhaps Persia. In this confession, the priest is not laughing, but he is smiling in a way that seems strange to the boy, who understood that the heavy grey face that followed him "desired to confess something. . . . It began to confess to me in a murmuring voice and I wondered why it smiled continually" (D 3). The priest's smile during this confession parallels his lonely laughter in the other confession box, reinforcing the connection between the two. In the light of Niebuhr's analysis of humor versus faith, I would argue that the priest's "sin," which he can only confess in a far-off country in the boy's subconscious mind, is that he has damaged the boy's ability to tolerate the profound incongruities that religion is designed to help us remember, and he has done so in the name of religion itself. He has taught the boy to judge, but not to care. His response to that is to laugh at his own impotence, and to ignore his neglected responsibilities, which he only confesses after death, in the dream of a boy he has taught, but also wronged.

Joyce's first published story, then, is about a man with his own name, James, who begins his life in faith and ends that life smiling and laughing to himself in a way that repulses the boy: "I wondered . . . why the lips were so moist with spittle" (D 3). When the boy can't pray as he kneels by the coffin, he imagines that the old priest is "smiling as he lay there in his coffin" (D 6). The smiles and laughter of this James, however, are far from funny; they are the stuff of nightmares. James Joyce went in the other direction; the comedy that animates the end of his life, Finnegans Wake, is a comedy of acceptance rather than derision. More unexpectedly, it is modeled on a sacred book, like the Bible or the Koran, a book that is not only a testament to the sacredness of the word, but also a celebration of a humor that is structurally the counterpart of that sacredness.

How, then, are we to understand the incongruity between *Finnegans Wake* as a sacred book and *Finnegans Wake* as a comedy? To prepare the ground for that discussion, it is useful to revisit what Niebuhr calls the "profound incongruities" (113), thinking of them in relation to the "Ithaca" episode of *Ulysses*. The profoundest incongruity of human existence is the contrast between the intensity of individual consciousness, aided by its ability to make symbols or "languages" to express such awareness, and the insignificance of a single mortal individual in the context of an immense universe. Niebuhr describes this contrast twice, first by quoting Edward Bellamy's description of it in *The Religion of Solidarity*: "On the one hand . . . is the personal life of man, an atom, a grain of sand on a boundless shore, a bubble of a foam flecked ocean, a life bearing a proportion to the mass of past, present and future, so infinitesimal as to defy the imagination. On the other hand is a certain other life, as it were a spark of the universal life, insatiable in aspiration, greedy of infinity, asserting solidarity with all things and all existence, even while subject to the limitations of space and time" (113–114). Niebuhr's way of translating this contrast into experiential terms is even more powerful. He contends that

> when man surveys the world he seems to be the very center of it; and his mind appears to be the unifying power which makes sense out of the whole. But this same man, reduced to the limits of his animal existence, is a little animalcule, preserving a precarious moment of existence within the vastness of space and time. There is a profound incongruity between the "inner" and the "outer" world, or between the world as viewed from man's perspective, and the man in the world as viewed from a more ultimate perspective. The incongruity becomes even more profound when it is considered that it is the same man who assumes the ultimate perspective from which he finds himself so insignificant. (114)

This is the profound incongruity that Niebuhr believes only faith can address; he sees it as too big for humor. It is also the contrast that Joyce addresses poignantly (not humorously) in the "Ithaca" episode of *Ulysses*, when Bloom apprehends the magnificent "heaventree of stars, hung with humid nightblue fruit" (*U* 17.1039). When recalling Bloom's handshake with the departing Stephen, the narrative, with its echoes of Christian catechism, adopts the "ultimate perspective" in its effort to describe the moments preceding, during, and following the contact and release of their hands as "bellchime and handtouch and footstep and lonechill" (*U* 17.1249). That ultimate perspective is one Bloom briefly experiences "alone," as he hears "the double reverberation of retreating feet on the heavenborn earth, the double vibration of a jew's harp in the resonant lane." He then feels "the cold of interstellar space . . . the incipient intimations of proximate dawn" (*U* 17.1242–1248). With "deep inspiration" (*U* 17.1270), Bloom returns home, the only home to which a perceptive and sensitive person can return: a sense of balance between the intensity of an individual's sensual and intellectual experience and the smallness of that vivid spark in a vast and mysterious universe that is largely unknown.

Joyce begins his career sternly, by carefully exposing the hypocrisies of the people around him and recording the pain they cause themselves through their own blindness. In *Dubliners,* he expresses sympathy for his characters, the ancestors of Beckett's pod-people, but he is not laughing. Humor in *Dubliners* does not serve to lubricate the friction that would otherwise be caused by the foibles and weaknesses of others: Joyce's anatomy of hypocrisy in *Dubliners* is serious. It does contain, however, an irony of perspective, an insistence on incongruity that is embryonic humor, and possibly the legacy of Joyce's waning faith. That ironic perspective grows throughout *A Portrait of the Artist as a Young Man,* but the humor of that book is something to which Stephen for the most part lacks access, and as a result readers have trouble picking it up because it flickers in the interspace between the text and the mythic contexts that help Joyce define Stephen's limitations. It isn't until Joyce writes an odyssey, *Ulysses,* that his work becomes fully comic, with a comedy that operates in two different registers. On the one hand, it stems from the foibles of the protagonists. We are prompted to laugh at the imperfections of Bloom, Stephen, and Molly, which is to say that we are asked to temper our judgment of their frailties with admiration for their very different virtues. We are teased to split our response, to balance accurate observation with sympathetic forbearance in a way that is incipiently humorous. That is the kind of humorous effect that Niebuhr analyzes, an effect that is both akin to a religious perspective and (for him) antecedent to it.

But there is another definition of Joyce's comedy that is almost identical to the religious perspective; it is the kind of comedy that animates Dante's *Divine Comedy.* In *Finnegans Wake,* Joyce meaningfully puns on comedy as "comeday" (*FW* 5.10), thereby stressing the relationship between the comic and the cyclic. Christianity, too, is a comedy in that the Fall of Eve (or eve) is reversed by the rise of the Son (or sun). A cycle, or odyssey, whether that cycle is diurnal or stretches across thousands of years, is implicitly both comic and religious in that it embraces the reality of opposite extremes by situating them in a rhythmic alternation that is both natural and super-natural, or spiritual. The Christian, ultimately, *is* the comic, if we understand comedy as a movement toward acceptance of everything that is, however heterogeneous, and to that extent very different from a comedy of derision.

This brings us "by a commodius vicus of recirculation" (*FW* 3.2) to the cyclical *Finnegans Wake,* Joyce's last comedy, which is not only circular but was designed as a kind of palimpsest of sacred scriptures from different faiths. It gives us a way of understanding why this book takes its inspiration and to some extent its enigmatic style from not one but many sacred texts: the Hebrew Scriptures, the Koran, the Egyptian *Book of the Dead,* the Kabbalah, the Scandinavian Eddas, perhaps the Upanishads, and the Christian Gospels, especially the version illuminated by Celtic monks and buried for a time to protect it from Viking raids: the Book of Kells. Is this blasphemy? Not only does it treat all sacred books in a comparative manner, but it regards them all as comic. Does that mean Joyce doesn't take them seriously? On the contrary. Joyce's comedy is built on the profound incongruities of religion, and it is above all else a comedy of acceptance that asks its readers to confront and embrace the painful incongruities of living, dying, and trying to communicate.

Joyce's works are all arguably "portal[s] of discovery" (*U* 9.229) for intrepid readers with the requisite amount of patience and commitment. A portal is, of course, a door, an opening, especially one of imposing appearance, and it can also designate the opening to a tunnel or mine.

Joyce's scripture, or writing, is focused on the challenge of how to open closed doors. What are the keys that will unlock the doors of the ear, the mouth, or another portal of the body that, if penetrated, might allow a woman to carry (or *porter*) a child? What prompts the mouth to open in speech, in laughter, or the ear to hear, or the heart to feel? This is a challenge central to religious thought, whether we are talking about the Egyptian *Book of the Dead,* with its ritual for the opening of the mouth, or whether we are thinking of the reason St. Stephen was stoned to death (the saint after whom Stephen Dedalus was named).

Let's start with the opening of the mouth in ancient Egypt, in which a statue or mummy was symbolically animated so that it could breathe, speak, eat, and drink after death. *The Book of the Dead* includes a spell for opening the mouth. It resonates with Psalm 51 of the Hebrew Scriptures, "O Lord, open thou my lips," and anticipates the stone that was magically moved to open the mouth of the tomb where Jesus's body had been laid:

> *My mouth is opened by Ptah* and what was on my mouth has been loosened by my local god. Thoth comes indeed, filled and equipped with magic, and the bonds of Seth which restricted my mouth have been loosened. Atum has warded them off and has cast away the restrictions of Seth.
>
> *My mouth is opened, my mouth is split open by* Shu with that iron harpoon of his with which he split open the mouth of the gods.[11]

We might call that "iron harpoon" a key. It is significant in this regard that the "heroes" of *Ulysses* are literally keyless, despite the fact that one of them is designing a "House of Keyes" featuring the crossed keys of Home Rule, or freedom.

But let us move on to St. Stephen. Most people know he was martyred for blasphemy, but many forget the actual words with which Stephen defended himself, when he accused his accusers of being incapable of listening or feeling: "You stiff-necked people, uncircumcised in heart and ears, you are forever opposing the Holy Spirit, just as your ancestors used to do" (Acts 7:51). This message is what prompts his listeners to cast Stephen out of the city and stone him: Stephen's charge that his listeners have "foreskin" over their ears and hearts.

I feel certain that Joyce gave his autobiographical character the name Stephen because of this verse. St. Stephen died trying to open the closed hearts and ears of his listeners. In *Finnegans Wake,* the names Earwicker and Porter both participate in a similar system of images: an earwig is said to penetrate the ears of humans in sleep and burrow into their brains to lay eggs there. An earwig, then, is a comic, insect version of the Holy Spirit, who as the divine Word penetrated the tympanum of Mary's ear and fertilized an egg. The name Porter draws attention to the fact that doors are important, and in combination with the name Earwicker reminds us that the body has several portals—the mouth, the vaginal opening, the anus, and the eyes as well as the ears. The aim of Scripture is to encourage readers (or listeners) to open or circumcise those portals by removing the foreskin; one of Joyce's many important innovations was to try to perform that circumcision with a comic pen, to understand that laughter, too, is an opening of the mouth.

Speak, laugh, listen, love—these are the imprecations of the strange scripture, written in tongues, that is *Finnegans Wake*. One "key" to the portal of the mouth is the tongue, a key that opens the door of the mouth in kissing and in speaking. In Dion Boucicault's *Arrah na Pogue*, the 1865 Irish melodrama from which Joyce took the name Shaun the Post, Arrah Meelish is engaged to be married to Shaun the Post, but she gets involved with a rebel, Beamish McCoul, who is later imprisoned. She, not Shaun the Post, ends up delivering a love letter that is the key to freedom. A kiss she gives Beamish McCoul when she visits him in prison contains a key and an escape plan. The opening of the mouth is here the key to freedom.

In *Finnegans Wake*, the "prankquean" who repeatedly knocks on the door of the Earl of Howth to get him to open it, asks, "Why do I am alook alike a poss of porterpease?" (*FW* 21.18–19) Why do I look like a pot of porter? Why am I stout, or pregnant? (because, like the Lass of Aughrim, she has opened her door to *him*, but he refuses to reciprocate). She wants him to open up, and when he refuses, she kidnaps a child with every failed attempt. In the end, he finally comes out through the arkway, which is also the rainbow of peace, and "the duppy shot the shutter clup. . . . And they all drank free" (*FW* 23.5, 7–8). She shut him up, they shut up shop, and drinks were on the house.

Finally, it is illuminating to take a brief look at the Book of Kells, which features so importantly in the letter episode (I.5) of *Finnegans Wake*, because it so aptly illustrates how the sacred and the comic intersect. The Book of Kells serves as a model for the sacred book that is both beautiful and comic. Like *Finnegans Wake*, it is elaborate both in the literal and in the etymological senses of the word: much labor went into its making. Interestingly, Colleen Jaurretche argues that "Kells arguably grew from the ancient monastic ritual of *Apertio aurium*, the opening of the ears,"[12] which would unexpectedly make it akin to the Egyptian Opening of the Mouth. Both the Book of Kells and *Finnegans Wake* combine the sacred and the profane. On what Joyce called the "tenebrous *Tunc* page of the Book of Kells" (*FW* 122.22), for example, *Tunc* (the Latin word for "then" or "at that time") is, as James Atherton noted many years ago, also an anagram of the word "cunt."[13] Atherton connects this with the lines in the "Night Lessons" episode (II.ii), "haul up that languil pennant, mate. I've read your tunc's dismissage" (*FW* 298.6), which indicate to him that "Joyce was claiming to have discovered an appositeness for the diagram as an illustration of a part of a woman's body named by an anagram of *Tunc*." The lines tell a boy to take in his member, because the woman's body has dismissed him. Literally, though, *tunc* means "tongue" here. Someone seems to have stuck out his tongue, and the speaker is telling him to pull it back because he's read its dismissive message. "Tunc," then, is first of all "tongue," a meaning reinforced by its description as "languil," meaning "long" and "languid" in context, but which also contains the French word *langue*. But "tunc's dismissage" also echoes a line from the book of Luke in the Vulgate translation: "nunc dimittis servum tuum [now you release your servant]" (Luke 2:29). Combined with an echo of one of the gospels, the word "tunc" evokes the famous page beginning with that word in the Book of Kells.

What Atherton did was to connect the protruding tongue (and *tunc*) of this passage with the geometrical diagram in the same episode. The twin boys draw the diagram to find where they came from: their mother's genitals, "the whome [home] of your eternal geomater [mother, earth, geometry]," *FW* 296.36–297.01). Whether or not one is convinced or simply amused by that reading, the Book of Kells contains "a thousand whimsical diversions, unconnected to the text, addressed to [the reader] alone— fantastic line-endings, monsters and grotesques, humorous figures playing in the margins, a world–full of incidents: children at their games, women at their work, nobles at their pleasures. So abundant [are] the decorations that they could not be seen all at once. Each day when the book was handled some new surprise would be discovered—and there would be enough to last for years—a lifetime of refreshing pleasure in a single book."[14] This is the kind of book *Finnegans Wake* was designed to be, a sacred and profane book, carefully and lovingly elaborated over many laborious years, designed not only to entertain the reader, but to train him or her in discernment. The illuminated manuscript, like the world, is full of diversions. How is one to find meaning in such a decorated and digressive world?

The Book of Kells is a very unusual manuscript written in what was at the time a foreign language in Ireland: Latin. Partly through the importation of a book, a larger world was brought to Ireland, along with a different, Christian, history that was both colorful and whimsical. In that sense the Book of Kells *is* a portal to the scriptural, simultaneously sacred and fun.

The first time I ever came to Ireland, which is over forty years ago now, I was sitting on a bus and found myself in conversation with the man next to me. When he found out what brought me to Ireland, he said, "We don't like your man over here. He ran his country down." I would have thought that the fact that I was sitting there because of Joyce might have been a refutation of the man's claim: Joyce had made me want to see Ireland firsthand as a complicated and expressive place rich in literature, history, and legend. But what that man really meant, I suspect, is that Joyce didn't kiss his country's ass. What he had done was far more ambitious and time-consuming: he had undertaken to *re-legere* Ireland, to reread its inhabitants and its religion in a way that ultimately produced a comic embrace of human difference throughout the world.

9 ▸ ON GLASS

One of the many metaphors for a book that Joyce understood thoroughly was its similarity to glass.[1] A book—like glass—serves as a lens through which a viewer or reader can have access to a bigger (or smaller!) world. Rudine Sims Bishop, in a highly influential essay, adds another metaphor, comparing a book to a sliding glass door through which the reader imaginatively enters another world.[2] Both these methods of looking or moving through the "glass" of a book are pleasurable and legitimate. But perhaps the most important way that a book can function as glass is when it is fashioned like a mirror, so that it reflects the reader and allows the reader to reflect upon himself. In Bishop's words, "Literature transforms human experience and reflects it back to us, and in that reflection we can see our own lives and experience as part of the larger human experience" (1). She argues that the reflective power of literature is a means of self-affirmation, which can be true, especially in the contexts she is discussing (the importance for minority groups to see themselves represented in books). But for Joyce the book as mirror performs another function as well: it allows readers to see themselves as others see them, affording them the opportunity to appreciate not only their potential but also their limitations, offering a balanced view of the self that may spur further development. The book becomes *a mirror not by happenstance, when, as Bishop puts it, "lighting conditions are just right" (1), but when glass is darkened so that it becomes reflective. In Joyce, the "glass" he increasingly darkened over the course of his career is the textual surface of his fiction. The "thickening" of the style with realistic details and unfamiliar words that make it harder to see through the narrative to the story, that make the reader look at the words on the page with incomprehension and eventually wonder, is one of the main stylistic mechanisms for allowing the reader to see herself by means of the text, and eventually to multiply her self-conception.*

In the "Ithaca" episode of *Ulysses*, the style playfully deploys different lenses, from the microscopic to the macroscopic, when responding to the narrator's questions. We move from a carefully detailed account of the distant source of the water that flows from Bloom's tap ("From Roundwood reservoir in County Wicklow of a cubic capacity of 1400 million gallons, percolating through a subterranean aqueduct of filter mains of single and double pipeage . . . to the 26 acre reservoir at Stillorgan . . ." [*U* 17.164–182]) to telescopic intimations of "the cold of interstellar space" and "the first golden limb of the resurgent sun perceptible low on the horizon" (*U* 17.1246, 1267–1268). Style can take us places we are unlikely to see with the naked eye— under the earth or into the heavens.

In addition to being a pair of glasses or an array of lenses, a book can also be a window. Readers can safely peer into other people's private lives without being seen themselves, protected by the separation of the "glass" page. As a window, the book again provides access to private spaces, offering readers the opportunity to widen and deepen their imaginative experience. Joyce, however, was acutely aware that using fiction as a window could also encourage readers to experience themselves as more powerful, more knowledgeable—superior—to the characters they were viewing.[3] Reading is more likely to kindle empathy when the reader enters the world—when the book is a door—than when the reader stays behind a window (think of Alice in Lewis Carroll's *Through the Looking Glass*).

Joyce, however, represents his semi-autobiographical avatar, Stephen Dedalus, as "disliking the aqueous substances of glass and crystal, distrusting aquacities of thought and language" (*U* 17.239–240), and there is evidence that Joyce felt the same way. He preferred to configure his books not as windows, but as mirrors. From *Dubliners*, which he described as a "nicely polished looking-glass," to *Ulysses*, which has affinities to the "cracked lookingglass of a servant" (*U* 1.154) that Stephen identifies as a symbol of Irish art, Joyce's books are designed not only to reflect the reader but to inspire self-reflection. Joyce is writing not only in the tradition of Oscar Wilde, who asserted, "It is the spectator, and not life, that art really mirrors," but also Robert Burns.[4] In "To a Louse," which both Bloom and Stephen recall at some point during the day, the speaker wishes, "O wad some Power the giftie gie us / To see oursels as ithers see us! / It wad frae mony a blunder free us, / An' foolish notion."[5] Being able to see oneself from the outside is not only a gift, but a power.

The engorged textual surface of *Ulysses,* bristling with detail and changing shape by the hour, is not just a sequence of "dirty" windows allowing partial access to a story. Rather, it functions as a series of mirrors designed to provoke and inspire new reflections in (and of) its readers. The reader experiences frustration when attempting to see through Joyce's text as if it were a window; in a sense, he struggles to "see through a glass, darkly" (1 Cor. 13:12). The question is why. Why did Joyce make it so difficult to see or follow what is going on? Why did he darken the glass? The answer—that it is a more realistic representation of vision—is partly suggested by that verse from Corinthians: in the mortal world, humans can only "see" imperfectly. Another answer is that it turns the window into a mirror: mirrors are made by silvering the back of a pane of glass so that it becomes reflective.

In the first episode of *Ulysses,* Buck Mulligan shows Stephen his own face in the cracked looking glass he pinched from a servant and then pulls the mirror away, attributing to Stephen "the rage of Caliban at not seeing his face in a mirror." He then clarifies the allusion: "If Wilde were only alive to see you!" (*U* 1.143–144). Mulligan's reference is to the preface of *The Picture of Dorian Gray,* in which Wilde defines both realism and romanticism by using the metaphor of a mirror. He defines the nineteenth-century dislike of romanticism as Caliban's rage at *not seeing* his own face in a glass (which Mulligan attributes to Stephen), and the dislike of realism as Caliban's rage at *seeing* his image (3). The implication is that all readers are savage and uncivilized Calibans, and they will be equally irritated if a writer shows them their (flawed) real image or replaces their image with an airbrushed, flattering one.

I would argue that Joyce revised Wilde's formulation of what readers want to see by opining that readers primarily look to literature (with appreciation rather than rage) for romanticized self-images. His view of heroism as a "damned lie" (*SL* 54) seems to suggest that in his view, when writers make their protagonists heroic they are pandering to the individual's desire to see the self as more admirable and capable than is likely or even possible. *Ulysses* gradually grew out of Joyce's effort to find an alternative to mere representation. Can literature somehow facilitate an increasingly expansive and multiple series of self-recognitions in its readers, recognitions that *evolve* over time? It isn't only religion that is designed to facilitate rereading; literature (like psychoanalysis) can offer readers the opportunity to reread the *self*. If literature is to give readers something more substantive than flattering self-images and distraction from everyday responsibilities, then it needs to engage with the *tension* between two contradictory experiences that are equally real: the intensity and apparent power that an individual feels in isolation, and the sense of being small and limited, especially when one sees oneself from the outside. Stephen succinctly sums up the problem this way: "Who helps to believe? *Egomen*. Who to unbelieve? Other chap" (*U* 9.1079–1080). Joyce's effort was to reconfigure the dominant fiction of subjective identity as predominantly admirable, and to replace it with a conception that is more porous and dynamic, modeled by the highly imperfect but nonetheless "good" protagonists of *Ulysses*. This reconfigured subject must repeatedly revise himself in response to an ongoing polylogue that takes place between individual attempts at self-expression and the many specialized discourses that frame (limit) any one person's efforts to signify. In theory, this reconfiguration could provide an individual with a way to relate meaningfully to other subjects in this modern Babel, helping to facilitate communication and even love.

If we look at Joyce's writing as a continuum, what started as an autobiographical exercise in defensive, defiant narcissism—a rejected essay on "A Portrait of the Artist" that turned into a thousand-page novel, *Stephen Hero,* asserting the heroism and superiority of the author—eventually germinated into something very different: a comic send-up of Stephen's self-importance that at the same time pays tribute to his extraordinary sensitivity and talent and sympathizes with the degrading effects of his environment. This book, *A Portrait of the Artist as a Young Man,* in turn produced a sequel: an encyclopedic epic celebrating the grandeur, pathos, and humor of human inadequacy, *Ulysses.* The trajectory from proud hauteur to the comic, even Rabelaisian, proliferation of discourses has misled several brilliant commentators—including Ezra Pound, John Cage, Sandra Gilbert and Susan

Gubar, and Leo Bersani—to the astonishingly wrongheaded conclusion that Joyce was a totalizing megalomaniac, a narcissistic humanist par excellence, vaunting the superiority of the ego of a male artist over the hoi polloi of women, colonized subalterns, and befuddled readers everywhere.

From Joyce's perspective, it is a waste of energy for an individual to fulminate against the individual's need to find self-worth amid the profusion of languages and differences that is the hallmark of modernity. The challenge is how to navigate or *read* a world in which fragments of specialized discourses and lexicons swirl at great velocity around a subject who may feel silenced, diminished, or isolated by the embarrassment of being unable to comprehend—encompass, or process—such a heterogeneous array of signifying systems, each with its own vocabulary and complex history: Catholicism, Jewishness, Irishness, law, medicine, mythology and folklore, classical literature and thought, and so on. How may the individual subject situate herself most flexibly and realistically, without megalomania or despair, in a world of proliferating discourses, in a global modernity characterized by an excess of competing, highly specialized languages and values? I am defining subjectivity as a fiction that gives shape and coherence to what is more precisely an embodied perceiving and expressive energy that develops in relation to a historically, culturally, and linguistically complex world. And I am suggesting that Joyce regarded the dominant fiction (or self-conception) of individual subjectivity as too simple, static, and unrealistic to be useful. One hundred years later, however, it is still the dominant view of the self that most readers bring to the reading process.

Readers are used to books that feature one admirable protagonist who ultimately prevails over misfortune (or dies), all with the sympathetic support of an omniscient narrator. In *Ulysses*, Joyce presents flawed but nonetheless extraordinary protagonists who model a different relation to their world and its excesses than most others in literature: they repeatedly revise their self-conceptions in response to the heterogeneous nature of their changing experiences. They understand that they must express themselves and recognize the limits of individual attempts at self-expression by turns. They see themselves as significant as well as recognizing the larger realities and discourses that frame any one person's efforts to signify. This alternation between self-assertion and the recognition of the limited nature of the self is often accented when a character glimpses his reflection in the mirror: Stephen, seeing his image in Mulligan's cracked mirror, with "hair on end.

As he and others see me. Who chose this face for me? This dogbody to rid of vermin" (*U* 1.136–137). Bloom, passing three mirrors at the beginning of Nighttown—concave, flat, and convex—that associate him with a gallant Admiral Nelson, Gladstone, and a piggish Duke of Wellington, respectively (*U* 15.144–149). The mirror in which Stephen and Bloom gaze together, which reflects not their own faces, but "*the face of William Shakespeare, beardless, . . . rigid in facial paralysis, crowned by the reflection of the reindeer antlered hatrack in the hall*" (*U* 15.3821–3824). Bloom and Stephen together produce the beardless, paralyzed, horned image of Shakespeare talking about Othello's deadly fear of having been cuckolded. The beardless face of Shakespeare is refeatured as the bearded face of Martin Cunningham, who is said to resemble him (*U* 15.3854–3855). There is the moment in "The Dead" when Gabriel Conroy passes from his frenzy of romantic desire to a view of himself from the outside, facilitated by a cheval glass that reflects his full-length image. He sees "his broad, well-filled shirtfront, the face whose expression always puzzled him when he saw it in the mirror and his glimmering gilt-rimmed eyeglasses" (*D* 219–220). A few minutes later, this image returns to him with a "shameful" coloring: "He saw himself as a ludicrous figure, acting as pennyboy for his aunts, a nervous well-meaning sentimentalist, orating to vulgarians and idealizing his own clownish lusts, the pitiable fatuous fellow he had caught a glimpse of in the mirror" (*D* 221).

Ulysses not only shows Stephen undergoing a critical change in his self-concept that draws him closer to Bloom, but it also stages a similar opportunity for the reader to be reflected objectively by the text. Readers begin the reading process (which is after all learned as part of the process of acculturation) by anticipating an encounter with an enhanced image of themselves. But *Ulysses*, through its monstrously excessive multiplicity of reflections, parodies the unconscious narcissism of such a desire. When the textual surface thickens and fractures, the book becomes less like a window through which one can observe life (as in Henry James's house of fiction), and more of a cracked looking glass in which a reader can see herself in multiple ways. In this sense, *Ulysses* is a genuine descendant of Wilde's view of art as mirroring the spectator rather than life.

A reconfigured subjectivity in which self-fictionalizations are periodically countered by objective reflections (whether those reflections are facilitated by a text or the perceptions of other people) prompts a more self-reflexive mode of reading. Such reading is neither voyeuristic nor condescending; the reader lacks the power of the hidden watcher in Jeremy Bentham's panopticon, and the author, too, has given up invisibility by inserting a younger and highly imperfect version of himself into his own text. The reader is being invited to practice a dialogical mode of interpretation that enhances and multiplies self-awareness. Such a practice, in which text and reader are equally important and in reciprocal relation, shows how the process of interpretation can help readers achieve the goal Stephen sets for himself in "Proteus": to avoid being either the "master of others or their slave" (U 3.295–296).

I will begin with an examination of how Stephen learns to see himself as others see him at the beginning of *Ulysses*, followed by an account of how this increased capacity for realistic self-assessment from the outside makes him more capable of sympathizing with others who differ from him, making him more similar to Bloom. Finally, I will outline how the book serves as a series of mirrors for the reader. *Ulysses* exposes the reader's desire to see herself portrayed in flattering ways that affirm her own importance, desirability, or perspicacity. While allowing such affirmation, Joyce's book also, like the cracked looking glass into which Stephen peers, comically "cracks" the photoshopped or airbrushed images of the self that readers may desire to find. Ultimately, the hardy reader may see her desire for self-worth, even superiority to others, side by side with her actual small size in an immense, even inspiring galaxy. *Ulysses* both reflects and exceeds the reader, by turns; the mirror is "framed." Theoretically, this rhythmic flux of affirmations, of the value of the individual and the immensity of a vast universe, allows the reader to evolve by multiplying his perspectives. This comedy of imperfection and worth, played out on a fluctuating scale ranging from the minute speck to the unimaginably complex operations of an immense cosmos, does not, like most literature, seek to divide people into two classes (the admirable and the contemptible). By presenting all individuals as both great and small, it removes the sting from inadequacy. And in so doing, it prepares readers to enjoy the proliferating differences of a newly global community instead of warring with them.

STEPHEN

It is tempting to gloss over what happened offstage between the end of *A Portrait of the Artist as a Young Man* and the beginning of *Ulysses*, but the

rupture between the two books is crucial. What was not narrated—
Stephen's mother's death and his refusal to pray for her—has punctured
Stephen's youthful ego, and he is in crisis. Stephen is no longer the brilliant
but heartless young aspiring artist who *flew* to Paris at the end of *Portrait,*
half Daedalus and half Jesus. Instead, Stephen represents himself as
defanged ("toothless Kinch" [*U* 3.496]) and also, less obviously, as dead. He
has undergone what psychoanalytic critics lamentably term castration, a
painful but important experience that challenges the subject's sense of self-
sufficiency, integrity, and potency. The subject must encounter the limits of
his or her power in some irrefutable way, which is what happened to
Stephen when he returned home to witness his mother's death. Interestingly, it is not his experience as a colonized subject that wrought this change
in Stephen, although he experiences the effects of Irish colonization more
sensitively in the wake of it. Stephen's guilt over denying his mother's dying
wish created a psychic division, represented by the crack in the mirror that
Buck holds up to him. He has been cut in two—the Stephen who stayed
true to his beliefs at the cost of his mother's peace of mind and the Stephen
who is haunted by having irreversibly hurt someone he loved.

Stephen's radically altered state—an emotional deadness expressed
through an identification with his dead mother—is most clearly illustrated through his double identification in "Proteus" with a dead dog
and with the drowned man whose corpse is expected to surface around
one o'clock that day. Stephen's feeling of being dead comes from his mother
(in whose body he had come to life), but his psychic imagery also registers
the possibility that he may resurface or be transformed through the offices
of a different kind of father.

Critics have pointed out that the two dogs in "Proteus," the dead dog and
the live pointer, have affinities with Stephen and Mulligan, respectively.
Mulligan called Stephen "poor dogsbody" in "Telemachus" (*U* 1.112), which
Stephen echoes when he refers to the image of himself in Mulligan's mirror
as a "dogsbody to rid of vermin" (*U* 1.137).[6] Stephen associates Mulligan
with the live dog in "Proteus" when he pictures the "blind bodies" of Mulligan
and Haines as those of a "panthersahib and his pointer" (*U* 3.277–278).
(Haines is the panther-hunter, Mulligan his hunting dog.) When the live
dog (associated with Mulligan) discovers the dead one, Stephen identifies
the dead dog with himself: "Ah, poor dogsbody! Here lies poor dogsbody's

body" (*U* 3.351–352). The dead dog is connected to the death-dealing sea via Stephen's fear of both dogs and water and his association of both with his mother. In a sense, Stephen could be said to have "drowned" in the amniotic sea of his dead mother's womb.

The relation between two dogs—one alive and one dead—is repeated in the connection between two men: the drowning man who was saved by Mulligan, and the drowned man whose corpse is expected to surface that afternoon. Mulligan is a hero who doesn't fear water and thinks death is just a mockery and beastly. When the live dog makes Stephen fearful, he contrasts that fear with Mulligan's bravery and he imagines Mulligan smiling on his fear. Stephen reflects, "He saved men from drowning and you shake at a cur's yelping" (*U* 3.317–318). He then worries about whether he could have done what Mulligan did: "Would you or would you not?" He recalls the "man that was drowned nine days ago off Maiden's rock. They are waiting for him now" (*U* 3.321–323). He thinks, "I would want to. I would try. I am not a strong swimmer. . . . If I had land under my feet. I want his life still to be his, mine to be mine. A drowning man. His human eyes scream to me out of horror of his death. I . . . With him together down. . . ." (*U* 3.323–329). And with the next phrase he thinks of his failure to save his mother: "I could not save her. Waters: bitter death: lost."

Stephen's mother's corpse is entangled in his mind with the corpse of the drowned man not only because he couldn't save either, but because he experiences both as objective correlatives or external reflections of a dead self, inundated by what he had feared, the sea of bile that Mulligan called "ouar great sweet mother" (*U* 1.78–79). But there are indications that Stephen is in the process of shifting focus from the mother to the father as a reflection of himself. This shift constitutes a transformation modeled on what happens to the drowning father that Ariel sang about in *The Tempest,* conjoined with the insistence in Milton's "Lycidas" that his friend Edward King, who had drowned in the Irish Sea, is not dead (*U* 3.474). These oddly twinned allusions raise the possibility that the drowned Stephen may yet undergo a strange resurrection or metempsychosis, comically heralded by the surfacing of the "saltwhite" corpse (*U* 3.472). Here, Stephen's fantasy of that corpse's sea change reflects *himself* as newly unmanned, his penis mere food for minnows: A quiver of minnows "flash through the slits of his buttoned trouserfly," having just fattened themselves on the "spongy titbit" within (*U* 3.476–481). Stephen, like his mother, the dead dog, and the drowned man, has died and suffered a sea change, one that heralds an encounter with a new kind of father.

At the end of "Proteus," we learn that Stephen has replaced Mulligan's view of the sea as "our great sweet mother" with a different epithet: "Old Father Ocean" (*U* 3.483). This replacement was anticipated in Stephen's two dreams of the night before, which he thinks were possibly part of the same dream: the nightmare that his mother is a ghoul trying to kill him and a fantasy about a Persian father who offers him a melon. "Open hallway. Street of harlots. Remember. Haroun al Raschid. . . . That man led me, spoke. I was not afraid. The melon he had he held against my face. Smiled: creamfruit smell. That was the rule, said. In. Come. Red carpet spread. You will see who" (*U* 3.365–369). Haroun al-Raschid (i.e., Aaron the Just) was the Caliph of Baghdad in the eighth century whose reign was marked by advances in science, art, music, and religion.[7] As critics have noted, Stephen's dream anticipates his encounter with Bloom in the "Circe" episode ("street of harlots"). Bloom, in the guise of an ancient Middle-Eastern caliph (neither Jewish *nor* Christian), offers Stephen the "creamfruit smell" of foreign fruits (which is what *melon* designated in Greek), a heterodoxy with earthy overtones of food and sex. Later, of course, he seems to tempt him with Molly (of the "melonous" rump [17.2242]).

Stephen's mother, in contrast, takes many forms. She is a nightmare—which is not only a bad dream but also a dark mare, or female horse, linked not only to Bloom (another dark horse) but also to the nightmare of history that threatens to give Stephen a "back kick" (*U* 2.379). In addition to being a mare, she is also the Latin *mare* ("sea") and French mère ("mother"), all of which (like her name, May) significantly evoke the name of Mary, the mother of Jesus.[8]

May Dedalus's connection to the Virgin Mary begins to show us something very important about Stephen, something revealed *not though the narrative* (which is a performance of Stephen's consciousness as it was at the time) but by Buck Mulligan. Buck not only holds a mirror up to Stephen, he also *acts* as a mirror himself: in Stephen's eyes, Buck's performances comically reflect and distort Stephen's pretensions (Stephen thinks, "He holds my follies hostage" [*U* 9.35]). Buck's initial "black mass" inverts and reflects Stephen's earlier desire to be a priest, and his performance of "The Ballad of Joking Jesus" (three times a day, after meals) parodies a much bigger folly,

Stephen's identification with Jesus. At the end of *Portrait*, Stephen styled himself not only after the father heralded by his patronym, the Greek inventor Daedalus, but also after Jesus, potential savior of Ireland. He cast his friend Cranly in the role of John the Baptist, who announced his advent (*P* 209). When he defied the Church by refusing to do his Easter duty, his defiance recalled Jesus's earlier challenge to the Pharisees, the leaders of his synagogue. In distancing himself from his mother (as well as Mother Ireland and Mother Church), Stephen mimicked the stance Jesus took toward *his* mother in Matthew 12:47–50. So, when Mulligan caricatures the story of Jesus by reducing his death to a cover story for what was really escapist flight, his performance effectively reflects and exaggerates Stephen's own heroic mirage, accenting its dishonesty and its ludicrousness. Buck capers before Stephen and Haines, "fluttering his winglike hands" and making "brief birdsweet cries" (*U* 1.601–602), chanting "in a quiet happy foolish voice":

> —*I'm the queerest young fellow that ever you heard.*
> *My mother's a jew, my father's a bird.*
> *With Joseph the joiner I cannot agree.*
> *So here's to disciples and Calvary.*

At the end of the ballad, Jesus flies away like his divine "bird" father and perpetuates a hoax on the world about his resurrection:

> —*Goodbye, now, goodbye! Write down all I said*
> *And tell Tom, Dick and Harry I rose from the dead.*
> *What's bred in the bone cannot fail me to fly*
> *And Olivet's breezy—Goodbye, now, goodbye!* (*U* 1.584–599)

Think of how a newly chastened Stephen must hear Mulligan's often-repeated caricature of divine father-son relations, especially as it relates to Stephen's own relationship with fathers. Recall the sheer number of bird-fathers with whom Stephen has engaged: there is Daedalus, the ingenious artisan exiled to Crete for killing his own nephew, who made wings for himself and his son Icarus to escape the labyrinth in Crete, like birds. There is Kevin Egan, the "wild goose," with whom Stephen had a drink in Paris, and his socialist rabbit of a son Patrice who doesn't believe in God. There is

Jesus, whom a drunken Stephen is still imitating in "Circe" when he hits the globe of the first gas light he encounters in Nighttown, "shattering light over the world" and proclaiming "*Salvi facti sunt* [and they are saved (or made whole)]" (*U* 15.98–100). Stephen must surely experience Mulligan's performance as a send-up of his own heroic pretensions.

The real problem besetting Mulligan's Jesus is that he can't get along with his earthly father, Joseph the joiner, so he flees (or literally "flies"). In the *Odyssey*, Telemachus could be described as being in a similar situation, although he has not one but many demanding would-be fathers, which is what drives him to go looking for Odysseus, risking his life in the process. Hamlet, too, is in a comparable bind: he can't get along with Claudius, his new stepfather, so he teams up with a ghostly father instead. In *Ulysses*, who is the ghost—Stephen or Bloom? It can be read either way, but Stephen is the ghost of Bloom insofar as Stephen has the capacity to evolve in Bloom's direction, a man who in many respects is Stephen's opposite, his anti-self. The person who is looking for an incorporeal father can paradoxically be read as a ghost himself, a not yet fully fleshed-out prediction of the fuller reality to come, whether that more powerful father is read as Odysseus or the Christian trinity or a Jew who is more Christian in his capacity for love than the characters who identify themselves with Christianity.

THE VIEWER AND THE REFLECTION, OR SHOT REVERSE SHOT

How has Stephen changed? His experience of intense loss has not only punctured and fragmented his ego, allowing him to alternate between projecting a fiction of himself that he would like others to believe (such as the idea that he is Jesus) and seeing himself as others such as Buck see him (as a Joking Jesus, risible in his lack of self-awareness). His ability to see himself objectively in turn enables him to imagine the experience of others *subjectively*, without judgment or derision. It is this second capability that is associated with the capacity to love. As the narrator says of Stephen in "Telemachus," "Pain, that was not yet the pain of love, fretted his heart" [*U* 1.102].

I would like to offer a particularly vivid example of the difference between a subjective, or internal, emotional expression of experience and one that looks at the subject from outside, objectively, which is not from *Ulysses*. The subjective account is from a journal entry written February 19, 2011, by a forty-five-year-old man incarcerated in a Texas treatment facility for men with misdemeanors or felonies due to drug or alcohol abuse:

> All my joints hurt. All my fingers feel like they are riddled with arthritis. My ankles and knees feel like theyre [*sic*] filled with a gravel and gasoline mixture. There are a dozen small knives being jabbed into my neck and shoulders every time I move my head. I have no idea how to describe the sensation from my elbows down through my forearms. Its like the tendons are being stretched to their limit and are about to pop. Is this being sober and old? Fuck that.

The metaphorically vivid roster of physical feelings ends with an expression of defiance that predicts the writer's future course of action after leaving the facility: he refuses to endure a version of himself that is decrepit and in pain, and he will again self-medicate as soon as he can.

Contrast this subjective account with an excerpt from the autopsy report of the same subject performed twenty-two months later:

> The body is that of a well-developed, well-nourished, white male clad in a gray sweatshirt, black underwear, white socks and brown shoes. The body weighs 198 pounds, is 68 inches in length, and appears compatible with the reported age of 47 years. The body is cold. Rigor is present to an equal degree in all extremities. . . . Tattoos are on the right buttock and right leg. . . . The heart weighs 430 grams. . . . The brain weighs 1325 grams.

The cause of death was ruled natural: hypertensive and atherosclerotic cardiovascular disease, although it was aggravated by "reported alcoholism."

This change of perspective illustrates what is known in film as a "shot reverse shot." Most subjects resist the reverse shot because it accents not their capacities but their limitations. If the subject attempts to balance his or her subjective perceptions with objective ones from an external perspective, it destabilizes the habit of privileging subjective perception, which in turn interferes with another habit, that of objectifying the other, to see the other primarily from the *outside*. The perceiver starts to project herself imaginatively into other people's experience, to see through the eyes of the other. This dynamic, rhythmic subjectivity complicates the impulse to be judgmental about the imperfections of others. It is this destabilized subjectivity (perhaps we should call it sub-objectivity or externalized consciousness) that Stephen is learning in the Telemachiad and that Bloom is already practicing, a practice Joyce seems to associate with the capacity to love.

Projecting oneself imaginatively into the experience of another not only destabilizes the opposition between subject and object, decentering the egocentric impulse, it also forestalls the impulse to prejudge the other (the literal meaning of the word "prejudice"). The exercise of imaginatively projecting oneself into the body of the other is the complement and corollary to the willingness to see one's own limits in an objective way. At the beginning of *Ulysses,* Stephen demonstrates a new capacity for imaginatively projecting himself into the experience of others, even those who are far removed. For example, he pictures the strand on which he walks as it was during the Viking era, a horde of Irish "dwarfs" running from the starving city to hack meat from a stranded school of whales. He then registers an intimate connection with them, despite the centuries that have intervened: "Their blood is in me, their lusts my waves. I moved among them on the frozen Liffey" (*U* 3.306–307). This capacity to look through the eyes of the other is one that Bloom has developed more fully, as we see on the first page of "Calypso" when he tries to see himself from the perspective of his cat: "Wonder what I look like to her. Height of a tower? No, she can jump me" (*U* 4.28–29).

Another intriguing example of Stephen's newly balanced assessment of others may be seen in his reaction to Mr. Deasy in "Nestor." Stephen clearly registers Deasy's errors of fact and his ugly prejudices against Jews and women, yet despite Deasy's limitations Stephen resolves to "help him in his fight" (*U* 2.430). He regards him in the end as harmless, a "toothless terror" like Stephen himself. Later, in "Aeolus," he is able to frame Deasy's denigrations of women with facts about Deasy's own marriage when he hears Myles Crawford describe Deasy's wife as "the bloodiest old tartar God ever made" (*U* 7.532–733).

Stephen's slowness to judge (or deplore) Deasy is balanced by the way he sees his students: his awareness of their toadying is met with a sharp understanding that he is no better. When he anticipates telling Haines his quip about Kingstown pier as a disappointed bridge, he realizes that he too will be playing the part of a "jester at the court of his master, indulged and disesteemed, winning a clement master's praise," a role not unlike the one that his own students perform for him in the classroom. So he goes on indulging but not esteeming the students who haven't memorized Milton's "Lycidas," and who have no idea who Pyrrhus was, registering their failings without condemnation. His self-awareness allows him to forge a connection with them, however unflattering that connection may be.

Stephen's metaphor for a more expansive sense of self that connects him to others is not unlike that of Mrs. Ramsay in Virginia Woolf's *To the Lighthouse*: it is a sense of shared darkness.[9] The opposed attitudes of Stephen and Deasy toward Jews pivot on their different views of darkness. Deasy thinks Jews have "sinned against the light" (*U* 2.361) but Stephen replies, "Who has not?" (*U* 2.373). Significantly, darkness or obscurity is also a stylistic technique. Stephen thinks of the "long look from dark eyes" that Jesus gives the Pharisees when they asked him whether they should pay tribute to Rome in connection with his reply, a "riddling sentence to be woven and woven on the Church's looms" (*U* 2.87). An enigmatic style is like a gift of darkness, and darkness, ignorance, and imperfection may have the effect of drawing people more closely together in sympathy and understanding. As Stephen thinks near the end of "Proteus," "You find my words dark. Darkness is in our souls do you not think?" (*U* 3.420–421). What turns a window into a mirror is a backing of darkness. This is what Joyce has done to his text: obscured it so that the reader can potentially see himself *in* it instead of judging others *through* it.

THE EPISODES (AND THEIR CHANGING STYLES) AS MIRRORS

To recap my argument: both Stephen and Bloom engage in the subjective mode of idealized self-expression that I am calling the projected mirage (a term Joyce used to describe the "meaning" of "Nausicaa" in the Linati schema), but they are also capable of correcting those projections by seeing themselves from the outside—a perspective that accents their limitations. Moreover, their egos have been fractured and thereby multiplied (which is what Stephen says happened to Shakespeare when he was seduced by Anne Hathaway). This fractured ego allows them to surpass the normal narcissistic stage of self-regard and instead imaginatively project themselves into the experience of others, both human and nonhuman.

What makes *Ulysses* so unusual, though, goes beyond what the characters do. Joyce designed the changing styles of the book to obstruct the reader's habits of regarding narration as a form of transparency. This is where textual obscurity—deriving from "excessive" specificity presented without explanation or context—becomes important, along with styles that flaunt their own artificiality and limitations. One cannot read *Ulysses* to lose oneself; instead, the book offers an opposite benefit: the possibility of finding one's predilections and habits *reflected* and parodied in the text. Joyce not only *represents* the comic energy of excess as the engine that drives and forms modern life, but he performs this operation on the reader by turning his novel into a multifaceted mirror, one that goes well beyond the "cracked lookingglass" that Mulligan stole from his aunt's servant Ursula.

Mirroring a reader in a potentially comic, affectionate way is a difficult feat, and it is even more impressive when those mirrors continue to work over a hundred years later. An example of how this may operate is the scene in "Calypso" in which Bloom defecates in the outhouse.

> He felt heavy, full: then a gentle loosening of his bowels. He stood up, undoing the waistband of his trousers. The cat mewed to him.
>
> ———Miaow! He said in answer. Wait till I'm ready.
>
> Heaviness: hot day coming. Too much trouble to fag up the stairs to the landing. A paper. He liked to read at stool. Hope no ape comes knocking just as I'm.
>
> . . . .
>
> He kicked open the crazy door of the jakes. Better be careful not to get these trousers dirty for the funeral. He went in, bowing his head under the low lintel. Leaving the door ajar, amid the stench of mouldy limewash and stale cobwebs he undid his braces. Before sitting down he peered through a chink up at the nextdoor windows. The king was in his countinghouse. Nobody.
>
> . . . .
>
> Quietly he read, restraining himself, the first column and, yielding but resisting, began the second. Midway, his last resistance yielding, he allowed his bowels to ease themselves quietly as he read, reading still patiently that slight constipation of yesterday quite gone. Hope it's not too big bring on piles again.
>
> . . . .

He tore away half the prize story sharply and wiped himself with it. Then he girded up his trousers, braced and buttoned himself. He pulled back the jerky shaky door of the jakes and came forth from the gloom into the air. (*U* 4.460–540)

I can report that most 18 to 22-year-old readers find this passage disgusting, despite the fact that defecation is a fact of life for everyone. That disgust can partly be explained culturally: elimination is considered a "dirty" act usually done in private. One could also argue that although everyone does it, not everyone is comfortable imagining themselves doing it, especially in such sensual detail. It is also something that readers are not expecting to see in great literature, much less the book that has been called the greatest novel of the twentieth century. This scene that readers find disgusting *reflects* a view of themselves as wanting to be represented in heroic or admirable or at least socially acceptable ways. They want a self-portrait of which they can be proud, delivered through a protagonist who is not actually realistic. Joyce reinforces the reader's aversion to seeing her own bodily reality represented in art when he depicts Bloom visiting the National Museum later in the day to ascertain whether the statues of classical goddesses have anuses. But the contrast between the reader's desire to see something better than bodily processes in great art and the detailed account of Bloom's thoughts and actions while defecating is funny. Moreover, if readers realize that they are trying to rewrite themselves as something *less* than they are through self-idealization, it puts them in an odd position: they may well seem less alive, more fictional, than the fictional characters in Joyce's book.

Of course, there is nothing particularly new about seeing literature as a mirror, in contrast to the "window" offered by popular forms of entertainment. The climax of Miss LaTrobe's pageant in Woolf's *Between the Acts,* for example, occurs when "riffraff" come from the bushes carrying candlesticks and cracked mirrors, to reflect the audience in "orts, scraps, and fragments."[10] The pageant represents Woolf's lifelong effort to produce works of art that culminate in a multiply reflective experience for a heterogeneous array of reader-spectators.

Joyce, too, multiplies the number of mirrors, but his "mirrors" are not literal ones. Instead, they are a function of style(s). He confronts readers with a series of stylistic obstructions that can make them aware of their unconscious desires by frustrating them. It is frustration that can trigger the reader to regard her own expectations from an outside perspective. The multiple stylistic mirrors of *Ulysses* all distort or fragment what they reflect in different ways, much like the three mirrors that Bloom encounters near the beginning of "Circe": concave, flat, and convex (*U* 15.143–149). The textual surface of *Ulysses* operates as a kind of fun house that exaggerates the features it selects, not unlike the mirrors at the end of Miss LaTrobe's pageant. The stylistic and informational excesses of the book, as Morgan Pulver notes, provide "a materiality against which thought comes to find a discernible orientation."[11] Excess prompts the reader to recognize her desire to have voyeuristic access to the errors of others behind a one-way window that protects her own ego, and it challenges her to reconsider her implicit view of herself as enlightened. Instead of a static subject gazing at a world of objects, she is challenged to transform herself into a "fluid point of contingency,"[12] which is the only way she can be touched by this seemingly discontinuous flux of details. *Ulysses* becomes meaningful when, through its "hyperbolic stylistic mischief," it makes the reader aware of "the interpretive frames within which [she] operates and through which [her] phenomenality and legibility are enabled" (to repurpose an observation made by Attell 125). It does this by multiplying those "frames," rendering them excessive.

In the "Aeolus" episode, for example, Joyce added headlines at a late stage of composition that interrupt the narrative and editorialize upon selected details. The headlines, which seldom resemble actual newspaper headlines, grow increasingly exaggerated and even outrageous (e.g., "Diminished Digits Prove Too Titillating for Frisky Frumps" [*U* 7.1169]), which is why they should not be read as "the voice of the press," but as an exaggeration and parody of that voice that serves a very particular rhetorical function. They not only deliberately disrupt the reader's attempts to lose himself in the story, but they also expel the reader out of the world he is vicariously inhabiting, forcing him to see it from the outside, an outside that makes fun of selected features of the narrative. Joyce is propelling the reader across "experiential or epistemological boundaries" (adapted from Attell 108), thereby inviting new awareness of the arbitrariness—the constructedness—of such boundaries through exaggeration. Joyce's art, like Shakespeare's (according to Stephen), is an "art of surfeit" (*U* 9.626), and the point of that surfeit is to remind the reader through the experience of reading that she, too, is constructed or limited not only by history, but also discursively and narratively through an unconscious and culturally mediated identification with fictions. What *Ulysses* offers its bored or outraged readers is a textual forum in which to recognize and exceed those fictional constructions of the subject, which can happen through an encounter with a highly material textual excess. To quote Wilde once again, "Nothing succeeds like excess."

10 ▸ ON LETTERS

Letters lie at the heart of literature, which was, "originally, 'writing formed with letters.'" "Letter" derives from the Latin littera, "'letter of the alphabet,' also 'an epistle, writing, document'" (Online Etymology Dictionary). Thinking about literature in relation to its component letters (in both senses) turns it from an abstract category into the sum of its everyday and often invisible parts. The power of those constituent parts is nowhere more apparent than in the use of four letters, not a name, to designate the divinity in the Hebrew Scriptures. The tetragrammaton (YHWH) is a sign of utmost power and holiness, not to be spoken aloud.[1] The letters inside words are also powerful in their immediacy and concreteness, as is apparent from the history of writing. Each a visual design and a sound, letters make communication possible. To look at fiction as something that began with the epistolary novel also recovers something now buried within it (although still present): an intimacy of address across distance. All fiction, Joyce suggests, is either a love letter or a message of defiance and resistance, and sometimes both.

Joyce was quite literally a man of letters. He wrote thousands himself, some notorious for their frank sexual content. He was even interested in the system of letter exchange, the post office, as is apparent in Finnegans Wake *through the*

*designation of Shem as a Penman and Shaun as a Postman (see chapter 4,
"On Writing by Hand"). The postal system—who or what controls (written)
communication—is an indication of who or what is in power, as the symbolism
of situating the 1916 Easter Rising at the General Post Office in Dublin helped to
underscore. The mailboxes all over Ireland were red, inscribed with the monogram (alphabetic letters) of the English monarch. Moreover, the pun on "mail"
and "male" helps to emphasize that men are the ones with the greatest public
control over communication. In* Finnegans Wake, *Joyce not only makes the
postal system central (anticipating what Thomas Pynchon would do in* The Crying of Lot 49*), but he also demonstrates a strong interest in letters in the other,
alphabetic (and numeric!) sense.*[2] *It is worth emphasizing that in* Stephen
Hero, *Stephen describes himself as putting "his lines together not word by word
but letter by letter" (SH 32). The main argument of this chapter is that letters
(like stories, and words) can be alive or dead, buried or resurrected. As Jed
Rasula once wrote, reading "l'etre" as "lettre,"* Finnegans Wake *saturates "language with ... animism,"*[3] *although it is important to note that Joyce also portrays the ease with which language can be deadened. Letters come back to life
when readers are forced to notice them—when they are used to create neologisms
or when their reorganization disrupts the look of a familiar word. Then, instead
of Shakespeare's* A Comedy of Errors *we encounter "a comedy of letters!" (FW
425.24).*

Literature may be admirable litter, as it was in the outhouse for Bloom
when he wiped himself with the story he called "smart" (U 4.515), or it can
be generative (as in a litter of puppies). A letter in the sense of a (usually
private) written communication between two people is a template for published literature, which is addressed not to one person alone (perhaps
named in the dedication), but to anyone who chooses to read it. An alphabetic letter, especially an illuminated one, slides across the boundary
between writing and visual art. Moreover, each one is a small body with a
power over meaning.

EPISTOLARY LETTERS

Joyce's life and work is full of significant, vibrant letters, beginning with the
sexy ones: from the "heliotrope envelope" Gabriel remembers caressing

with his hand in "The Dead" (*D* 214) to Joyce's sexually explicit 1909 letters to Nora (*SL* 157–196), which are possibly more widely read than his fiction. Molly Bloom in *Ulysses* also sees letters as erotic, remembering how she posted them to herself in Gibraltar and recalling the excitement generated by Bloom's strangely provocative letters to her: "his mad crazy letters my Precious one everything connected with your glorious Body everything underlined that comes from it is a thing of beauty and of joy for ever something he got out of some nonsensical book that he had me always at myself 4 and 5 times a day sometimes" (*U* 18.1176–1179). The "Penelope" episode was originally intended to be written as a series of letters by Molly, loosely modeled on Nora's letters to Joyce.[4] Bloom is having a virtual affair via an erotically charged, furtive letter exchange with Martha, who answered an ad for someone to help him "with literary work." The privacy of those letters, and the eroticism intensified by that privacy, is something Bloom comically protects. He has three letters from Martha in his drawer, together with her address, written in code, specifically "in reversed alphabetic boustrophedonic punctated quadrilinear cryptogram (vowels suppressed) N. IGS./WI. UU. OX/W. OKS. MH/Y.IM" (*U* 17.1774, 1799–1801).[5] If sexy letters are alive and secret, the dead letter is "public" (conveyed by wireless) and intensified by a misprint. Stephen's blue French telegram is a "curiosity to show," reading, "Nother dying come home father" (*U* 3.198–199). The fact that it is a French letter (slang for condom) and blue (meaning "obscene"[6]) suggests that this death-dealing letter is an inversion—perhaps perversion—of the sexually alive letters.

In *Finnegans Wake,* with its overriding concern with death and resurrection, the understanding of literature as stemming from letters becomes historical and artistic as well as personal. At the heart of *Finnegans Wake* (itself a "radiooscillating epiepistle" [*FW* 108.24]) is a letter that stands for all letters. That letter (and the book it represents) is a palimpsest of several different kinds of communications that have been melted together by history. It takes several forms in the book, but all are attempts to communicate with someone at a remove, shaped by love, grief, defiance, defensiveness, and a desire for deliverance. When Biddy Doran, the "original hen" (*FW* 110.22), scratches up this compound letter from the orange-flavored mudmound or "fatal midden [wasteheap]" (*FW* 110.25) of the past, some "gloompourers . . . grouse that letters have never been quite their old selves again since . . . Biddy Doran looked ad literature" (*FW* 112.24–27).

This first "resurrected letter," found at twelve o'clock in bleak January, is defaced and inscrutable, like anything from the distant past. Its unearthing is compared to the Ardagh chalice (*FW* 110.35) and later to the Book of Kells, both of which were also found in the ground.[7]

> [It] looked for all this zogzag world like a goodish-sized sheet of letterpaper originating by transhipt from Boston (Mass.) of the last of the first to Dear whom it proceded to mention Maggy well & allathome's health well only the hate turned the mild on *the van* Houtens and the general's elections with a *lovely* face of some born gentleman with a beautiful present of wedding cakes for dear thankyou Chriesty and with grand funferall of poor Father Michael don't forget until life's & Muggy well how are you Maggy & hopes soon to hear well & must now close it with fondest to the twoinns with four crosskisses for holy paul holey corner holipoli whollyisland pee ess from (locust may eat all but this sign shall they never) affectionate largelooking tache of tch. The stain, and that a teastain . . . marked it off on the spout of the moment as a genuine relique of ancient Irish pleasant pottery . . . (*FW* 111.8–23)

This stained letter ("it has acquired accretions of terricious matter whilst loitering in the past" [*FW* 114.28–29]) is itself compounded of more than one missive. At one level it is a letter from Boston addressed to Maggy (a seeming distortion of His Majesty), signed with a "teastain," which suggests that it is about the revolutionary Boston Tea Party of December 16, 1773. This version resembles John Andrews's letters to his brother-in-law-William Barrell in Philadelphia on the shipment of tea to Boston harbor and what it portended. The letter most like the hen's is dated December 18, 1773, two days after the Tea Party: "The tattered letter showed the wear and tear of having passed through many hands."[8]

At another level the letter seems to have been written by a woman who is drinking a cup of tea while she writes to her friend Maggy, who is the mother of twins (like ALP). The writer says they are all in good health except that the heat soured the milk in the van Houten's cocoa. It makes reference to a wedding *and* a funeral (another reference to literature as concerned with both life and death) It ends with four "crosskisses" and a "pee ess." This, too, is presumably signed with the tea stain, although here tea means not revolution but domestic sociability.

Biddy is a version of ALP, and we discover a little later that she has not only found a letter but is writing one herself. Her letter is a defense of her husband and his sexual "sins." Like Joyce's throughout *Finnegans Wake*, her aim is "not . . . to dizzledazzle" with portmanteau words from Latin and Greek (*FW* 113.1–2), but simply to tell the truth about HCE:

All schwants (schwrites) ischt tell the cock's trootabout him. . . . He had to see life foully [fully] the plak [old] and the smut [sick], (schwrites). There were three men in him (schwrites). Dancings (schwrites) was his only too feebles [two foibles]. With apple harlottes. And a little mollvogels. Spissially (schwrites) when they peaches. Honeys wore camelia paints. Yours very truthful. Add dapple inn. (*FW* 113.11–18)[9]

ALP's letter in defense of HCE's weakness for the delicious but forbidden fruit (apples and peaches) that he sees embodied in young women (a sexual sin reminiscent of the Fall) is being penned by her son Shem (the Penman) and delivered by his twin brother Shaun (the Post). Some critics have suggested that the whole book is a massive expansion of that letter. One of the letter's main lines of defense rests on HCE's multiplicity: "there were three men in him." What is true of HCE is also true of the hen's letter dug up from the mudmound: "Closer inspection of the *bordereau* [a detailed statement] would reveal a multiplicity of personalities inflicted on the document or documents" (*FW* 107.23–25). Many other writers have left their mark on the letter.

The "Nightlessons" episode (II.ii) ends with what might be yet another version of the letter, and this one is also about death and renewal ("youlldied" and "Incarnation"). It is an Oedipal communiqué written to the mother, father, and all their forebears by their three children, titled "NIGHTLETTER":

With our best youlldied greedings to Pep and Memmy and the old folkers below and beyant, wishing them all very merry Incarnations in this land of the livvey and plenty of preprosperousness through their coming new yonks from jake, jack and little sousoucie [also JJ&S: John Jameson and Son] (the babes that mean too). (*FW* 308.20–29)

In the left margin is a drawing of someone thumbing his nose and below it a skull and crossbones, commented on in the footnotes by Issy. This is a

Christmas letter to the parents ("youlldied [Yuletide/you'll die] greed-ings") that also contains the taunt that the parents will die. It expresses both good wishes (for reincarnation) and defiance (thumbing the nose and the image of poison). The double meanings recall the references to both a wed-ding and a funeral in the letter to Maggy.[10]

In *Finnegans Wake*, then, the letter-as-epistle is a smaller version of litera-ture. Its content ranges from the domestic to the political, encompassing trivia, defiance, and a grand apologia. It is not simple or easily decoded, because it is muddied from accretions from the past and contains the imprint of multiple personalities. It celebrates a tea party, which is both a polite social meal symbolic of community and an incendiary act of sinking a shipment of British tea in Boston harbor that signifies rupture and impend-ing revolution.

The tea stain with which the hen's letter was signed, called "the tea-timestained terminal" (*FW* 114.29–30), is "a cosy little brown study" all in itself (*FW* 114.31). On the one hand, it resembles the letter itself: "This old-world epistola of their weatherings and their marryings and their buryings and their natural selections has combed tumbled down to us fersch and made-at-all-hours like an ould up on tay" (*FW* 117.27–30). On the other hand, "tea" is also the letter "T," just as "pee," associated with the "rain" and "reign" of the prankquean, is also the letter "P." The word "twins" is spelled as "twoinns," or two "N"s. Ann spells her name "Add dapple inn" at the end of her letter (*FW* 113.18), which is "A" with a "double N" added. The epistle or missive is also, viewed another way, an alphabetic character. As the narrator tells us early in the book, "(Stoop) if you are abcedminded [absentminded, alphabet-minded], to this claybook [book of earth/key], what curios of signs (please stoop), in this allaphbed [alphabet, a bed for Allah and alpha]! Can you rede (since We and Thou had it out already) its world?" (*FW* 18.17–19).

The main text in "Nightlessons" (II.ii) sums up the ubiquity of letters in a kind of "posy cord" or post card: "All the world's in want and is writing a letters. A letters from a person to a place about a thing. And all the world's on wish to be carrying a letters. A letters to a king about a treasure from a cat" (*FW* 278.13-17). In the left hand margin, Shem illuminates the meaning of this passage: the first letter is a domestic one from big uncle to small neice, "Uncle Flabbius Muximus to Niecia Flappia Minnimiss." The second one is about ambition and revolution, raising a ladder (*FW* 278.19–20) and razing a leader (*FW* 278.21). The reference to a king and a cat refers to a proverb about equality: "even a cat can look at a king." Shem has annotated the second kind of letter with a reference to *Julius Caesar*: "Dear Brotus, land me arrears [lend me your ears]." Letters, then, are primarily concerned with love or protest, sex or violence.

ALPHABETIC LETTERS

Not only is a novel a collection of letters; so, too, are words. A word can be deadened in many ways: by repetition, overuse, or excessive abstraction, as when children repeat the same word over and over until it returns to nonsense (semantic satiation). A word "dies" when the reader stops reacting to it as anything other than a means to an end, when it fails to generate intellectual or emotional engagement or response. Advertisers play with words to make them come alive again (so as to draw the consumer's attention and sell products). One of the many examples of this in *Ulysses* is the ad for James Rourke's city bakery that Bloom (a canvasser for ads) remembers. The "melody" for the ad is "Tell me where is fancy bred, / Or in the heart, or in the head?" from Shakespeare's *Merchant of Venice* (3.2.63–64). The bakery ad keeps the meter but changes the spelling of the last word in the first line to set up the ad: "O tell me where is fancy bread, at Rourke's the baker's, it is said" (*U* 16.58–59). Here, the reader is set up by "literature" (here Shakespeare) to visit a bakery by an unexpected pun that has resurrected and redirected the word. "Nother dying come home father" (*U* 3.199) works the same way through error rather than intent. The telegram is a "curiosity to show" because of the unanticipated appositeness of the error, which links a dying mother to others who have died in Stephen's family. This is the principle that brings words alive in *Ulysses*, but especially in *Finnegans Wake*: inventing neologisms, puns, intersections of meaning and sound, crossings between languages.

In *Ulysses*, Stephen imagines writing books using individual letters for titles: "Have you read his F? O yes, but I prefer Q. Yes, but W is wonderful. O yes, W" (*U* 3.139–140). In addition to "entitling" the letter in Stephen's fantasies, Joyce pays homage to the magic with which a deletion or addition of one or two letters can transform the meaning of a word: minus an "l," "Bloom" becomes "Boom," as it does in the newspaper account of Dignam's funeral. With the deletion of an "m," "Bloom" becomes "bloo" ("blue" and the "boo" of "boo hoo" as well as "Bloom who?") when he is designated "Bloowhose" (U 11.149), an apt designation of the sadness of Bloom in "Sirens." With the addition of a few letters, "Bloom" becomes "bloomers," in which he has an obsessive interest. Molly thinks, "I suppose theyre called after him" (U 18.840). Joyce's interest in the transposition or deletion and addition of letters and how they transform meaning was anticipated years earlier by Lewis Carroll, who on Christmas day 1877 invented a game called "word ladder."[11] (Here "letter" is "ladder," which accords well with the ladder that the mason Tim Finnegan was climbing when he fell to his apparent death.)

"Character" can refer to a personage in a literary work or an alphabetic letter. It originated in the fifteenth century as "a symbol marked or branded on the body," and it gradually expanded to designate a defining characteristic of a person and eventually to a "person in a play or novel" (1660s). Just as writing emerged out of the invention of letters, so did the idea of a character as "the sum of qualities that define a person" (Online Etymology Dictionary). Character in both senses is a symbol, whether for an individual or for a sound. In Finnegans Wake, Joyce plays with the double meaning of character (recall the two meanings of "letter") by having his two main personages be identified by three letters (HCE, ALP), a thread that connects them when they appear under different names.[12] Each of their signatures is a constantly recombined trio of alphabetic letters—sometimes discernible as acrostics. The nature of identity, often said to be narrative, is here literal: a set of "variously inflected, differently pronounced, otherwise spelled, changeably meaning vocable scriptsigns" (FW 118.26–28. For an extended aside on individual letters in the alphabet, both Greek and Roman, see FW 119–122). To put it another way, we usually refer to the self with a single letter: "I."[13] Joyce expands the self into a changing trinity of letters instead. There are at least three people in all of us.

Written letters were said to have mythical origins. They were represented as magical (which perhaps helps to account for the double meaning of "spell" as both orthographic and witchy).[14] Early in the writing of Finnegans Wake, Joyce took notes from a book on the history of writing, Edward Clodd's The Story of the Alphabet. Clodd pays homage to letters as "earpictures" that were regarded as both magical and divine. He recounts that the Greeks credited the Phoenician Cadmus with giving the alphabet to the

Greeks, whereas the Egyptians attributed the gift as coming from the god Thoth. According to Irish legend, Ogham, the script in which Irish Gaelic was first written, was introduced by Ogmios, the Gaelic Hercules.[15] The Celts associated Ogham with the double magic of tree and stone, which serve as representations of Shem and Shaun, Paul and Peter, in *Finnegans Wake* (combined, they make "Tristan"—tree/stone).

The alphabet that Cadmus was said to have brought to Greece was Phoenician and consisted of thirteen consonants.[16] (Alexander and Nicholas Humez say sixteen, to which the Greeks added another ten).[17] Herodotus gave credit for importing these *grammata*, or letters, to Cadmus, whereas Plato attributed their invention to the Egyptian god Thoth.[18] There is something Promethean about Cadmus's gift, in that (like fire) it was both a blessing and a curse.[19] (See the "Night Lessons" episode of *Finnegans Wake* (II.2), where Cadmus is written in the margin next to the title, "Should Spelling?" [*FW* 307.25, left margin]). He comes nine lines after "Prometheus," identified as "Santa Claus," another gift-giver [*FW* 307.16].) Cadmus features in many different stories in mythology, including one in which he kills a dragon and then plants its teeth, which sprout up as armed warriors that help him found Thebes. But the most relevant fact about Cadmus is that he and his family are cursed, and eventually he and his wife are turned into dragons themselves. The implication seems to be that these major gifts— whether of fire or letters—bring punishment to the donor. Perhaps the most important fact about Cadmus the letter-bringer for Joyce is that he comes from Phoenicia. In a lecture Joyce gave in Trieste, he argued that Phoenicians settled in Ireland (more on this below).

Thoth, with the head of an ibis and crowned with a crescent moon, was thought to have invented not only letters but also numbers, two related symbolic systems. The mythic stories about Thoth also include a warning that letters can be harmful as well as beneficial, which helps to explain why it is important to make them hermetic (from "Hermes"), or difficult to decipher. Significantly, Hermes was linked with Thoth to form the "thrice great" Hermes Trismegistos.[20] Thoth is therefore not only the inventor of writing, but of esoteric or hermetic writing, which helps safeguard letters from being easily appropriated and used. Those who would decode hermetic writing must earn understanding through labor and openness of mind. This is an important principle behind the difficulty of *Finnegans Wake*. As we learn when traveling along the traintracks of the dead, milestones are provided by "Brahm and Anton Hermes!" (*FW* 81.7; Anton was Hermes's son, "Brahm" alludes to the Hindu god Brahma, and Hermes mediates between life and death). In the "Night Lessons" episode, we get a reference to Hermes Trismegistos's "emerald canticle" (*FW* 263.22), or the Emerald Tablet, on which he carved a number of principles (ten or four-teen, depending on what you consult).[21] Later, when Shaun the Post has given his "fireless" (fearless but also unimpassioned) soapbox speech, we read that "our greatly misunderstood one we perceived to give himself some sort of hermetic prod or kick to sit up and take notice, which acted like magic" (*FW* 470.1–3). Here Shaun rouses himself in the manner of Hermes Psychopompus, who prods the dead with his staff.[22]

Joyce emphasizes Thoth's connection to libraries and books as well as letters. His first allusion to Thoth is in *A Portrait of the Artist as a Young Man*, when standing on the steps of the National Library, Stephen begins to fear the unknown, with its "symbols and portents." One such symbol or portent is "Thoth, the god of writers, writing with a reed upon a tablet and bearing on his narrow ibis head the cusped moon" (*P* 225). In *Ulysses*, Stephen once again recalls Thoth, this time inside the library:

> Coffined thoughts around me, in mummycases, embalmed in spice of words. Thoth, god of libraries, a birdgod, mooncrowned. And I heard the voice of that Egyptian highpriest. *In painted chambers loaded with tilebooks.*
>
> They are still. Once quick in the brains of men. Still: but an itch of death is in them, to tell me in my ear a maudlin tale, urge me to wreak their will. (*U* 9.352–358)

Stephen here seems to equate Thoth's "magic" books with the ghost of Hamlet's father: dead themselves, they work to keep the dead alive by speaking to the living and persuading them to do what they tell them. In *Finnegans Wake*, Thoth seems to have the power (through his letters) to bring the dead back to life. Letters, together with the words they spell and respell, have the power to resurrect the dead.

Moshe Gold, in his discussion of Thoth and Cadmus in *Finnegans Wake*, argues that printing (books, letters, words) was not only a mode of repro-duction, it was also violent (letters are always associated with death as well as increase).[23] Gold stresses how the "teeth" of the printing press recall the dragon's teeth that Cadmus sowed in the earth to "birth" armed warriors. According to Gold, Joyce often associates the name Thoth with "tooth" (as well as "truth"), which connects both mythological figures (Cadmus and Thoth) not only with violence but with Johann Gutenberg's invention of movable type.

In *Phaedrus*, Socrates illuminates the creative and destructive power of writing by recounting a conversation between Thoth (Theuth) and the Egyptian king Thamus.[24] He explains that although Thoth's most important invention was letters, he also invented "number and calculation, geometry and astronomy, not to speak of draughts and dice." Thoth tells Thamus that, in letters, he has discovered an elixir of "memory and wisdom," but Thamus disagrees, arguing that letters will in fact produce the opposite: forgetfulness. Essentially, they will serve as a crutch for memory, so that it will be possible for humans to gain merely the appearance of wisdom rather than its fully internalized essence. Most accounts agree, though, that the origin of letters was considered divine. E. A. Wallis Budge, author of the *Egyptian Hieroglyphic Dictionary*, refers to Thoth as "lord of sacred words," which he interprets as words written in hieroglyphs, and "lord of the divine Word" (quoted by Gold 205). Significantly, Thoth is associated with "the ceremony of 'opening the mouth' of the deceased," enabling posthumous speech (see "On Religion," above). Thoth's position in the funeral rite seems to suggest symbolically that written letters allow the mouths of the dead to open again and speak to the ears of the living. This is the gift of letters; the curse is that they can also convey dead knowledge, drained of personal experience and feeling.

In his discussion of the "Proteus" episode of *Ulysses*, Stuart Gilbert provides narrative evidence for preserving the secrecy of Thoth's magic. He argues that the story of Proteus in the *Odyssey* is connected with an Egyptian story from the Ptolemaic period about the importance of keeping the Book of Thoth hidden. In "Setne Khamwas and Naneferkaptah," the Book of Thoth is a magic book containing spells that was originally kept at the bottom of the Nile, locked inside a series of boxes guarded by six miles of serpents.[25] In a sense, the Book of Thoth anticipates the Book of Kells, since both were buried and recovered, not unlike HCE himself.[26] The Book of Thoth is found and taken but Setne ends up having to return it to obscurity and death, here Naneferkaptah's tomb, which seems to confirm that the

FIGURE 13. Full-size polychrome vignette of Hunefer in judgement scene, in the Egyptian Book of the Dead (c. 1275 B.C.), frame 3 . © The Trustees of the British Museum.

wisdom of writing is the wisdom of the dead. This helps to contextualize Stephen's sense that books contain "coffined thoughts."[27]

Joyce's interest in the history of writing, and in Phoenician or Egyptian origins of the alphabet, dates from early in his career.[28] In "Ireland: Island of Saints and Sages," a lecture he gave in Italian on April 27, 1907, Joyce claims that the Irish language has been identified "by many philologists with the ancient language of the Phoenicians." He argues that as seagoers, they "established a civilization in Ireland which was in decline and had almost disappeared before the first Greek historian took up his quill." Furthermore, "The religion and civilization of that ancient people, later known as Druidism, were Egyptian."[29] Joyce, then, regarded the Irish as descendants of the Egyptians and Phoenicians, and therefore closely connected with the origin of letters. In the "Ithaca" episode of Ulysses, after Stephen and Bloom have exchanged information about the ancient Irish and Hebrew languages, the narrator recounts that their mutual reflections merge in a discussion of different ways of writing: "The increasing simplification traceable from the Egyptian epigraphic hieroglyphs to the Greek and Roman alphabets and the anticipation of modern stenography and telegraphic code in the cuneiform inscriptions (Semitic) and the virgular quinquecostate ogham writing (Celtic)" (*U* 17.770–773; virgular: made up of thin lines or strokes; quinquecostate: having five lines or ribs).

Ogham appears again in *Finnegans Wake*. As Joyce wrote to Harriet Shaw Weaver at the beginning of 1925, "The Irish alphabet (ailm, beith, coll, dair etc) is all made up of the names of trees."[30] "Ailm," the sixteenth letter of the Ogham alphabet, means "pine"; "beith" or "B" means "birch," and it is the first letter. "Coll" is "hazel" and "dair" is "oak." The second letter of the alphabet, "luis," is "rowan," or the mountain ash tree, from which Joyce took the name of his semi-autobiographical protagonist in *Exiles*. It corresponds to the letter "l." According to Celtic mythology, the first woman was supposed to have been a rowan. (Joyce also knew that Hebrew letters signify things in the world. When he is describing the procession of different generations, the narrator exclaims, "It's as as semper as oxhousehumper!" [*FW* 107.34]. Ox, house, and camel—here "humper" because of its hump—are the first three letters of the Hebrew alphabet, aleph, beth, and gimel; see Clodd 136. See another rendering as "olives, beets, kimmells," *FW* 19.8-9).

It is difficult to ascertain exactly what Joyce knew about Ogham, since knowledge of the writing system has greatly increased in recent years, as is apparent in the "Ogham in 3D" project spearheaded by Nora White at the Dublin Institute for Advanced Studies.[31] The stones that survive are found mostly in Munster,[32] and they date from the early medieval period, from the fifth to the seventh centuries, although the alphabet was probably created earlier. Ogham possibly emerged as a "uniquely Irish" alphabet designed to be "the preserve of the learned" (O'Sullivan and Downey 28). It was influenced by runes and Latin, and was designed to represent approximately eighty sounds from the Gaelic language.[33] John Sharkey sees the monogram page of the Book of Kells as a visual counterpart to Ogham, with its "dense, luxuriant world of hidden meanings, pictures, and designs."[34] Nigel Pennick, too, classes Ogham with the "Western Mystery Tradition" as "a means of preserving and transmitting knowledge."[35] He says that initiates "could read the arts and sciences of the world" from the letters on stones (58). These records were both literal and symbolic in esoteric ways.

Ogham inscriptions "have been described as Ireland's oldest documents, surviving from an otherwise undocumented age" (O'Sullivan and Downey 26). As O'Sullivan and Downey go on to explain, letters doubled as meaningful words, and "the largest single semantic category of letter names was the arboreal one, such as *beithe* (birch tree)" (26), which is what Joyce was referring to in his letter to Weaver quoted above. The name for letters is *feda*, which is the plural of *fid*, which means "tree," and the letters themselves resemble trees with horizontal "branches" (a single stroke is called *flesc*, "a twig") that extend out from the *druim*, or "edge."[36] The inscriptions are read from bottom to top (the way one would climb a tree). Ogham was used to train poets and scholars, who would use the *aicme* (groups of letters named for the first letter in the group) to create lists for memorization: there was a bird Ogham in which the birds were listed in the order of the alphabet: *besan* ("pheasant"), *lachu* ("duck"), etc., as well one listing inland harbors and one for churches (Swift 5).

The origins of Ogham cannot be established with any certainty. James Bonwick quotes Dr. G. Moore as follows: "The grammatical distinction of the letters indicates that—the oghams came from a southern and an oriental land," but others trace it to runes, to the wedge letters on the angles of Babylonian bricks, or to the Phoenician alphabet.[37] The derivation of the name Ogham is also "unsettled." One writer derives it from *oe, ogh*, or *ogha*, a circle. Another connects it with *ghuaim*, or the wisdom of birds (Bonwick 313). Some say the letters were invented by Ogma Mac Elathán of the Tuatha Dé Danaan, who was called Grianann, or "belonging to the sun." According to the manuscripts, "The Biblical narrative of the creation of linguistic diversity inspired the invention of the ogham system of writing and the Irish language" (O'Sullivan and Downey 29), whereas others think it was derived from numerals used to tally amounts, making it an early mathematical system, or else from a secret manual gesture alphabet used by pre-Christian Druids. Pennick suggests, "It is possible that ogham also reproduces a form of bodily sign language, being written across the edge of a stone with strokes that could signify fingers" (59). As Swift elaborates, "Adaptations of Cistercian sign language are found in *Cossogam* (Footogham) or *Sronogam* (Nose-ogham), which spell out individual letters using one to five fingers arranged around the shin or on either side of the nose (one finger on the right of the nose represents 'b' and two represents 'l,' while a finger laid on the nose is an 'a' and two fingers an 'o')" (5). Sharkey links Ogham to the Druids' practices of divination. They told the future "from bird calls, from the paths of animals, and from casting yew sticks: divination was inseparable from the nature lore of the forest" (90).

In a book published in 1894 that Joyce might therefore have known, James Bonwick summarizes the views of different scholars on the nature of Ogham. Some believe that writing could not have been known prior to the Christian period, and that Patrick was believed to have introduced Roman letters. The fifteenth-century Scottish philosopher Hector Boece says of the old Irish, "in all their secret business they did not write with common letters used among other people, but with cyphers and figures of beasts" (quoted in Bonwick 310–311). As John Toland wrote in his *History of the Druids* (1726):

> The use of letters has been very ancient in Ireland, which at first were cut on the bark of trees, prepared for that purpose; or on smooth tables of birch wood, which were called *Taibhe Fileadh*, poets' tables; as their characters were in general named *Feadha*, twigs and branch letters, from this shape. Their alphabet was called *Beth-luis-nion*, from the first three letters of the same, B, L, N, *Beth, Luis, Nion*,—Birch, Quicken, and Ash; for the particular name of every letter was, for memory sake, from some tree or other vegetable. (cited by Bonwick, 311)

It's possible Joyce had Ogham in mind when he refers to "woodwordings" (*FW* 280.4); the punning substitution of wood for word occurs rather often ("You is feeling like you was lost in the bush, boy? You says: It is a puling sample jungle of woods" [*FW* 112.3–4]). His love for the name Sylvia Beach as a double tree reference might also be connected to his interest in the ancient Irish tree-alphabet, since "Sylvia" means "woods," and beech (a homonym of "Beach") is a tree.

Ogham as a system of writing is importantly associated not only with trees but also with sacred stones, because the tree-letters were inscribed on both wood *and* stones. Irish writing itself began as a kind of magical, esoteric tree-stone, which helps to illuminate Joyce's repeated references to "tree-stones" throughout the *Wake*. Deep in the esoteric "runes" of *Finnegans Wake*'s seemingly incomprehensible jumble of letters is an awareness of the hermetic interconnectedness of all things.

What, then, is a letter, and why is it so important to the construction of *Finnegans Wake*? What is the significance of the alphabet (or *allaphbed* [bed for Allah as well as *aleph*], or "allforabit"? (*FW* 18.18, 19.02), and why—or

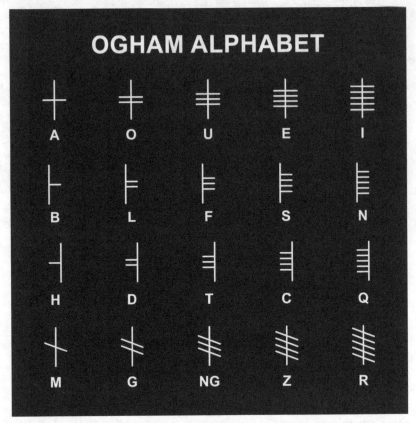

FIGURE 14. Ogham alphabet. Ali DM /Shutterstock.com.

how—are alphabets so central? They are the units through which one creates the important epistles, the prototype for all literature: "When men want to write a letters. Ten men, ton men, pen men, pun men, wont to rise a ladder. And den men, dun men, hen men, hun men wend to raze a leader. Is then any lettersday from many peoples, Daganasanavitch?" (*FW* 278.13–23). This passage conflates a letter (in the singular) with letters (in the plural), which draws attention to the alphabetic letters that make up the epistolary letter. It also is about numbers as well as writing. *Finnegans Wake* is implicitly a "lettersday from many peoples."

In *Finnegans Wake*, the correspondences made possible by letters presuppose a now-forgotten overlap between letters, numbers, and musical notation—even colors.[38] Moreover, several of these systems seem to have once had a close relation to parts of the human body.[39] The links between numbers, letters, and music is apparent in a passage in the "Night Lessons" episode (II.2), when the twins are "cudgeling" about "some a rhythmatick or other over Browne and Nolan's divisional tables" (*FW* 268.7–9) while Issy sits and knits on the suggestively musical "solfa sofa" (*FW* 268.14). This is where we hear what she has learned from "gramma's grammar" (*FW* 268.17). Although the references play on the rules of grammar, the most important word is neither "grammar" nor the reference to her grandma, but the emphasis on the Greek word *gramma*. *Gramma* means "that which is drawn; a picture, a drawing; that which is written, a character, an alphabet letter, written letter, piece of writing," and finally, "learning" itself (*Online Etymology Dictionary*, "-gram").[40] When the text (I'll call it a corpus, just to keep the body theme in the foreground) talks about grammar, it is often assuming connections between writing, geometry, music, and sex as systems of reproduction that rely upon the interpenetration of opposites (such as death and life, burial and resurrection). We see it first in the assertion that "if there is a third person, mascarine, phelinine or nuder, being spoken abad it moods prosodes from a person speaking to her second which is the direct object that has been spoken to, with and at" (*FW* 268.17–22). In other words, if a speaker is talking to another person about a third person, that third person proceeds from the two who are having the conversation (or "intercourse"). As Issy notes, This is the law of increase, the "law of the jungerl [jungle/young girl, and Jung!]" (*FW* 268n.3).

The word *gramma* is also proximate to "gamma," the third letter of the Greek alphabet and the ancestor of the roman "c", for "every letter is a godsend" (*FW* 269.17). "Gamma" points us to a view of the alphabet as what we might call sexed: the consonants (or stops) are male and the vowels (which are open) are female. Together, they make words capable of millions of permutations. This process is seemingly described as follows: "Where flash becomes word and silents selfloud (selbstlaut: vowel). To brace congeners [things or persons of the same kind or category], trebly bounded and asservaged twainly. Adamman, Emhe, Issossianusheen and sometypes Yggely ogs Weib. Uwayoei!" (*FW* 267. 16–21). Vowels are associated with beginnings or genesis, as we see by the rendering of "aeiou and sometimes y or w" as Adam, Eve, Issy, Ossian, and Yggely or Woman (Ger. *Weib*).

The alphabet, moreover, seems to have grown out of the number system. The numerical system is decimal (based on 10), probably because it was inspired by the body, with its ten fingers and toes. Many other measurements are based on the body, as well; the height of a horse is measured in hands, a foot is a foot, a span is the distance from the tip of the thumb to that of the little finger, a cubit is the distance from the tip of the middle finger to the elbow, a fathom is the length of rope that a sailor can stretch from one hand to the other across his back.[41] Humez and Humez assert that both Semitic letters and the elements of the Greek alphabet "found themselves being used as a primitive though by no means unsophisticated form of mathematical notation: Different letters and combinations of letters stood for different numbers" (8).[42] This reinforces what is believed to be true of Ogham, as well.

Roman numerals are also closely connected with the body, as Roland McHugh notes when glossing Issy's penultimate footnote in FW II.2. Developed when the limitations on counting on one's hands became too great, a system of adding and subtracting seven symbols was developed in 900–800 B.C. that was based on the hand.[43] One of the symbols, a single line (I), designated one unit or finger, and another, the V, represented the five fingers through the V shape made by the thumb and forefinger. X (10) signified two hands: the illustration of crossbones in Issy's last footnote is a skeletal version of how that works. Several of the other symbols in Roman numerals—notably M, C, and L—evolved not from numbers but from Greek letters: phi, theta, and psi, respectively, but the relation between letters and the body seems to work somewhat differently.

Musical notation has a more mediated relation to the body: the seven letters of the scale are another kind of language, printed on the page as a combination of "male" and "female" lines and circles. As Joyce so amply demonstrated in the "Sirens" episode of Ulysses, the body is also an instrument; music is produced by the body. Music is written using notes that are shaped like lines and circles, ones and zeroes, both black and white. The relation between notes, numbers, and letters is dramatized in the left-hand margin of FW 272 when B.C. and A.D. are drawn as musical notes on a treble clef, while also being anagrams of the beginning of the alphabet. History emerges as another kind of music, variously and melodically voiced: "storiella as she is syung [sung, sighing, FW 267.7-8]."

If we see letters and numbers as evolving from parts of the body, one of the results is that the distance between epistemology and carnality is lessened. Joyce's original contribution to this way of resolving the mind-body problem is to represent all these systems as *sexed*. All three of the Earwicker children (and the book itself) understand the number 10 as a generative conjunction of male and female sexual bits. In a 10, the one is a line (length without breadth), a penis in fact, and the zero (or zeroine) is female, the o of the vaginal opening and a homonym of "eau," the water that is always associated with sexually mature women. HCE is "the upright one" and ALP "that noughty besighed him zeroine" (*FW* 261.23). Letters, too, are what we might call sexed: the consonants (or stops) are male and the vowels (which are open) are female. Together, they make words capable of millions of permutations.[44]

At least four different writing systems can be said to come out of an interrelation of opposites based on the body: numbers, the alphabet, music, geometry. The alphabetic letter is first a visible shape that signifies a sound, what Clodd called an "ear-picture" (10). It can resemble a chicken scratch (this is how Joyce describes the beginning of literature when the original hen, Biddy Doran, starts from scratch).[45] But individual letters also have bodily connections that are apparent through puns and anagrams. The word "tea," for example, is an anagram of "eat," but it is also a homonym for the letter "T," despite the fact that Joyce has fun with "T" and tea throughout *Finnegans Wake*. Everyone knows that "P" is a homonym for "pea" and "pee," and that HCE finds this erotic (micturition is something he likes to see, or "C," young girls engaged in). This gets alluded to in II.2, which speaks appreciatively of "briefest glimpse from gladrags, pretty Proserpronette whose slit satchel spilleth peas" (*FW* 267.10–11). But peeing and tea-ing are connected as two kinds of wetting (to wet the tea is to conceive a child, as we hear more than once, most memorably in III.4 when HCE and ALP are delighted that he didn't "wet the tea" because he was wearing a condom). "X"s mean kisses, another bodily connection. "O"s stand for hugs. We are back to the connection between letters and gestures that was integral to Ogham as well.

Finnegans Wake, among many other things, pays homage to the history and variety of alphabetic letters. Letters can be arranged to flow in different directions on the page. Writing from left to right favors right-handed readers, but Semitic scripts move right to left, Ogham from bottom to top, and Japanese and Chinese are still sometimes written top to bottom. Perhaps the most interesting is Boustrophedon, an early Greek system for writing as the ox plows: when the end of a line is reached, the writing turns and goes back the other way. This conserves paper (it was not until 300 B.C. that the left-to-right Ionic script was adopted across Greece (Humez and Humez 10). As discussed earlier, in *Ulysses* Bloom used boustrephedon when writing Martha's name and address (*U* 17.1779–1800).

Individual letters and alphabets also vary widely, from the Cyrillic alphabet of Russia to the cursive Arabic Abjad. Whether carved into wood or stone as a memorial or whether representing gestures or trees, letters are associated not only with blessings or curses, but also, by extension, life and death. The Book of Kells, for example, as mentioned above, participated in the pattern of burial and resurrection that is also part of its content: the death and resurrection of Jesus. Its reenactment of that story testifies to the fact that Christianity is structurally comic (not humorous, but ending redemptively, like Dante's *Divine Comedy*). The sacred (here closely related to the sacrificial) is compatible with the profane, diurnal, or comic. The content of Kells is sacred (the Christian Gospels), but a "comic" and profane element may be found in the fanciful and colorful decoration of its majuscules, or capital letters. These illuminations make it come alive; the animals and vines and fantastic creatures animate the "dead" letters, showing how spiritual truth is intertwined with the profane world of living creatures. The book, then, is a thing that can come to life, but only in the imagination of the viewer. Illuminated letters also had a personal significance for Joyce, since his daughter Lucia designed colorful decorations of letters in special early editions of parts of *Finnegans Wake*: *The Mime of Mick, Nick, and the Maggies* and *Storiella as She Is Syung*.[46] She also designed and illuminated lettrines in *A Chaucer ABC*.[47]

The power of death and rebirth in the Irish imaginary is historically illustrated by the Easter Rising of 1916, which was designed to reenact the hope of resurrection through death that its timing (at Easter) gestured toward. Can the dead come back to life? Could an independent Ireland be resurrected? In this case, the Rising played a role in the eventual establishment of a modified form of Home Rule in Ireland less than a decade later. But Joyce treats it differently; for him, the Rising is woven into the very structure of his last and most Irish (as well as most international) work of literature. *Finnegans Wake* is all about falling and rising, from the fall and rise of the sun every day, to the rise and fall of the male penis to the fall and rise of Tim Finnegan, Jesus, and the hope that Ireland will rise again. The fact that Easter contains the word "east" reinforces all these connections: Jesus is the

FIGURE 15. Illumination of the letter "Q" by Lucia Joyce for the poem "Queen of Comfort" in *A Chaucer ABC* by Geoffrey Chaucer. Paris: Obelisk Press, 1936. Used by permission from the Estate of James Joyce. Image courtesy of the Poetry Collection of the University Libraries, University at Buffalo, State University of New York.

son/sun who falls and rises, and his rising happens in the East(er). The book's sleeping and flawed protagonist, HCE (Humphrey Chimpden Earwicker or Here Comes Everybody) is called the "King of the Yeast." HCE as Humpty Dumpty falls, too, and the book rests on the comic hope that he will rise again (in the morning, from sleep). Letters and books participate in this rhythm.

There is another crucial aspect of the book's structure that is based not on the timing of the Rising but on its location: the General Post Office. Joyce seems to have read this as an indication that resurrection can be understood to be a matter of control over "letters." (In this sense it is significant that Patrick Pearse and Thomas MacDonagh were both literary men.) Throughout, the pattern of spiritual deliverance is overlaid onto the diurnal process of delivering letters, reinforcing the centrality (in every sense) of the General Post Office. Interestingly, "to deliver" (meaning to "disburden," or to "hand over," as in delivering a child or a letter) can also mean "to liberate," "to save," or "to preserve." This takes us back to the Book of Kells, with its burials and exhumations. Even the creation of the book itself as a high-quality scribal transcription of the Gospels illuminated by beautifully executed, whimsical art is a way of "preserving" the gospels and "handing [them] over," thereby *translating* them, or carrying an enhanced version of them across space and time. That is also what the rebels of the Easter Rising did as well: they tried to *deliver* something—themselves, their country—thereby resurrecting or preserving its "life." Life here is not biological life, but the power to have impact on others across time and space. It is in the eye of the perceiver because it can only have that impact on those who are aware of its history and construction. It is magical in that it deploys imagination and craft to resurrect a dead time, dead words, and lost meanings. This is also what *Finnegans Wake* itself attempts to do: to demonstrate the power of the (hermetic) letter to renew both life and meaning. It isn't the Word that is divine and capable of incarnation, but the letter. Joyce might be said to have replaced the biblical claim that "The letter killeth, the spirit giveth life" (2 Corinth. 3:6) with a new formulation: The letter killeth, the letter giveth life.

11 ▸ ON CLOSING AND OPENING

As noted earlier, another name for the Earwicker family is the Porters, and among its other meanings, a porter is the guardian of a door. Doors can allow or prevent egress; shut, they signify an ending that can change, opening into whatever lies beyond the threshold. This is the kind of reading of Joyce's corpus that I have been demonstrating in this book. The book is ending, but the process itself can continue indefinitely, with new topics. It begins with a willingness to engage with unknown particulars, in all their seemingly chaotic profusion. While incomprehensible at first, "hermetic" writing can also ignite a curiosity about particular words and histories that open previously occluded connections. The multitude of new details in turn stimulates the need for a nonreductive synthesis. The web of new connections that is formed re-creates or modifies old categories. What readers usually do is to assume the existence of reductive categories into which individual particulars are classed and by which they are flattened (race, sex, ethnicity, religion, class, etc.), and then to fit each new particular into them.

Perhaps I can best demonstrate how easily this process of reading can be continued—by myself and others—by doing it once more: running the idea of the present moment through Joyce's fiction to see what emerges.

ON THE PRESENT

We know that one of the virtues for which Athena valued Odysseus was "presence of mind." The phrase serves almost as an epithet for Odysseus (e.g., "Odysseus, with his usual presence of mind" [bk.7, l. 320]; "Odysseus, with his great presence of mind" [bk. 8, l. 511]). Moreover, it is an attribute he shares with his wife, Penelope, who tells the "stranger" who is Odysseus in disguise that he will never find out whether she surpasses "all other women / In presence of mind" if he sits down to dinner unbathed in her hall (bk. 19, ll. 360–362). Presence of mind is both a gift and a discipline; it is the ability and determination to anchor oneself in the present moment. For Joyce, the present is, as another meaning of the word implies, a gift. That gift is the gift of momentary release from the consciousness of time's inexorable progression. The present is a gift *from* the past, a gift *to* the future, but it is neither past nor future. It is untimely, unique, a repository of possibilities, few of which will be realized. Joyce's style is a succession of such presents, conceived by the sublimation of his body until that sublimation produces "one continuous present tense integument" designed to slowly unfold "all marryvoising moodmoulded cyclewheeling history" (*FW* 186.1–2). In *Finnegans Wake*, HCE, ALP, and Shaun carry these presents on or even in their backs. HCE has a hump, ALP has a "nabsack" (*FW* 11.19) and Shaun a mailbag full of letters. These various mounds of presents morph into St. Nicholas's bag of Christmas gifts, a tumulus full of corpses, and a womb full of 111 children (a number that read differently designates three children: Shem, Shaun, and Issy). Above all, though, the present is what Joyce repeatedly, continuously offers the reader: a succession of narrative presents or moments each of which changes after it has been experienced.

It is surprisingly difficult for a reader to live in the present while reading; to apprehend the disappearing gift of an imaginative presence mediated and facilitated by words. Part of the problem is with habit: for most readers, reading fiction means a habitual submission to a chain of events, in which the present is just one link in the chain, not a world of sensual and cognitive possibilities in itself. The difficulty is compounded by another obstacle: readers have learned to understand a writer's gifts as part of a system of exchange (this is also a problem with the dominant understanding of gift-giving). We tend to evaluate writing in relation to a prior expectation; we unconsciously expect something—a certain kind of story, or constellation of thoughts or feelings, that corresponds to those we have encountered before—and our response closely correlates to whether that expectation was gratified, exceeded, or frustrated. It is apt, then, that a gift is also known as a "present," because the problem of the gift (especially as it was outlined by Jacques Derrida[1]) is also the problem of the present in relation to time: as the link between past and future, it gets caught up in the web of experience and expectation, memory and desire, and once it is simply a mediating device, it disappears as anything other than a link in a chain, a means to an end. Like a gift, which ceases to be a gift when it has been expected or reciprocated (because it is then a transaction, an exchange, a bargain, and not a free offering or expression of feeling), the present moment also implodes when it is seen as merely a link between past and future, when its function is to ensure continuity rather than acting as an end in itself, or an anchor for sensory, material, and relational possibilities.

What would a present moment be like if it could stand outside the flow of time? How is a textual present different from one that is lived in the world? Did Joyce understand Odysseus's "presence of mind" as the rare ability to attend to the present as an end in itself? Is this how Joyce's books were designed to be read, as disruptions to the set of expectations that condition most communication? Are *Ulysses* and *Finnegans Wake*, then, not constructions (attempts to approximate some totalized meaning) but extended and increasingly fragmented efforts to disrupt the textuality—the socially mediated quality—of seamless experience in a "civilized" world? Could they be seen as different experiments in stopping the clock? Did Joyce hear the word "lock" in "clock"?[2]

In the "Scylla and Charybdis" episode of *Ulysses*, Stephen seems to understand the present as a kind of olive tree to which one can cling—like Odysseus—so as not to be sucked into the whirlpool of time when he thinks, "Hold to the now, the here, through which all future plunges to the past" (*U* 9.89). The present moment is given immediacy by its sensuality: Stephen registers the importance of this when he tries to bring Shakespeare back to life by using Loyola's "composition of place" to evoke the sights, sounds, and smells of Shakespearean London. Stephen models a way of reading here: when we read *Ulysses*, as he read Shakespeare, we need to try to see, smell, and taste the "presence" of a day that (a) never existed and (b) was said to have happened over a century ago. Readers who visit the Martello tower or who hunt for traces of Nighttown, readers who breakfast on pork kidney or mumble seedcake or smell opoponax or look for blooming rhododendrons on the Hill of Howth are all trying to realize a part of Joyce's fictional "present" through the senses, and these efforts are consistent with what *Ulysses* directs its readers to do: read with greater immediacy, with the body as well as with the mind.

What presents and the present time have in common is an emphasis on bodily reality and immediacy. A present, in the sense of a gift, dates from the early thirteenth century, and it depended upon "bringing something into someone's presence" (*Online Etymology Dictionary*). Only around 1500 did the word come to mean "this point in time," and again, the idea is that the present time is the one in which the subject has actual presence (as opposed to past and future, when the subject is remembered or imagined). But presence of mind is not only the willingness to immerse oneself in a network of sights, sounds, tastes, smells, and textures; it is relational in not only a sensual but also an intersubjective way. Many years ago, when I was finishing a dissertation on Joyce, I was struggling to articulate the most important differences between Stephen and Bloom. What I didn't quite have the language to say then is that these differences have more to do with intersubjectivity than they do sensuality. Stephen may be cerebral in his relation to the world around him, but his imagination of Shakespeare is highly sensual: he paints for his listeners in the library a day in mid-June in the late sixteenth century, complete with the growling of a bear named Sackerson in a pit near the bankside and sailors chewing sausages among groundlings (*U* 9.154–158). He knows that such sensual details make his listeners into his "accomplices" (*U* 9.158). But what Stephen cannot do is look through the eyes of other living beings with that sensual immediacy. He lacks Bloom's curiosity about how his cat sees him: "Wonder what I look like to her" (*U* 4.29–30). Stephen romanticizes, even idealizes the sensual touch of a prostitute, experiencing the pressure of her lips and tongue as "darker than the swoon of sin, softer than sound or odor," whereas Bloom tries to imagine what prostitution might be like for a new recruit: "Aho! If you don't answer when they solicit must be horrible for them till they harden" (*U* 13.869–870).

When he observes a flock of pigeons flying before "the huge high door of the Irish house of parliament," he imagines them having a postprandial conversation about whom to "do it on": "I pick the fellow in black. Here goes. Here's good luck." Then he imagines what it is like to defecate while flying: "Must be thrilling from the air" (*U* 8.401–403). When he looks down over O'Connell Bridge, he imagines how it must have felt to be Reuben J. Dodd's son, who had thrown himself into the River Liffey and had to be pulled out: "Must have swallowed a good bellyful of that sewage" (*U* 8.52–53).

In the sense I am using it here, physical presence is not something that authorizes the authenticity of an utterance or brings it closer to speech. Nor is presence of mind simply the capacity to remember (the opposite of absent-mindedness); instead, presence of mind has to do with how attention is deployed, which is why it is as relevant to the reader as to the characters or author. When a character or reader has presence of mind, he or she has a degree of self-awareness that allows her to isolate the present moment from its brothers and sisters in the past and future, and to see, hear, taste, and feel it as unique, transient, and unexpected. The moment has imaginative immediacy, and yet the experience of the moment is not controlled or dominated by the perceiver; attention can ricochet from the perceiver to the perceived so that the perception becomes mutual, reciprocal, as in Bloom's view of the prostitute or the pigeons or the cat. Seen through this lens, the gift of the present is its power to disrupt habit, since as Kierkegaard has argued in *Works of Love*, habit may be defined as that which cannot perceive itself: "Of all enemies habit is perhaps the most cunning, and it is cunning enough never to let itself be seen, for he who sees the habit is saved from the habit. Habit is not like other enemies which one sees and against which one strives and defends himself. The struggle is really with oneself in order that one sees it" (50–51). Habit only preys upon the sleeping, and presence of mind is the active, imaginative, sensual alternative to sleep. Moreover, habit is systemic, or perhaps systematic; it leads the perceiver to believe that nothing has changed, that nothing *can* change; it lulls, reassures, and slowly and invisibly deadens the mind and the body to the world around it.

Presence of mind does have a danger, however. If it isn't exercised as a continuous discipline, the moments of heightened, even exquisite sensitivity, reciprocity, and immediacy it can foster (we might call them, with a nod to Virginia Woolf, moments of being) can overshadow all other moments, making them seem lifeless by contrast. This is what happened for Bloom and Molly on the Hill of Howth when they exchanged erotically charged seedcake, a moment sensually recalled by Bloom in "Lestrygonians," enacted briefly in "Circe," and ecstatically, painfully reexperienced in memory by Molly at the end of the book. As familiar as this passage is, it is nonetheless worth analyzing how it becomes hauntingly super-present in a way that transforms the moment from a gift into a memory that is simultaneously a delight and (because it was transient but unforgettable), a burden. Framed by the flies stuck on the pane, brought back to life by the taste of burgundy wine on Bloom's tongue, the memory is evoked in a Proustian way by the sensual stimulus of touch and taste: "Touched his sense moistened remembered" (U 8.899). Bloom recalls that there is no sound, and that the colors of the bay change as it nears the shore from purple to green to yellow-green with lines of faint brown. He recalls the earwigs in the heather; Molly's hand "coolsoft with ointments" touching him (U 8.894–895). But the dominant sense was taste, appealing to an appetite that both fed and was fed in equal measure: she gives him in his mouth "the seedcake warm and chewed" and he eats it with "joy." We understand without being told that he has or shortly will return her gift of seed to her body in another way. He thinks, "She kissed me. I was kissed." And he repeats, "Kissed, she kissed me" (U 8.915–916). In its sensual reciprocity, with "gumjelly" (U 8.909), seedcake, and currant overtones, this experience of shared appetite becomes overpowering, incapable of being replicated.

For Bloom, the moment becomes spectrally powerful because of its balancing of appetites, but for Molly the dominant note is not food but flowers, not sweetness and warmth, so much as scent, blossoms, and youth. She sees this moment as the pinnacle of her blooming:

> the rosegardens and the jessamine and geraniums and cactuses and Gibraltar as a girl where I was a Flower of the mountain yes when I put the rose in my hair like the Andalusian girls used or shall I wear a red yes and how he kissed me under the Moorish wall and I thought well as well him as another and then I asked him with my eyes to ask again yes and then he asked me would I yes to say yes my mountain flower and first I put my arms around him yes and drew him down to me so he could feel my breasts all perfume yes and his heart was going like mad and yes I said yes I will Yes. (U 18.1601–1609)

THE RHYTHMIC APERTURE, OR A PHOENIX FINISH

As I began writing the last chapter of my first book on Joyce, I had a startling realization that revolutionized my understanding not only of Joyce's corpus, but also of language.[3] Joyce regarded language as a "poetic" record of the interconnections linking different aspects of seemingly unrelated experience, and he used that understanding to shape his fiction. Language, then, is a collective art, created not by an individual writer, but by billions of anonymous users. The English language, or "jinglish janglage," as Issy calls it in *Finnegans Wake* (FW 275n.6), extends its feelers not only through time, but also across the entire globe, containing traces of many other languages within it.[4] Finally, language is something that can be both seen and heard; it is visual (when written) and aural (when spoken). The soundtrack of language creates a "musical" web of interconnections among different words through homonyms, rhymes, and alliteration.[5] A noninstrumental approach to language such as Joyce's—I refer to it as poetic, although it also might be called "archaeological" in its attentiveness to etymology—highlights the ways in which words echo or call out to one another over or under the aegis of conscious intention and reason. Imbued with the past, words are also open to present and future needs or desires as people adapt them for new purposes. Collective, participatory, sensual, and abstract, language is perhaps the ultimate work of art. Rather than creating a work of art that rivals the intricacies of language, Joyce studied language in order to "play" it in his fiction. Although it was not written collectively (unless we understand Joyce's engagement with the works of so many previous writers as collective), Joyce's work is best *read* with other people, because groups give a more immediate appreciation of the richness of his use of words.

Joyce's view of language also seems to have been seasoned by his immersion in Catholic theology. To take Communion is to "communicate," which puts an unexpected spin on the usual ways of thinking about communication. Ordinarily, spoken words come out of the mouth, but in Communion, the Word (in the form of the bread and wine that has been transformed into Christ's body and blood) is put *into* the communicants' mouths in the hope that as it is incorporated into their bodies it will also be integrated into their lives. Life feeds off death, as it always does in the act of eating, but in the sacrament of Communion the death of Jesus is also a gift of everlasting life—the bread and wine become more than food. They are infused with spirit and with a kind of life that cannot be extinguished by death. The word is eternal, as the famous beginning of the Gospel of John indicates: "In the beginning was the Word [*Logos*], and the Word was with God, and the Word was God" (John 1:1). The word, then, is divine. When Jesus is identified as the Word, the metaphor suggests that language operates much like incarnate divinity. Or, to put it the way Joyce thought of it when writing *Dubliners*, language can be arranged to enable an *epiclesis*, or invocation of the divine spirit to transform the ordinary into something more meaningful. It is specifically used to transform the bread and wine of the Eucharist into the body and blood of Christ. This process of capturing the eternal and the ordinary in the same substance exemplifies what Joyce intentionally tried to do with his language.[6]

Language facilitates the possibility of communication and communion, but it is also (more often?) an agent of miscommunication. Initially, when he was writing *Dubliners*, Joyce chafed at the limitations of characters who refused to see their mistakes as an opportunity to access different levels of understanding. But by the time he wrote *Finnegans Wake*, he saw those misunderstandings as comic. "*Hirp! Hirp! for their* [*and our*] *Missed Understandings! chirps the Ballat of Perce-Oreille* [Fr. "earwig," lit. "pierce the ear"]" (*FW* 175.27–28). Joyce's appreciation for misunderstanding as comedy is supplemented by his interest in what we now call Freudian slips, which so often provide access to suppressed meaning.

Differences—whether of sex, race, ethnicity, nationality, or language—resemble "mistakes": they, too, are portals of discovery opening out into the social and global. Throughout his work, Joyce portrays people who are regarded as "different" as opportunities to gain a more comprehensive understanding of the world, to move closer to something like social justice. Language facilitates the navigation of difference through its democratic quality. Although accents and argots and idioms indicate differences of class or profession, "alley english spooker" [all English speakers]" (*FW* 178.6) rely on the same linguistic base. With its openness to foreign influence and its roots in many other languages—both ancient and modern—Joyce's use of language serves as a model for social interaction unbounded by the parochialism of a single nation or religion. Language is enriched and rendered more flexible by difference, as society can be. When readers encounter unfamiliar words, that very unfamiliarity is a solicitation to learn.

Musical and participatory, open and ever-evolving, language is "a chorale in canon, good for us all for us all us all all" (*FW* 222.5–6).

This book on Joyce's playful attentiveness to many different aspects of the English language aims to address a disappointment that Leopold Bloom recalls in *Ulysses* when he looked to the works of William Shakespeare "for the solution of difficult problems in imaginary or real life." The narrator asks, "Had he found their solution?" only to reply, dejectedly, "In spite of careful and repeated reading of certain classical passages, aided by a glossary, he had derived imperfect conviction from the text, the answers not bearing in all points" (*U* 17.384–391).

What are the stakes of reading literature this way? My hope is that it constitutes a refinement of literary criticism as a mode of reasoning in and about the world, that it exhibits formidable literary power, that it draws on other disciplines without being beholden to them. These effects are possible because of the importance of interpretation as a social act that balances discipline and freedom, thought and feeling.[7] Joyce's works are such a good site for demonstrating how to interpret because of his insistence on respecting the reader's freedom to make connections and to make mistakes, both of which are valuable. Writing from the position of a colonial subject, Joyce contests the notion that freedom can be reduced to political autonomy; instead, he presents the ability to interpret, with both detachment and compassion, as the root of all freedom. As Stephen Dedalus drunkenly proclaims in *Ulysses*, pointing to his forehead: "In here it is I must kill the priest and the king" (*U* 15.4436–4437). A test of cognitive freedom is how inclusively and incisively one can read—or peruse—language, literature, and life. Joyce provokes readers to read his fiction with a precision and passion that matched his own.

Joyce is also exemplary for his understanding of reading as an activity with the potential to create communities (as interpreting Scripture has done for religions of the book). In place of private storytelling, in which the author-narrator recounts events (along with their meaning) to a listener, Joyce presents enigmatic scripts with the capacity to foster collaborative problem-solving among its readers. Instead of being plot-centered, Joyce's fiction highlights the highly sensual texture and history of language, its reach across space and time, and its capacity to create networks of meaning as well as communities of readers.

Near the end of *Finnegans Wake,* a voice asks, "Are we for liberty of perusiveness?" (*FW* 614.23). Joyce was an Irish Catholic writer who believed that freedom for the Irish was not only a matter of freeing Ireland from English control, or from the doctrinal strictness of the Catholic Church. Fundamental freedom (the kind that cannot be taken away) is the disciplined and joyous process of perceiving and interpreting stimuli sharply and independently. It was to encourage this kind of "comic" freedom (operating, as all freedom must, within carefully defined parameters) that Joyce devoted his life to crafting a different kind of literature, one that rewards those willing to explore and to practice interpretive autonomy.

Fin(n): Again!

EPILOGUE
The Everyday

The title of this book, *The Joyce of Everyday Life,* attempts to address the question of what to do with our lives through its echo of two other phrases: the *joys* of everyday life and *The Psychopathology of Everyday Life.*[1] By conjoining the two phrases, I hope to suggest that the joys inhere *in* the psychopathology (or suffering, if we read "pathology" etymologically), in the errors, forgetfulness, and malapropisms that serve as symptoms of dis-ease in daily existence. To the extent that errors are experienced as shameful or embarrassing, that diminishes their capacity to produce joy, and joy is what authorizes the work of both Joyce and Freud (Joyce liked to say that his name meant the same thing as Freud's since *Freude* is the German word for "joy"). It is fitting, then, that Joyce's books reward us for practicing the movements of mind that Freud explained theoretically.

Freud's book applies the technique of interpretation he had developed for dreams to everyday, apparently insignificant mistakes. The book is full of examples that illustrate how the unconscious mind works through forgetting, association, and displacement to save individuals from bringing unpleasurable thoughts to consciousness. In other words, the ease (as opposed to the joy) of everyday life stems from avoidance; it is produced by our capacity to slide symptoms of dis-ease along an associative axis that is often verbal (Freud calls this a "superficial" linkage).[2] The unconscious mind substitutes a word or name with a similar sound for the one the subject would like to forget; what seems to be a meaningless error or momentary lapse is actually an expression of (unintentionally disavowed) feeling. One of the many examples of how this works in Joyce can be found in the "Ithaca" episode of *Ulysses,* when the narrator asks about Bloom, "Which domestic problem as much as, if not more than, any other frequently engaged his mind?" The answer is "what to do with our wives" (*U* 17.657–659). Bloom's solutions to this question range from tiddlywinks and knitting to mandolin and "the clandestine satisfaction of erotic irritation in masculine brothels" (*U* 17.668). However, if we listen closely to the problem that engages Bloom, we realize, from the sound of the word "wives" and from the expectation generated by the structure of the phrase, that his underlying worry actually concerns what to do with our *lives,* and that playing tiddlywinks isn't a satisfactory answer. For easily understandable reasons, Bloom thinks the problem is more focused than it actually is; he has transferred his own dilemma over what to do with his life onto what to do with his wife. Such a substitution simultaneously relieves him of the responsibility *and* the power to find an answer. Concern with his wife disguises his worries over a much bigger concern: his life.

From an early age, Joyce delighted in slips of the tongue, which we now associate primarily with Freud. One early example of this from his adolescence occurred when he was dancing with Mary Sheehy, the daughter of the MP David Sheehy.[3] She was having difficulty following his lead because he held her so limply, so he told her to "Hold my thumb." Mishearing, she asked how she could do that, and Joyce repeated, "My thumb!" When she explained, "I thought you said your tongue," Joyce shouted with laughter, then resumed his detached dancing.[4]

Associative movements of mind are often unconscious, and what makes Freud's book so important is that like its precursor *The Interpretation of Dreams,* it outlines and illustrates a deeper layer of thought that subtends and often undermines the rational and sequential efforts of deliberate, conscious planning. The joys of everyday life exist in precarious relation to the pains and fears of daily existence, and both are registered in words and images that we learn to dismiss as coincidental. Freud's demonstration of how we make unconscious associative connections every day, as well as every night, makes those connections ordinary. Moreover, if we make the decision to examine instead of to discard the signs of what is repressed, the *Erlösung*, or release of tension, that results is often surprisingly pleasurable, even joyful. Instead of insisting upon a division between the sacred and the profane, between the irrational and the rational, between feeling and thought, literature and science, we may choose to "read" more comprehensively, more courageously, with the recognition that at the deepest levels of apprehension, these opposites are importantly and intimately interconnected. Such reading leaves no room for the "bad" everyday, which is characterized by predictability and sameness.

The theory of everyday life that I am proposing inheres in its practice, as demonstrated in the chapters of this book. Chapter 5, "On Fat," for example, enriches the morning act of spreading butter or margarine on toast by illustrating how Joyce has gendered the difference between the natural and the synthetic by way of the history of margarine and Shakespeare's *Julius Caesar*. I would nonetheless like to frame that practice by examining three other approaches to the everyday that help to contextualize those of Joyce. The first is that of Henri Lefebvre, who derives his understanding of the everyday as reliant upon language from Joyce. The second shares Joyce's view that art is a mirror. Xavier de Maistre's *Voyage around My Room*, a copy of which Joyce owned in Trieste, redefines the epic not as sweeping and vast, but as diurnal and circumscribed: the small and the everyday can be regarded as epic. Finally, Maurice Blanchot describes the everyday in terms that effectively capture what it is like to read Joyce: it is a churning chaos, lit up by moments of unexpected and intense illumination.

One of the best treatments of the everyday in Joyce in relation to language is that of Henri Lefebvre in *Everyday Life in the Modern World*.[5] Lefebvre's book begins with a discussion of *Ulysses*, which he reads as a symbol of "universal everyday life" that rescues "each facet of the quotidian from anonymity."[6] According to Lefebvre, the publication of *Ulysses* represented a "momentous interruption of everyday life into literature," or, to put it more precisely, it occasioned a new awareness of everyday life for readers, generated by "the medium of literature or the written word" (2). Lefebvre appreciated Joyce's use of the resources of language to illuminate, even animate, the "wealth and poverty of everyday life" (3). The disruption or adulteration of ordinary language can also recomplicate the reader's connection to the everyday. Lefebvre describes things and people in Joyce's narrative as magnificently unstable in themselves and in relation to one another: "They [people and things] are not static, they change, expand, contract; the seemingly simple object before us dissolves when subjected to the influence of acts and events from a totally different order" (3). *Ulysses,* then, transfigures everyday life "not by a blaze of supernatural light and song but by the words of man [*sic*], or perhaps simply by literature." The "hero" of the book (like those that precede and follow it) is language, language pushed to—and perhaps past—its limits, propelled into music, art, and history. Joyce, then, invites readers to discover the hidden possibilities of everyday life by deploying a capacious, dynamic language that regards subject and object as protean, dynamic, and reciprocally related through the potential for silent "conversation." Lefebvre anticipates John Updike's appreciation of Joyce's gift for "tuning plain language to a perfect pitch."[7]

Despite the fact that *Ulysses* seems to be modeled on a Homeric epic, Joyce's emphasis on microscopic changes of awareness and practice, changes to the texture of everyday life, is not typically associated with that typically sweeping genre.[8] In deciding to focus on the complexity of mundane, everyday experience, Joyce may well have been influenced by a very different, "miniature" epic, Xavier de Maistre's *Voyage around My Room.*[9] De Maistre, who is called "the Sterne of polite society" in the preface to the 1908 edition, describes his book as a kind of travel narrative, in which "the minutest particulars are carefully described" (47). He charmingly takes his reader on a forty-two-day tour of his room in Turin, in which he was imprisoned at the end of the eighteenth century. His tour becomes the occasion for exquisitely precise description enlivened by philosophical reflection, political and social commentary, and romantic sentiments. He discusses poverty, his dog, the French Revolution, his infatuation with a woman called Madame de Hautcastel, his library, his servant, art, breakfast, and the contents of his desk. He dreams of Aspasia and Hippocrates, and he meditates on the influence of clothes on the minds of those who wear them.

De Maistre's technique anticipates Joyce's (as well as Proust's) in several particulars, the most important of which is the significance of attending carefully to one's immediate surroundings. His determination to restrict his focus to his room resembles Joyce's decision to confine his modern odyssey to a single day in one city: both restrictions make it necessary to reimagine the everyday. Moreover, by giving his room the same kind of intense scrutiny he would give any other travel destination—Mont Blanc or the tomb of Empedocles (47)—de Maistre is able to encourage the reader moving along "life's hard path" to gather the delights that "are placed within our reach" (16). Some of de Maistre's comic touches are remarkably similar to Joyce's in the "Ithaca" episode of *Ulysses,* as when he identifies the latitude in which his room is situated (16); Joyce also specifies the longitude and latitude on which Bloom and Molly lie (*U* 17.2303–2304). And de Maistre's inventory of the contents of his bureau drawers (88–89) parallels Joyce's listing of the contents of the shelves in the Blooms' kitchen dresser (*U* 17.298–318) and the contents of Bloom's drawers (*U* 17.1774–1823, 1854–1867). In a world in which value is determined primarily by tradition and consensus, things frequently overlooked may come to have the force of a revelation, like the crowd of half-naked, wretched children de Maistre sees lying under the porticos outside his window. Thinking of the contrast between the comparatively luxurious room in which he is imprisoned and the cold and miserable children outside, de Maistre fervently wishes that "this page of my book were known throughout the universe!" (80). In contrast to these poor creatures, his "rose and white bed, with its two mattresses, seemed to rival the magnificence and effeminacy of Asiatic monarchs" (82).

De Maistre's focus on his immediate surroundings produces a sharper awareness of the external world, but it also highlights his inner life, evoking what we might describe as a psychological self-awareness that from a present-day perspective is almost humorous. He is attentive to the subconscious part of his mind, which he likens to an animal, such as his dog, Rose, with "its own tastes, inclinations, and will" (22). He illustrates the disunion of what he calls the "spiritual" and the "animal" faculties by analyzing his response to a work of art. When he reads, for example, his "soul" (or higher faculty) will sometimes go off with an agreeable idea, whereas the "animal" will mechanically follow the words and lines without remembering what it reads (22). Similarly, while the soul is contemplating a fine painting, the animal, left to its own devices, may well decide to take itself to the door of a beautiful woman (25). The animal has the job of preparing breakfast and doing other sensually appealing tasks. The irrationality of love is comically attributed to "animal magnetism," a relation underscored by way that the lady the narrator admires (Rosalie) incorporates the name of his adored dog (Rose) (46, 33). Most strikingly, perhaps, de Maistre embraces a Swiftian notion of art very like the one that Joyce uses to characterize *Dubliners*: he would like to see a kind of art that could function as a "moral mirror, in which all men might see themselves, with their virtues and their vices," although he is careful to caution, anticipating Wilde's Calibanesque view of readers, "What would a moral mirror avail? Few people would look at it, and no one would recognize himself" (73–74).[10]

Like de Maistre's, Joyce's approach to everyday life redirects the reader's attention to the micromovements of thought, perception, and behavior. Joyce's efforts to capture the motion of thought—often triggered by subconscious responses to language—might be described as an extended anatomy of attention: not only does he attempt to record, with exquisite precision, how and why the attention of his characters changes focus, he also anticipates how the attention of the reader will operate. He is able to predict where that attention has been trained to go—toward the overview or big picture, unfolded sequentially through plot or residing in the overall "meaning"—and he strategically defers the reader's access to those privileged vantage points. What happens as a result is that readerly attention is solicited by the apparently insignificant aspects of experience normally overlooked by adults: a man's momentary hunger for a woman's thighs; the half-read story in a newspaper before a man wipes himself with it in the outhouse. Most unusually, we are enjoined to look through the eyes of characters that are immensely admirable in some respects and blind or helpless in others, which helps us understand—often after much resistance—that such "inconsistent" characters are relatively rare among literary protagonists.[11] Joyce's characters are modern equivalents of the old tragic heroes in one specific way: they are both superb and flawed, with flaws that are far from fatal but which nevertheless compromise the quality of their interactions with others, and cast intriguing shadows over their lives.[12]

If we approach the everyday from yet another angle, such as the one taken by the French theorist Maurice Blanchot, it emerges as a space in which something significant may always happen. For Blanchot, in everyday life the individual is unmarked, unnamed, unheroic: "The individual is held, as though without knowing it, in human anonymity."[13] The everyday is elusive, inexhaustible, uneventful, even boring. It is "the inaccessible to which we have always already had access" (20). Because it is what most people take for granted, its essential trait is that "it escapes": "The everyday is what we never see for a first time, but only see again, having always already seen it by an illusion that is, as it happens, constitutive of the everyday" (14).[14] Blanchot is careful to present both sides of the everyday. On the one hand, he sees a "secret destructive capacity . . . at play in it, the corrosive force of human anonymity" that not only "challenges heroic values" but "impugns all values" (19). On the other hand, he understands the everyday as a "connected movement . . . by which we are *continually* (though in the mode of discontinuity) in relation with the indeterminate totality of human possibilities" (19). "The everyday is our portion of eternity" or "eternullity" (20); it is the collective experience and denial of a hole that is also whole.

The everyday, then, is for Blanchot "what we are first of all, and most often" (12): a faceless blur caught in the machinery of society. It is like the fertile chaos that preceded creation: it is a state in which "nothing happens" that nevertheless suggests "something essential might be allowed to happen" (15). Most readers feel themselves to be in such a space when reading Joyce's novels: nothing seems to be happening, but something very different might happen (in another register) at any moment. Joyce's works produce in *readers* a state of "quotidian confusion" (16) in which everything seems adulterated, interpenetrating into everything else, and nothing seems to blossom into "real life." Blanchot's description of such confusion could be fruitfully applied to describe the experience of reading Joyce's works:

> Seeming to take up all of life, it [the everyday, the text] is without limit and it strikes all other life with unreality. But there arises here a sudden clarity. "Something lights up, appears as a flash on the paths of banality . . . it is chance, the great instant, the miracle." And the miracle "penetrates life in an unforeseeable manner . . . without relation to the rest, transforming the whole into a clear and simple account."[15] By its flash, the miracle separates the indistinct moments of day-to-day life, suspends nuance, interrupts uncertainties. (16)

This is what the process of reading Joyce entices readers to experience— the tension between quotidian confusion and sudden, intermittent flashes: the unexpected insight that seems to light up the banal, an illumination that cannot be sustained. Such moments are unpredictable, but they can only happen if one remains attentive to the uneventful specificity of the ordinary. Paradoxically, the extraordinary appears only when observers regard "ordinary" things as capable of yielding surprising insights.[16]

In the process of reading Joyce, attentiveness to the "everyday," and to seemingly insignificant detail, gives rise to flashes of insight. My method *in The Joyce of Everyday Life* works in reverse: flashes of insight derived from Joyce—ones that illuminate the hidden stories subtending the surface of his texts—are used to draw attention back to the everyday as the "ground" of all meaning. The autonomous, associative, hermetic practice of reading I practice cannot be done quickly, or easily; it improves with time, effort, and repetition, and it is enhanced by research. I have attempted to illustrate its results and rewards.

ACKNOWLEDGMENTS

I want to begin by thanking the acquisitions editor, Suzanne Guiod, and the series editor, Anne Fogarty, at Bucknell University Press for their expert handling of my manuscript. I am also grateful to the many different places that invited me to give talks that developed into chapters of the books: the University of Otago in Dunedin, New Zealand; the James Joyce Foundation in Zurich; the James Joyce Foundation for invitations to Dublin and Austin; The University of Chicago; the James Joyce Summer Schools in Dublin and Trieste; Northwestern University and its Carol and Gordon Segal Distinguished Professorship in Irish Literature; and the University of Birmingham in the United Kingdom, to name the most recent. I am also indebted to Fordham University Press and the *Joyce Studies Annual* for permission to use "Love, Race, and *Exiles*: The Bleak Side of *Ulysses*" (2007).

I could not have written this book without the support of numerous friends and colleagues, including Joanne Ahearn, Scott Browning, Ron Bush, Meredith Gamer, Sara Gordon, Norman Hjelm, the late Tim Mahaffey, Wendy Truran, and Joseph Valente. I would like to extend my thanks for the contributions of two talented artists, Dennis Haugh and Christina Valente, and the gifted photographer, Morgan Gerace. And finally, I owe so much to the encouragement, writing talent, and critical acumen of my wonderful daughters, Amanda Dennis and Laura MacMullen.

This volume is lovingly dedicated to the person who helped me face my past, J.E.R., and to my lively grandson Conor, who is helping me embrace the future.

NOTES

INTRODUCTION

1. Frank Budgen, *James Joyce and the Making of* Ulysses (Bloomington: Indiana University Press, 1960), 175.
2. James Joyce, *Ulysses*, ed. Hans Walter Gabler with Wolfhard Steppe and Claus Melchior, afterword by Michael Groden (New York: Vintage, 1986), 14.141–143. Hereafter cited parenthetically in the text as *U*, followed by the episode and line numbers.
3. James Joyce, *Dubliners*, with an introduction and notes by Terence Brown (New York: Penguin, 1992), 105. Hereafter cited parenthetically in the text as *D*.
4. A phrase taken from Michael Fried, *Menzel's Realism: Art and Embodiment in Nineteenth-Century Berlin* (New Haven, CT: Yale University Press, 2002), 159.
5. On the "case" in "A Painful Case," see Paul K. Saint-Amour and Karen R. Lawrence, "Reopening 'A Painful Case,'" in *Collaborative Dubliners: Joyce in Dialogue*, ed. Vicki Mahaffey (Syracuse, NY: Syracuse University Press, 2012), 238–260.
6. James Joyce, *A Portrait of the Artist as a Young Man*, ed. with an introduction and notes by Jeri Johnson (Oxford: Oxford University Press, 2000), 213. Hereafter cited parenthetically in the text as *P*.
7. For additional perspectives on this phrase in *Ulysses*, see Cleo Hanaway-Oakley, "'See Ourselves as Others See Us': Cinematic Ways of Being and Seeing in *Ulysses*," in *Roll Away the Reel World: James Joyce and Cinema*, ed. John McCourt (Cork: Cork University Press, 2010), 122–136; and Kimberly J. Devlin, "'See Ourselves as Others See Us': Joyce's Look at the Eye of the Other," *PMLA* 104, no. 5 (October 1989): 882–893.
8. As Kant explained in 1784, "*Immaturity* is the inability to use one's understanding without guidance from another." See "An Answer to a Question: What Is Enlightenment?," in Immanual Kant, *Perpetual Peace and Other Essays on Politics, History, and Morals*, trans. Ted Humphrey (Indianapolis: Hackett Publishing, 1992), no. 1.
9. Richard Ellmann, in his list of the books in Joyce's Trieste Library, erroneously attributes *A Journey around My Room* to de Maistre's older brother, Joseph. See Richard Ellmann, *The Consciousness of Joyce* (New York: Oxford University Press, 1977), 118.
10. Oscar Wilde, *The Picture of Dorian Gray: Authoritative Texts, Backgrounds, Reviews and Reactions, Criticism*, ed. Donald L. Lawler (New York: Norton, 1988), preface.
11. See Hugh Kenner, *Joyce's Voices* (McLean, IL: Dalkey Archive Press, 2007).
12. Theodor W. Adorno, *Aesthetic Theory*, ed. Gretel Adorno and Rolf Tiedemann, trans. Robert Hullot-Kentor (London: Continuum, 1997), 8–9.
13. James Joyce, *Finnegans Wake* (New York: Viking Press, 1967), 560.20. Hereafter cited parenthetically in the text as *FW*, followed by the page and line numbers. *Finnegans Wake* is divided into four books, three of which are further divided into chapters. The

chapters themselves will be identified by book and chapter number, as follows: I.8 refers to book I, chapter 8.

14. Jane Bennett, *Vibrant Matter: A Political Ecology of Things* (Durham, NC: Duke University Press, 2010), viii. Hereafter cited parenthetically in the text.

15. Hugh Kenner, "The *Portrait* in Perspective," *Kenyon Review* 10, no. 3 (Summer 1948): 366.

16. Jane Bennett, *The Enchantments of Modern Life: Attachment, Crossings, and Ethics* (Princeton, NJ: Princeton University Press, 2001), 4–5. Hereafter cited parenthetically in the text. Bennett roots her claim that joy can be a source of ethics in Nietzsche's *Also Sprach Zarathustra,* in which Zarathustra discloses that he always seems "to have done better" when he "learned to feel better joys." He asserts that feeling too little joy "is our original sin," concluding that "learning better to feel joy, we best unlearn how to do harm to others and to contrive harm." Cited in Bennett, *The Enchantment of Modern Life,* 12–13.

17. Thomas Moore, *The Re-Enchantment of Everyday Life* (New York: Harper Collins, 1996), x.

18. Bennett's *Enchantment* is an effort to explore the effect of a "mood of enchantment" on ethics. She sees enchantment as the effect produced when the world comes alive.

19. *OED Online.* All subsequent references to the *OED* will be indicated parenthetically in the text.

20. See Vicki Mahaffey, "Changing Perspective: Why Style and Structure Matter in *Ulysses,*" in *Joycean Possibilities: A Margot Norris Legacy,* ed. Joseph Valente, Vicki Mahaffey, and Kezia Whiting (New York: Anthem, 2023), 189–204.

21. Derek Attridge, *Peculiar Language: Literature as Difference from the Renaissance to James Joyce* (Ithaca, NY: Cornell University Press, 1988), 109. Hereafter cited parenthetically in the text.

22. See, for example, Heidi-Maria Lehtonen, Henri Penttinen, Jukka Rauhala, and Vesa Valimaki, "Analysis and Modeling of Sustain-Pedal Effects, *Journal of the Acoustical Society of America* 122, no. 3 (2007): 1787–1797. My thanks to Alex Kessler for this reference.

23. A fun fact about an earwig that is *not* a myth is that the male has two penises, in case one breaks off.

24. *Online Etymological Dictionary,* etymonline.com. All subsequent etymologies are from this source unless otherwise noted.

25. See James Joyce, "Oscar Wilde: The Poet of *Salomé,*" in James Joyce, *Occasional, Critical, and Political Writing,* ed. Kevin Barry (Oxford: Oxford University Press, 2000), 151: "It is the truth inherent in the spirit of Catholicism: that man cannot reach the divine heart except across that sense of separation and loss that is called sin."

26. Typologically, the main reversal of the fall into babble that resulted from the attempted erection of Babel is Pentecost, in which the disciples could understand the meaning of what was spoken in many different tongues.

27. Berber Bevernage, "Time, Presence, and Historical Injustice," *History and Theory* 47 (May 2008): 163. Hereafter cited parenthetically in the text.

28. Bevernage labels these two views the "time of history" vs. the "time of jurisprudence," arguing that history and justice depend upon different conceptions of time as reversible or irreversible. "The time of jurisdiction [promoted by Walter Benjamin] frequently assumes a *reversible* time in which the crime is . . . still wholly present and able to be reversed or annulled by the correct sentence and punishment." Nietzsche's history, in direct contrast, "makes use of a fundamentally *irreversible* time," emphasizing its inalterability. "It is unthinkable that perfect justice can be realized within the realm of history, because even a perfectly just society can never compensate for the misery of the past." If time is inevitably irreversible, history "can offer only the slender consolation of truth and remembrance in the face of the worst atrocities of the past" ("Time, Presence, and Historical Injustice," 153, 157).

29. This phenomenon, akin to the Bergsonian *durée* of 1910, was discussed by Ernst Bloch as early as 1932 as "nonsynchronism." See Ernst Bloch, "Nonsynchronism and the Obligation to Its Dialectics," *New German Critique* 11 (1977): 22–38.

30. Jacques Derrida, *Specters of Marx: The State of the Debt, the Work of Mourning, and the New International,* trans. Peggy Kamuf (New York: Routledge, 1994), 1–3, 48. Derrida uses this quotation as an epigraph.

31. William Butler Yeats, "Per Amica Silentia Lunae," in William Butler Yeats, *Mythologies* (New York: Collier-Macmillan, 1959), 362.

32. William Butler Yeats, *The Collected Works of W. B. Yeats,* vol. 1, *The Poems,* ed. Richard J. Finneran (New York: Macmillan, 1989). All subsequent citations of Yeats's poetry are from this edition.

33. T. S. Eliot, "Burnt Norton," *Four Quartets* (London: Faber and Faber, 1959), 13.

34. "In Memory of W. B. Yeats," 1939. W. H. Auden, *Collected Shorter Poems, 1927–1957* (New York: Random House, 1966), 143. The historical moment in which he was writing, as Europe was poised on the brink of World War II, gave additional passion and urgency to Auden's account of how global war is linked to intellectual and emotional poverty in the individual.

35. Maurice Maeterlinck, *Wisdom and Destiny,* trans. Alfred Sutro (London: George Allen, 1898), 31. Hereafter cited parenthetically in the text. In *Ulysses,* Stephen slightly abridges and reverses the quotation in a way that suggests Joyce may be quoting from memory: "*If Socrates leave his house today he will find the sage seated on his doorstep. If Judas go forth tonight it is to Judas his steps will tend* " (U 9.1042–1044). Maeterlinck develops his point by arguing, "There comes no adventure but wears to our soul the shape of our everyday thoughts; and deeds of heroism are but offered to those who, for many long years, have been heroes in obscurity and silence" (*Wisdom and Destiny,* 31).

CHAPTER 1   ON BEDS

1. Richard Ellmann, *James Joyce* (New York: Oxford University Press, 1982), 394. Cited by Maud Ellmann, "Lotus Eaters," *The Cambridge Centenary* Ulysses: *The 1922 Text with Essays and Notes,* ed. Catherine Flynn (Cambridge: Cambridge University Press, 2022), 131.

2. Virginia Woolf, *To the Lighthouse*, foreword by Eudora Welty (New York: Harcourt Brace Jovanovich, 1955), p. 23. Hereafter cited parenthetically in the text.

3. Joseph Shipley explains that "litter" was first a bed, and that its meaning of "rubbish" is an extension of the straw that used to be used for bedding. Joseph T. Shipley, *The Origins of English Words: A Discursive Dictionary of Indo-European Roots* (Baltimore: The Johns Hopkins University Press, 1984), p. 59: "deph."

4. *The Oxford Dictionary of English Etymology*, ed. C. T. Onions with the assistance of G.W.S. Friedrichsen and R. W. Burchfield (Oxford: Clarendon Press, 1966).

5. Homer, *Odyssey*, trans. Stanley Lombardo, intro. Sheila Murnaghan (New York: Hackett Publishing, 2000), bk. 23, l. 178. Hereafter cited parenthetically in the text by book and line numbers.

6. Joyce compares Boylan's method of riding a woman to his treatment of a mare, which Molly registers when she remembers how he slapped her arse when he left: "I didnt like his slapping me behind going away so familiarly in the hall though I laughed Im not a horse or an ass am I" (*U* 18.122–124).

7. ALP jingles in a comparable way, as Joyce stresses when he associates her with the end of the nursery rhyme: "With rings on her fingers and bells on her toes, she will have music wherever she goes." To mark the publication of the Anna Livia Plurabelle chapter of *Finnegans Wake*, Joyce wrote a little rhyme to the tune of "Ride a Cock Horse to Banbury Cross." Intended for the dust jacket, it included the lines "Sevensinns in her singthings, / Plurabelles on her prose, / Sheashell ebb music wayriver she flows." See Herbert Gorman, *James Joyce* (New York: Rinehart and Company, 1939; 1948), p. 343. The rhythm of the nursery rhyme can be heard in "specks on her eyeux, and spudds on horeilles and a circusfix riding her Parisienne's cocknese," for example (*FW* 102.12–13).

8. In *Finnegans Wake*, Joyce consistently opposes the stone to the tree, seeing these opposites as united in the name Tristan (tree-stone). They become associated with Shem and Shaun, and with Paul and Peter, a connection reinforced by the connection between Peter and "rock."

9. Gloria Bertonis, *Stone Age Divas: Their Mystery and Their Magic* (Bloomington, IN: Author House, 2011), 72. Interestingly, the siglum for Anna Livia Plurabelle in *Finnegans Wake* is such a triangle. Bertonis notes that the cuneiform of Sumeria (modern day Iraq) dates from 3100 B.C., when it was primarily used for administrative records, and by 2500 B.C. it had become more sophisticated and literary. Cuneiform survives on clay tablets, which were impressed with a wedge-shaped stylus ("cuneiform" means "wedge-shaped"), 87.

10. Max Hunt, "Cunt: A Cultural History of the C Word." Since Hunt's death, the essay originally accessed has been taken down.

11. See *Odyssey*, bk. 8, ll. 265–365.

12. For more on Joyce's treatment of Kevin, see Mahaffey, "'Ricorso': The Flaming Door of IV," in *Joyce's Allmaziful Plurabilities: Polyvocal Explorations of* Finnegans Wake, ed. Kimberly J. Devlin and Christine Smedley (Gainesville: University Press of Florida, 2015), 296–298.

13. Carol Ann Duffy, *The World's Wife* (London: Picador, 2000), 30.

14. Aristotle, *Physics,* translated by Robin Waterfield, with introduction and notes by David Bostock (Oxford: Oxford University Press, 1996). Plato, *Republic,* translated Roblin Waterfield (Oxford: Oxford University Press, 1993).

15. This is what Aristotle has famously called a "final cause," arguing that it is implicitly moral.

16. *The Complete Poems of Emily Dickinson,* ed. Thomas H. Johnson (Cambridge, MA: Harvard University Press, 1983), poem 829.

CHAPTER 2   ON DIRTY SHEETS

1. See Joyce's letter to Nora of December 3, 1909, in James Joyce, *Selected Letters,* ed. Richard Ellmann (1966; New York: Viking, 1975), 182–183. Hereafter cited parenthetically in the text as *SL.* See also Brenda Maddox, *Nora: A Biography of Nora Joyce* (New York: Fawcett Columbine, 1988), 27.

2. Robert Tweedy, *The Story of the Court Laundry* (Dublin: Wolfhound, 1999), 22.

3. Interestingly, although we think of a sheet as white, it is aurally linked with the blackness of excretion through a homonymic kinship with "shit." As Phillip Herring explained, in Old Saxon, our modern word "shit" had a long vowel, so that it was pronounced "sheet"; gradually, in Britain, the vowel shortened until it was pronounced "shit." He points out that "shit" is still pronounced "sheet" in Low German, which is still used as slang all over North Germany (email message to the author, summer 2004).

4. This is how ALP wants to present HCE in her letter, as a man determined to see all of life, its beauty, and its ugliness: "All schwants (schwrites) ischt tell the cock's trootabout him. . . . He had to see life foully the plak and the smut (schwrites)" (*FW* 113.11–14). She tries to do the same thing in her letter about him: to present his larger-than-life qualities as well as his frailties, especially his weakness for young girls. The connection between paper and excrement can be surprisingly close as well. In Thailand, I visited a local business that made paper from elephant dung, which contains thick fibers that produce strong paper.

5. See the reference to ALP's "litter" of children: "But it's quite on the cards she'll shed more and merrier, twills and trills, sparefours and spoilfives, nordsilikes and sudsevers and ayes and neins to a litter" (*FW* 201.36–202.2).

6. Margaret Mary Alacoque also appears in *Dubliners,* in the story "Eveline." And "Clay" should also be mentioned in relation to laundry. For more information on the history of this important subject and the "rehabilitative" function of laundries for women, see James M. Smith, *Ireland's Magdalene Laundries and the Nation's Architecture of Containment* (South Bend, IN: University of Notre Dame Press, 2007), as well as the films *The Magdalene Sisters* (2002) and *Philomela* (2013).

7. P. W. Joyce, *A Social History of Ancient Ireland,* 3rd ed., vol. 2 (Dublin: M. H. Gill, 1920), 429. See also Seumas MacManus, *The Story of the Irish Race: A Popular History of Ireland,* rev. ed. (Old Greenwich, CT: Devin-Adair, 1921), 21.

8. See Shari Benstock, "Sylvia Beach and Adrienne Monnier: Rue de l'Odéon," in *Women of the Left Bank: Paris, 1900–1940* (Austin: University of Texas Press, 1986), 194–229.

9. "Banshee" literally means female *sidhe*, or what we would now call a fairy from the mound, although the *sidhe* in Irish folklore were the gods and goddesses of ancient Ireland, the Tuatha de Danaan, who went into the hillside when they died and are still to be felt in the wind. A banshee is thought to herald an imminent death, usually by keening or shrieking.

10. Margot Norris, *Joyce's Web: The Social Unraveling of Modernism* (Austin: University of Texas Press, 1992), 139–163. Hereafter cited parenthetically in the text.

11. Sheldon Brivic, *Joyce's Waking Women: An Introduction to* Finnegans Wake (Madison: University of Wisconsin Press, 1995), 37.

12. Maddox, *Nora*, 94, 111; and Norris, *Joyce's Web*, 149–150.

13. As Norris points out, in the first draft Joyce identified the food they'd run out of as "horsemeat," which was later changed for "horsebrose" (a mash of oats used to feed horses (*Joyce's Web*. 157).

14. Joyce started marking his notes in colored crayons when writing *Ulysses*. See Luca Crispi, "A First Foray into the National Library of Ireland's Joyce Manuscripts: Bloomsday 2011," in *Genetic Joyce Studies*, issue 11 (Spring 2011): "he habitually crossed through the words he had incorporated into his writings with variously coloured crayons." https://www.geneticjoycestudies.org/articles/GJS11/GJS11_Crispi

15. In one of his most beautiful letters to Nora, Joyce also describes her effect on him as having transformed him from a pearl into an opal, firing him, filling him with color (Joyce, *Selected Letters*, 161).

CHAPTER 3   ON SALMON

1. Eliot, "Little Gidding," *Four Quartets*, 59.

2. "From Work in Progress," by James Joyce, *The Transatlantic Review* I, no. 4 (April 1924).

3. James MacKillop points out that Finn MacCool was also seen in different ways, as a villain as well as a hero. An example of his villainous side is his pursuit of Diarmuid and Grania, as emphasized in Yeats and George Moore's play of that title. As MacKillop puts it, "To some people, Fionn mac Cumhaill was a hero and to others he was a fool." James MacKillop, *Fionn mac Cumhaill: Celtic Myth in English Literature* (Syracuse, NY: Syracuse University Press, 1986), xiii. Hereafter cited parenthetically in the text.

4. James Joyce, "Oscar Wilde: The Poet of *Salomé*," in James Joyce, *Occasional, Critical, and Political Writing*, ed. Kevin Barry, 151. This is also the meaning of Yeats's short story, "The Tables of the Law," which Joyce knew by heart.

5. Although Joyce would probably have used the King James version of the Bible, I am using the Revised Standard version throughout for its more contemporary idiom.

6. For a fuller account of Finn MacCool stories spanning six hundred years, see MacKillop, *Fionn mac Cumhaill*, esp. his chapter on *Finnegans Wake* (163–193).

7. Jeremiah Curtin, "Birth of Fin MacCumhail," in *Myths and Folk-lore of Ireland* (1890; New York: Weathervane Books, 1975), 204–220. Hereafter cited parenthetically in the text.

8. T. P. Cross and C. H. Slover, eds. *Ancient Irish Tales* (New York: Henry Holt, 1936), 384. As MacKillop notes, Danis Rose and John O'Hanlon showed how extensively Joyce used Cross and Slover's translations of Old Irish texts. See Danis Rose and John O'Hanlon, "Finn MacCool and the Final Weeks of Work in Progress," *A Wake Newslitter* 17, no. 5 (October 1980): 69–87. The Buffalo notebooks consist of Joyce's many workbooks for "Work in Progress" and *Finnegans Wake,* housed at the University of Buffalo in their James Joyce Collection. They will be cited as B (for Buffalo) followed by VI (for *Finnegans Wake*) and then the number of the notebook and the page. For a description of notebook 30, for example, see https://library.buffalo.edu/jamesjoyce/catalog/vi -finnegans-wake/vib30/. Some of the notebooks have been published and cross-referenced by Brepols Publishers, edited by Vincent Deane, Daniel Ferrer, and Geert Lernout: https://www.brepols.net/series/FWNB.

9. Quoted in Cross and Slover, *Ancient Irish Tales,* 365.

10. Quoted in Rose and O'Hanlon, "Finn MacCool"; see also Cross and Slover, *Ancient Irish Tales,* 384.

11. Rose and O'Hanlon, "Finn MacCool."

12. In *FW* I.8, one of the washerwomen refers to ALP's many children as "aleveens" (*FW* 201.27).

13. In *Finnegans Wake,* a reference to a "redd" can be found on 58.31; "parr" on 36.06, 170.28, 205.02; "smolt" on 170.28; "fry" on 35.14 and 446.12.

14. "Waking Early Sunday Morning," in Robert Lowell, *Collected Poems* (New York: Farrar Straus and Giroux, 2007), 383.

15. Quoted in Rose and O'Hanlon, "Finn MacCool," 69.

16. Lady Gregory and William Butler Yeats, *Gods and Fighting Men: The Story of the Tuatha de Danaan and the Fiana of Ireland* (1904; London: Wentworth Press, 2016), 14–15.

17. Transcribed by Brian Fox with the help of Wim Van Mierlo from the Hans E. Jahnke Bequest at the National Library of Ireland and cited in Brian Fox, *James Joyce's America* (Oxford: Oxford University Press, 2019), 115. The original can be viewed on the National Library of Ireland website: catalogue.nli.ie/Record/vtls000576137.

18. Luca Crispi, "Storiella as She Was Wryt: Chapter II.2," in *How Joyce Wrote Finnegans Wake: A Chapter-by-Chapter Genetic Guide,* ed. Luca Crispi and Sam Slote (Madison: University of Wisconsin Press, 2007), p. 239: "the genetic evidence indicates that it too was not a structurally or thematically significant source."

19. Lionel Trilling, "The Greatness of *Huckleberry Finn,*" in *Huckleberry Finn: Text, Sources, and Criticism,* ed. Kenneth S. Lynn (New York: 1961), 192, 193; from Lionel Trilling, Introduction to *Adventures of Huckleberry Finn,* by Mark Twain (New York: 1948). Cited by Emory Elliott, Introduction, *Adventures of Huckleberry Finn,* ed. Emory Elliott (Oxford: Oxford University Press, 1999), xxxviii.

20. Mark Twain, *Adventures of Huckleberry Finn,* ed. Emory Elliott (Oxford: Oxford University Press, 1999), 247. Hereafter cited parenthetically in the text.

21. Roland McHugh, *Annotations to Finnegans Wake* (Baltimore: Johns Hopkins University Press, 1991), 3.

CHAPTER 4   ON WRITING BY HAND

1. Maddox, *Nora,* 27. 1 am grateful to several people for contributing information to this chapter: Luca Crispi, Ramona Curry, Penelope Fielding, Gregory Steirer, and Christina Walter. I also wish to thank the film librarians at the Library of Congress.

2. Ovid, *The Metamorphoses of Ovid,* trans. Mary M. Innes (Harmondsworth, England: Penguin Books, 1955), bk 8, ll. 185–186.

3. David Hayman, *The "Wake" in Transit* (Ithaca, NY: Cornell University Press, 1990), 190: the "insufficiently despised notetaker" had become "Jim the Penman."

4. This phrase is attributed to Philip Vernon in James Greene and David Lewis, *The Hidden Language of your Handwriting* (London: Souvenir Press, 1980), 18. The reference is to G. W. Allport and P. E. Vernon, *Studies in Expressive Movement* (New York: Macmillan, 1933).

5. According to Greene and Lewis, "As the ability [to write cursively] becomes increasingly effortless and automatic the child begins to develop a style which differs from that taught in school. With increasing maturity, personality and other factors exert far more influence on the character of the handwriting than the early classroom-taught letter shapes. What emerges is an absolutely unique arrangement of line and loop, form and flow that distinguishes each individual's handwriting" (*The Hidden Language of Your Handwriting,* 17). Jacques Derrida examines this paradoxical quality of the signature more closely in "Signature Event Context," in Jacques Derrida, *Limited Inc,* trans. Samuel Weber and Jeffrey Mehlman (Chicago: Northwestern University Press, 1988), 1–21. As Niall Lucy explains in *Debating Derrida* (Carlton South, Victoria: Melbourne University Press, 1995), "In order for every signature-event to be unique, singular, self-identical, each has to conform to a general structure. This is what Derrida calls the "enigmatic originality" of the signature. . . . No less than any other mark, in order to be what it "is" (singular, functional, present) a signature must be iterable, able to be forged. To be original, it must be reproducible. . . . To be authentic, a signature must be able to be counterfeited, stolen—misused" (43).

6. Greene and Lewis, *The Hidden Language of Your Handwriting,* 18.

7. Cf. *The Trial of Jim the Penman* (James Townsend Saward), ed. George Dilnot (London: Geoffrey Bles, 1930). Dilnot argues that Jim the Penman was "the first to make forgery an organized business, to devise a technique to guard against discovery which in most of its essentials has been followed ever since" (12). The historical James Saward was "a man of good birth, of culture and education, and a barrister of considerable legal attainments" (12). He had "suave and polished manners" and "remarkable keenness and penetration in conversation," but according to Dilnot his downfall was "his ill-disciplined indulgence of his passions. . . . By a curious perversity he sought his boon companions among the lowest and most degraded sections of society" (13). At his trial, he was found guilty in five minutes and sentenced to transportation for life, and he seems to have died in exile. It is quite possible that Joyce saw Jim the Penman's story as an ironic counterversion of his own defiant and heroic self-exile from Ireland.

8. I have not located a published version of the play. The copy I used was a microfilm of a typed playscript, complete with changes, deletions, and handwritten additions to the

stage directions located in the University of Pennsylvania's Van Pelt Library. Subsequent citations use the microfilm pagination. However, E. J. Phillips cites the play as having a rather late publication date (1912).

9. George C. D. Odell, *Annals of the New York Stage,* vol. 13 (New York: Columbia University Press, 1942), 217. The stars of the first New York performance were Agnes Booth (as Jim's wife) and E. M. Holland (as the detective). E. J. Phillips played Lady Dunscomb. See "Jim the Penman," Life and Times of Actress EJ Phillips, last modified August 25, 2020, https://www.maryglenchitty.com/jimthepenman.htm.

10. James Joyce, *James Joyce's Letters to Sylvia Beach, 1921–1940,* ed. Melissa Banta and Oscar A. Silverman (Oxford: Plantin Publishers, 1987), 41.

11. *New York Times,* April 10, 1914, p. 5. The aim of this list, according to the announcement that accompanied it, was to aid the self-education of the Catholic playgoer, in the hope that "he may be saved from exposing those near and dear to him to the dangers of contamination."

12. See Act 1 of the play, in which Jim's wife Nina asks who Jim the Penman is, and one of her guests answers, "An invisible, intangible entity" (12).

13. Note that here, as is often the case, a "pen name" allows the author to change not only her name but also her sex.

14. Dick Donovan, *Jim the Penman* (1901; London: George Newnes, n.d. [1917]), 4. Hereafter cited parenthetically in the text. The first edition had a subtitle: "The Life Story of One of the Most Astounding Criminals That Have Ever Lived."

15. In the novel version Jim's wife is cold and calculating. She sets him up for a life of forgery by her expensive habits, then introduces him to an Englishman who offers to pay him if he will use his abilities as a chemist to erase writing from checks and then rewrite them. Unlike the play, this forger doesn't have a particularly good heart; the question is whether the sins of the fathers must be visited upon the children. As the daughter asks near the end, "Must the children for ever suffer because their parents sinned?" (*Jim the Penman,* 252). This novel, unlike Ibsen's *Ghosts,* answers "no." Unlike her parents, Jim's daughter remains innocent and good, and is ultimately able, after much suffering, to live a fulfilling noncriminal life. She frees herself from the sin of her parents, which was "too great a love for money" (19).

16. This is the kind of comment that Joyce parodies in *Finnegans Wake* when the narrator jibes (playing against the first line of the song "Araby": "Sing us a song of Araby"), "Sing us a song of alibi" (*FW* 190.30).

17. Compare Stephen's insistence that Shakespeare's genius is rooted in sin, "the original sin that darkened his understanding, weakened his will and left in him a strong inclination to evil" (*U* 9.1006–1007), a sin that gave him the imaginative range to become all the parts in all of his plays. He is the ghost and the prince in *Hamlet,* and "in *Cymbeline,* in *Othello* he is bawd and cuckold" (*U* 9.1021). In this respect, he is like God, "the lord of things as they are," who "is doubtless all in all in all of us" (*U* 9.1048–1050).

18. Joyce's essay on *When We Dead Awaken,* "Ibsen's New Drama," was first published on April 1, 1900, in the *Fortnightly Review.* It is reprinted in *James Joyce: Critical Writings,* ed. Richard Ellmann and Ellsworth Mason (New York: Viking, 1959), 66, 54.

19. See "Jim the Penman."

20. According to Kenneth W. Munden, ed., *The American Film Institute Catalog of Motion Pictures Produced in the United States: Feature Films, 1921–1930* (Berkeley: University of California Press, 1971), "The camera used contained two lenses separated by the distance between a normal pair of eyes. The two films produced were tinted red and green. Spectators at the exhibition wore two-color glasses to view the film" (F2.2805). Wisconsin has a still from this 1915 Famous Players Film company version (distributed by Paramount Pictures). The film, directed by Edwin S. Porter, starred John Mason as James Ralston and was released on June 3, 1915.

21. The film was produced by Whitman Bennett, distributed by Associated First National Pictures, and released in April of 1921; Kenneth Webb was the director (Munden, *The American Film Institute Catalog*, 1971). *Jim the Penman.*

22. Printed music for *Jim the Penman* (for piano or organ) is available at the Library of Congress, Performing Arts Reading Room (LC Classification M176.J)..

23. Promotional material distributed by First National (April 1921), microfilm.

24. Farnum is identified in the promotional material as "one of the best known in the country." As the *Los Angeles Times* reported on July 19, 1921, noting one of the ways in which the film was even more "absorbing" than the play, "The stage didn't show us the herd of shrieking conspirators drowning in the cabin of the yacht" (3.4).

25. According to the promotional material, this indomitable fidelity to his wife and daughter is what is most admirable about Jim (along with his manual dexterity and genius at escaping detection): "When the happiness of his wife and daughter is threatened he takes the brave man's course and gives his life to protect them."

26. A review in the *Los Angeles Times* of July 19, 1921, identifies Jim's wife as "the unfortunate girl he loved so deeply that he committed an unforgivable crime to win her." The *Chicago Daily Tribune* of April 3, 1921, emphasizes the love angle even more strongly: "He forges the name of the girl he loves on a dance program so that the last watch [*sic*; error for "waltz"] shall be his. Because he loves her he forges a check to save her father from disgrace. And that's the beginning" (F3).

27. A not very favorable review of the film in *Variety* dated March 25, 1921, refers to the plot as a "chain of evidence leading up to the wife's realization that her husband is a criminal."

28. This is one of the captions of the film in Part 3.

29. This line was included as one of the "Catchlines for Programs, Teasers and Lobby Cards" in the First National promotional material.

30. "This absence is not a continuous modification of presence, it is a rupture in presence, the 'death' or the possibility of the 'death' of the receiver inscribed in the structure of the mark" (Derrida, "Signature Event Context," 5).

31. Jacob Boehme, *Boehme's "Signatura Rerum" and Other Discourses*, introd. Clifford Bax (London: Dent, n.d.). Boehme's *Signatura Rerum* was originally published in German in 1621; first published in English in 1649. Hereafter cited parenthetically in the text.

32. In First National's promotional material for the release of *Jim the Penman,* in an article titled "Science Balks Forgeries Where the Naked Eye Is Easily Deceived," the signature (as a guarantee of authenticity) is traced to the ancient use of tokens: "In the very early days chiefs and kings had a token of some kind by which they were known and the messengers were given these tokens to carry with them that the receiver of the message might know that the message was genuine." Proof that people forged these tokens exists in early records of executions for the offense.

33. New Revised Standard Version.

34. Nick Groom, *The Forger's Shadow: How Forgery Changed the Course of Literature* (London: Picador, 2002), 1.

35. Tom Davis, "Forged Handwriting," in *Fakes and Frauds: Varieties of Deception in Print and Manuscript,* ed. Robin Myers and Michael Harris (Winchester, England: St Paul's Bibliographies, 1989), 131–132.

36. Tom Davis explains that "a skilled writer works to a rhythm: . . . he or she takes the same amount of time to do similar component actions, with a resulting economy of movement and uniformity of shape" ("Forged Handwriting," 129). This is possible because "skilled handwriting is not done piecemeal, letter by letter, but in bursts: packages of information are sent down from the brain for realization by the muscles of the hand and arm" (132). Signatures, especially, reside in the memory as a pattern that is executed automatically with little intervention from the conscious mind. This is possible because there are two ways of "correcting" or monitoring what we do as we write: one is "proprioceptive" (which literally means that the muscles are self-observing; this is what I would call muscle memory), and the other is visual (133–134). Once we have learned the skill of writing and it has become a habit, we rely primarily on proprioceptive feedback, which allows us to write in a smooth, uninterrupted wavelike motion. A forger, however, is often forced to fall back on "the visual rather than the proprioceptive feedback mechanism" (135), which produces defects in line quality. An excellent forger would have had to have practiced the signature until he or she could execute it automatically, which is what we see Jim the Penman doing in the film when he writes "Nina Bronson" over and over on a sheet of paper.

It is interesting to note that "handwriting is a free-form activity, and there are an infinite number of ways to write even the simplest letter combination. It is highly unlikely that any person will write his or her own name exactly the same way twice in an entire lifetime." See Emily J. Will, "Theory: Handwriting and Signatures—Some Basic Facts and Theory," Emily J. Will, D-BFDE, accessed February 4, 2024, https://qdewill .com/theory.html. Readers interested in the history of handwriting may wish to consult Jonathan Goldberg, *Writing Matters: From the Hands of the English Renaissance* (Stanford, CA: Stanford University Press, 1990), esp. the chapters on "Signatures, Letters, Secretaries: Individuals of the Hand" and "The Hand in Theory."

37. James Joyce, *Stephen Hero,* ed. Theodore Spencer, John Slocum, and Herbert Cahoon (1944; New York: New Directions, 1963), 184. Hereafter cited parenthetically in the text as *SH.*

38. This is the famous ending of the penultimate diary entry in Joyce's *A Portrait of the Artist as a Young Man*: "Welcome, O life! I go to encounter for the millionth time the reality of experience and to forge in the smithy of my soul the uncreated conscience of my race" (213). For additional overtones of the author as blacksmith/forger associated with Wieland the Smith, see Vicki Mahaffey, "Wagner, Joyce and Revolution," *James Joyce Quarterly* 25 (Winter 1988): 237–247.

39. In the "Circe" episode of *Ulysses*, Stephen, after chanting the bloodoath from Wagner's *Götterdammerung* (The Twilight of the Gods), shatters the chandelier in Bella Cohen's brothel with his ashplant, which he calls "*Nothung*" after Siegfried's sword in *The Ring of the Nibelungen*. See *U* 15.3650–3653 and 4242. *Nothung* means "necessity."

CHAPTER 5   ON FAT

1. Maddox, *Nora*, 198. For more on why Joyce made Molly fat, see Vicki Mahaffey, "Who Resembles Molly Bloom?," *Joyce Studies Annual* (2022): 361–377.

2. Jacques Lacan, "God and the *Jouissance* of the Woman," in *Feminine Sexuality: Jacques Lacan and the* école freudienne, ed. Juliet Mitchell and Jaqueline Rose, translated by Jacqueline Rose (New York: Norton, 1982, 137–148, especially 144 and the introduction to the essay, "'The Woman' does not exist, in that phallic sexuality assigns her to a position of fantasy." This is one of the central chapters of *Seminar XX, Encore*, given in 1972–1973.

3. Margaret Visser, *Much Depends on Dinner: The Extraordinary History and Mythology, Allure and Obsessions, Perils and Taboos of an Ordinary Meal* (New York: Macmillan/ Collier, 1986), 84–85. Hereafter cited parenthetically in the text.

4. Sigmund Freud, *The Interpretation of Dreams,* translated and edited by James Strachey (New York: Avon; reprint of Vols. IV and V of the *Standard Edition* (London: Hogarth Press, 1953). For condensation, see 312–339, 634–636; for displacement, 342–343, 627–628, 634–636. In *Finnegans Wake*, Joyce refers to the "intrepidation of our dreams" (*FW* 338.29).

5. See the German-based passage, "*Der Haensli ist ein Butterbrot, mein Butterbrot! Und Koebi iss dein Schtinkenkot! Ja! Ja! Ja!*" (*FW* 163.5–7). Roland McHugh renders this as follows: "Little Hans is eating bread and butter, my bread and butter, and Jacob's eating your ham sandwich" (*Schinkenbrot*), rendered as *Schtinkenkot,* or stinking shit—from the German verb *stinken* ("to stink") and *Kot* ("shit"). McHugh, *Annotations to Finnegans Wake,* 163.

6. *Ulysses,* too, is interested in the correlation between the political desire of Ireland for Home Rule and the desire of men to rule their own homes.

7. Dante Alighieri, *The Divine Comedy: Inferno,* trans. Charles S. Singleton (Princeton, NJ: Princeton University Press, 1970), 365.

8. On the economics of the dairy industry, see Philip Keel Geheber, "Assimilating Shem into the Plural Polity: Burrus, Caseous, and Irish Free State Dairy Production," *European Joyce Studies* 24 (2016): 127–139. As Geheber argues, "The Burrus and Caseous tale reveals how economic and political power resists assimilating difference into its systems, offering a cautious vision of a plural polity that values difference within the body politic but remains ambivalent about the polity's ability to equitably integrate difference" (127).

9. "Margarine: Types and Properties," M. Vaisey-Ginser, in *Encyclopedia of Food Science and Nutrition*, 2nd edition, ed. Luiz Trugo and Paul M. Finglas (Elsevier Science Ltd., 2003), 3704–3709.

10. See also Visser on butter's war against margarine (*Much Depends on Dinner*, 102–114). She notes that in German towns of more than five thousand people, those who wanted to buy margarine had to use a different entrance to go to a separate section of a food shop for those who bought cheaper, imitation butter (106).

11. Siert F. Riepma, *The Story of Margarine* (Washington, DC: Public Affairs Press, 1970), 109.

12. Riepma, *The Story of Margarine*, 29.

13. McHugh, *Annotations to Finnegans Wake*, 167.

14. Donagh MacDonagh, *The Hungry Grass* (London: Faber and Faber, 1947).

15. See Christine Smedley's exploration of famine images in "Shem the Penman" (I.7), which she calls "a chapter thematically structured around the alimentary processes of an ailing Irish body—eating, drinking, and defecating." Christine Smedley, "Shem's 'Strabismal Apologia': The Split Vision of the Famine in I.7," in *Joyce's Allmaziful Plurabilities: Polyvocal Explorations of* Finnegans Wake, ed. Kimberly J. Devlin and Christine Smedley (Gainesville: University Press of Florida, 2015), 117. James Joyce, *Giacomo Joyce*, Introduction and Notes by Richard Ellmann (New York: Viking Press, 1968), 12.

16. For more on the meaning and politics of hunger, see Maud Ellmann, *The Hunger Artists: Starving, Writing, and Imprisonment* (Cambridge, MA: Harvard University Press), 1993.

17. For the links between hunger and violence, see Smedley, "Shem's 'Strabismal Apologia,'" esp. 123–124.

CHAPTER 6 ON ADULTERY AND VIRGINITY

1. See Laura Pelaschiar, "'My Story Being Done, / She Gave Me for My Pains a World of Sighs': Shakespeare's *Othello* and Joyce's *Ulysses*," in *Joyce/Shakespeare*, ed. Laura Pelaschiar (Syracuse: Syracuse University Press, 2015), 38–55.

2. Barbara Leckie, *Culture and Adultery: The Novel, the Newspaper, and the Law, 1957–1914* (Philadelphia: University of Pennsylvania Press, 1999), 1.

3. Paul de Kock, *Le Cocu* (Boston: Jefferson Press, 1903–1904).

4. Tony Tanner, *Adultery in the Novel* (Baltimore: Johns Hopkins University Press, 1979). Hereafter cited parenthetically in the text.

5. For recent scholarly work on Joyce and Flaubert, see Scarlett Baron, *'Strandentwining Cable': Joyce, Flaubert, and Intertextuality* (Oxford: Oxford University Press, 2012).

6. James Joyce, *Exiles: A Play in Three Acts, including Hitherto Unpublished Notes by the Author, Discovered after His Death, and an Introduction by Padraic Colum* (1918; New York: Viking, 1951), 126–127. Hereafter cited parenthetically in the text as *E*.

7. Molière, *The School for Husbands and The Imaginary Cuckold, or Sganarelle,* trans. Richard Wilbur (New York: Theatre Communications Group, 2009).

8. Gustave Flaubert, *Madame Bovary,* trans. Lydia Davis (New York: Penguin, 2010): "Emma was rediscovering in adultery all the platitudes of marriage" (257). Hereafter cited parenthetically in the text.

9. Lydia Davis, "Flaubert and Point of View," in Lydia Davis, *Can't and Won't* (New York: Picador, 2014), 267–268.

10. Oscar Wilde, "The Soul of Man under Socialism," in *The Soul of Man Under Socialism and Selected Critical Prose,* ed. Linda Dowling (London: Penguin, 2001), 132.

11. For more on the "Nausicaa" episode, see Vicki Mahaffey, "Nausicaa," in *The Cambridge Centenary Ulysses: The 1922 Text with Essays and Notes,* ed. Catherine Flynn (Cambridge: Cambridge University Press, 1922), 473–483.

12. Angela Carter, *The Sadeian Woman: An Exercise in Cultural History* (New York: Penguin, 1979), 69. Hereafter cited parenthetically in the text.

13. See Julia Kristeva, "Stabat Mater," in *The Female Body in Western Culture: Contemporary Perspectives,* ed. Susan Suleiman (Cambridge, MA: Harvard University Press, 1986), 99–118.

CHAPTER 7   ON LOVE

1. Søren Kierkegaard, *Works of Love: Some Christian Reflections in the Form of Discourses,* trans. Howard and Edna Hong (New York: Harper and Row, 1962), 36.

2. A version of this chapter appeared as Vicki Mahaffey, "Love, Race, and *Exiles*: The Bleak Side of *Ulysses,*" *Joyce Studies Annual* (2007): 92–108.

3. Interestingly, Kierkegaard antedates Joyce on the subject of passion. "Erotic love and friendship are related to passion, but all passion, whether it attacks or defends itself, fights in one manner only: either—or: 'Either I exist and am the highest or I do not exist at all—either all or nothing'" (*Works of Love,* 59).

4. Contrast Kierkegaard: "'Only law can give freedom.' Alas, we often think that freedom exists and that it is law which binds freedom. Yet it is just the opposite; without law freedom does not exist at all, and it is law which gives freedom" (*Works of Love,* 53).

5. Robert M. Adams, "New Light on Joyce's *Exiles*? A New MS, a Curious Analogue, and Some Speculations," *Studies in Bibliography* 17 (1964): 86.

6. Samuel Beckett, *Waiting for Godot* (New York: Grove Press, 1954), 8–9.

CHAPTER 8   ON RELIGION (AS REREADING)

1. I have explored a related idea featuring other Irish authors in a recent essay, "Irish Christian Comedy," in *The Edinburgh Companion to Irish Modernism,* ed. Maud

Ellmann, Siân White, and Vicki Mahaffey (Edinburgh: Edinburgh University Press, 2021), 284–298.

2. Lernout, for example, argues in his thoroughly researched *Help My Unbelief: Joyce and Religion* that "James Joyce was an unbeliever from the start of his life as a writer, that he never returned to the faith of his fathers and that his work can only be read properly if that important fact is taken into account." Geert Lernout, *Help My Unbelief: Joyce and Religion* (London: Continuum, 2010), 2. Gottfried calls it "misbelief," defined as faith in a carefully constructed heresy informed and inspired by the history of heresy. Roy Gottfried, *Joyce's Misbelief* (Gainesville: University of Florida Press, 2008). For Joyce's position in *Finnegans Wake*, see Chrissie Van Mierlo, *Joyce and Catholicism: The Apostate's Wake* (London: Bloomsbury Academic, 2017).

3. Beryl Schlossman, *Joyce's Catholic Comedy of Language* (Madison: University of Wisconsin Press, 1985), ix.

4. See Chrissie Van Mierlo's fascinating account of the Catholic Church's constraints on individual and secular interpretation of the Scriptures. She shows that the restraints were loosened somewhat by Pope Leo XIII's 1893 encyclical *Providentissimus Deus* concerning the Study of Holy Scriptures, which "appears to allow Catholics more freedom to study Scripture than had been enjoyed at any time since the Reformation" (14).

5. Reinhold Niebuhr, *Discerning the Signs of the Times* (New York: Scribner's, 1946), 11–131.

6. Oscar Wilde, "The Truth of Masks," in *The Soul of Man Under Socialism and Selected Critical Prose*, ed. Linda Dowling (London: Penguin, 2001), 304.

7. Cleanth Brooks, *Irony as a Principle of Structure*, PDF file, 1971, https://static1 .squarespace.com/static/5441df7ee4b02f59465d2869/t/588e94e446c3c4023d8c80ae /1485739236785/Irony+as+a+Principle+of+Structure.pdf.

8. Friedrich Nietzsche, *Thus Spake Zarathustra*, trans. Walter Kaufmann, in *The Portable Nietzsche*, edited by Walter Kaufmann (Harmondsworth, England: Penguin, 1976), pt. II, 3.

9. The original photograph appeared in "Stark Display Offers Critique," *Spokesman-Review*, December 23, 2007, https://www.spokesman.com/stories/2007/dec/23/stark -display-offers-critique/. There is apparently an urban legend that this motif originated in Japan in the years after World War II, although no evidence survives to support it. This particular display was created by a man named Art Conrad in Bremerton. He photographed the image to make Christmas cards with the caption "Santa died for your MasterCard."

10. For more on "The Sisters," see the article I coauthored with Michael Groden, "Silence and Fractals in 'The Sisters,'" in *Collaborative Dubliners: Joyce in Dialogue*, ed. Vicki Mahaffey (Syracuse, NY: Syracuse University Press, 2012), 23–47.

11. Spell for the "Opening of the Mouth" ceremony, *The Ancient Egyptian Book of the Dead*, translated by Raymond O. Faulkner, edited by Carol Andrews (Austin: University of Texas Press in cooperation with British Museum Publications, 1972), 51–52. See also John Bishop, "Inside the Coffin: *Finnegans Wake* and the Egyptian Book of the Dead," in *Joyce's Book of the Dark* (Madison: University of Wisconsin Press, 1986), especially 114–116.

12. Colleen Jaurretche, "Joyce's Common Reader: A Primer for Sensory Consciousness in I.5," in *Joyce's Allmaziful Plurabilities*, ed. Kimberly J. Devlin and Christine Smedley (Gainesville: University Press of Florida, 2015), 83.

13. James S. Atherton, *The Books at the Wake: A Study of Literary Allusions in James Joyce's Finnegans Wake* (New York: Viking, 1960), 65.

14. The Walters Art Gallery, *Illuminated Books of the Middle Ages and Renaissance: An Exhibition Held at the Baltimore Museum of Art, January 27–March 13* (Baltimore: Trustees of the Walters Art Gallery, 1949), xi.

CHAPTER 9   ON GLASS

1. For a vivid account of the growth of glass manufacturing in the nineteenth century, see Isobel Armstrong, *Victorian Glassworlds: Glass Culture and the Victorian Imagination, 1830–1880* (Oxford: Oxford University Press, 2008).

2. Rudine Sims Bishop, "Multicultural Literacy: Windows, Mirrors, and Sliding Glass Doors," *Perspectives: Choosing and Using Books for the Classroom* 6, no. 3 (Summer 1990): 1–2. The essay has been reproduced multiple times; see, for example, https://scenicregional.org/wp-content/uploads/2017/08/Mirrors-Windows-and-Sliding-Glass-Doors.pdf.

3. See Joyce's use of the term "perverted commas" for inverted commas, or quotation marks. So-called scare quotes are arguably ways of elevating one's own view over what other people say. *Letters of James Joyce*, vol. 3, edited by Richard Ellmann. (New York: Viking Press, 1966), 99. Hereafter cited parenthetically in the text.

4. Oscar Wilde, "The Preface," in *The Picture of Dorian Gray*, ed. Donald L. Lawler (New York: Norton, 1988), 3. Hereafter cited parenthetically in the text.

5. Robert Burns, "To a Louse, upon Seeing One on a Lady's Bonnet at Church": https://www.scottishpoetrylibrary.org.uk/poem/louse-seeing-one-ladys-bonnet-church/

6. Mulligan is using the slang meaning of the word, a man "upon whom the wearisome errands and unwelcome jobs devolve," Eric Partridge, *A Dictionary of Slang and Unconventional English*, 8th ed., ed. Paul Beale (London: Routledge, 2002), "dog's body."

7. Interestingly, Haroun was one of those historical personages who so captured the imagination that he became a literary figure. He plays a legendary role in *A Thousand and One Arabian Nights*, and Yeats wrote a poem about him a year after *Ulysses* was published ("The Gift of Harun al-Raschid"). Tennyson and Salman Rushdie are among those who have also written about Haroun al-Raschid.

8. In "Who Resembles Molly Bloom?," *Joyce Studies Annual* (2022): 361–377, I argue that May Dedalus is the antithesis of Molly Bloom, a difference underscored by their shared names, both variants of Mary.

9. Stephen's understanding of the ethical importance of accepting a shared darkness helps explain his inversion of the pronouncement in John's Gospel. John refers to Jesus as the light shining in darkness, and the darkness comprehendeth it not (1:5),

whereas Stephen inverts the phrase when he thinks of "Averroes and Moses Maimonides, dark men in mien and movement, flashing in their mocking mirrors the obscure soul of the world, a *darkness* shining in *brightness* which *brightness* could not comprehend" (*U* 2.158–160, my emphasis).

In *To the Lighthouse*, Mrs. Ramsay ruminates on the freedom, peace, and stability that comes from shrinking to "a wedge-shaped core of darkness" that could go anywhere. Such darkness is what lies beneath "our apparitions, the things you know us by"; it is "spreading" and "unfathomably deep" (62).

10. Virginia Woolf, *Between the Acts* (New York: Harcourt Brace Jovanovich, 1969), 188.

11. Morgan Pulver, "Folds of Nonsense: Explorations of Style in Joyce" (MPhil thesis, University of Queensland, 2013), 53.

12. Kevin Attell, "Of Questionable Character: The Construction of the Subject in *Ulysses,*" *Joyce Studies Annual* 13 (Summer 2002): 112. Hereafter cited parenthetically in the text.

CHAPTER 10   ON LETTERS

1. In the "Ithaca" episode of *Ulysses*, it is revealed that Bloom felt remorse for having treated with disrespect certain beliefs and practices, including "the ineffability of the tetragrammaton" (*U* 17.1900–1901).

2. For just a few examples of critical articles on Joyce and letters, see Matthew Bevis, "Joyce's Love Letters," *James Joyce Quarterly* 44 (Winter 2007): 354–357; and Scarlett Baron's "Joyce and the Rhythms of the Alphabet," in *New Quotatoes: Joycean Exogenesis in the Digital Age*, ed. Ronan Crowley and Dirk Van Hulle (Leiden: Brill/Rodopi, 2016), 18–44.

3. Jed Rasula, "*Finnegans Wake* and the Character of the Letter," *James Joyce Quarterly* 34, no. 4 (Summer 1997): 522. As Rasula notes, "The spell of Joycean spelling animates many more letters than other texts do and thus lends character to the grammatological landscape, as on a relief map" (521).

4. Maddox, *Nora*, 273.

5. For more on this, see Bevis, "Joyce's Love Letters," 355; and Baron, "Joyce and the Rhythms of the Alphabet," 34n.53.

6. "blue, adj." *OED*, 2.10.b. Perhaps from *La Bibliothèque Bleue*, a series of French books. See Eric Partridge, *A Dictionary of Slang and Unconventional English*, 8th ed., ed. Paul Beale (1937; London: Routledge, 2002).

7. The chalice was discovered in 1868. Two young men, Jimmy Quinn and Paddy Flanagan, were digging potatoes in the village of Ardagh (County Limerick) that they had planted inside a ring fort, perhaps in the hope that it would protect the potatoes from blight. They unearthed the Ardagh hoard, which consisted of the beautiful chalice, and (inside it) four brooches and a stemmed cup. Quinn's mother sold the hoard to the bishop of Limerick for the ridiculously low sum of 50 pounds (the bishop later sold it for 500 pounds). As the narrator puts it in *Finnegans Wake*, "What child of a strandlooper

[beachwalker] but keepy little Kevin in the despondful surrounding of such sneezing cold would ever have trouved up on a strate that was called strete a motive for future saintity by euchring the finding of the Ardagh chalice by another heily innocent and beachwalker whilst trying with pious clamour to wheedle Tipperaw raw raw reeraw puteters [potatoes] out of Now Sealand" in sight of the massacre of most of the Jacobites (*FW* 110.31–111.4).

8. "John Andrews Informs Philadelphia of the Trouble with Tea in 1773," New England Historical Society, accessed February 5, 2024. https://www.newenglandhistoricalsociety .com/john-andrews-informs-philadelphia-of-trouble-tea-1773/.

9. One of the many titles of the "untitled mamafesta" announces the content of this letter as follows: "*First and Last Only True Account all about the Honorary Mirsu Earwicker, L. S. D., and the Snake (Nuggets!) by a Woman of the World who only can Tell Naked Truths about a Dear Man and all his Conspirators how they all Tried to Fall him Putting it all around Lucalizod about Privates Earwicker and a Pair of Sloppy Sluts plainly Showing all the Unmentionability falsely Accusing about the Raincoats*" (*FW* 107.1–7). Here the accusation against HCE seems to be that he exhibited his privates beneath a raincoat (Redcoat?) to two young women—that is the "naked truth."

10. In Book 4, or the *ricorso*, ALP seems to write yet another letter, this one to Dear Dirty Dublin: "Dear. And we go on to Dirtdump. Reverend. May we add majesty?" (*FW* 615.12–13)

It runs for four pages and is signed "Alma Luvia, Pollabella" followed by a P.S. (*FW* 619.16–19). The section that immediately follows seems to be oral. It is the River Liffey speaking to the city: "Soft morning, city!" (*FW* 619.20). These two concluding episodes of Book 4 were originally part of the "Letter" episode (I.5). Fuse calls this relocated part of the letter the "Revered Letter." See Mikio Fuse, "The Letter and the Groaning: Chapter I.5," in *How Joyce Wrote* Finnegans Wake: *A Chapter-by-Chapter Genetic Guide*, ed. Luca Crispi and Sam Slote (Madison: University of Wisconsin Press, 2007), 98–123.

11. Also called Doublets, word-links, change-the-word puzzles, laddergrams, and word golf. A word ladder begins with two words, and the challenge is to create a chain of words to link the two in which two adjacent words can only differ by one letter. See Lewis Carroll, *Doublets: A Word Puzzle* (London: Macmillan, 1879).

12. As both Rasula and Baron point out, ALP is also the beginning of the word "alphabet."

13. See Baron on this in relation to Stephen's play with letters in *Ulysses*: A. E. I. O. U. (*U* 9. 203–212) ("Joyce and the Rhythms of the Alphabet," 30–32). She also makes intriguing observations about George Russell's letter name—AE for Aeon—in relation to his own interest in correspondences for individual letters.

14. Rasula's formulation is particularly felicitous, and it includes not only magic and orthography but also a pun on the German *spiel* ("to play") and the meaning of "spell" as a verb: "to give respite." "So you need hardly spell me how every word will be bound over to carry threescore and ten toptypsical reading throughout the book of Doublends Joined" (*FW* 20.13–16). See Rasula, "*Finnegans Wake* and the Character of the Letter," 521.

15. Edward Clodd, *The Story of the Alphabet* (London: George Newnes, 1900), 10, 16–17. Ogmios was a god of eloquence, described in Lucian as having a smiling mouth from which long chains dangled from his tongue, connecting him to the ears of his listeners. Clodd also discusses the origin of writing in Chinese (attributed toTs'ang Chien), Hindu (Brahma), Scandinavian (Odin), and Assyrian (Nebo) legends. The "dragon-faced, four-eyed sage Ts'ang Chien" saw the footprints of birds in the stars of heaven and modeled written characters on them, together with the marks on the back of the tortoise (16). The handwriting of Brahma can be seen "in the serrated sutures of men's skulls" (17). As Baron recounts in "Joyce and the Rhythms of the Alphabet," Joyce ordered the book in September 1926 and recorded approximately 139 notes from it in three notebooks (VI.B.15, VI.B.35, and VI.B.49b). See also Vincent Deane, "Claybook for *Finnegans Wake*," *A Finnegans Wake Circular* 3, no. 2 (Winter 1987): 21–39; Danis Rose, "Clodd One and Two: Corrigenda and Agenda," *A Finnegans Wake Circular* 3, no. 3 (Spring 1988): 53–56; and Danis Rose and Vincent Deane, "Clodd in VI.B.49.b," *A Finnegans Wake Circular* 3, no. 3 (Spring 1988): 57–60.

16. One source for this story seems to be Herodotus. Cited by Moshe Gold, "Printing the Dragon's Bite: Joyce's Poetic History of Thoth, Cadmus, and Gutenberg in *Finnegans Wake*," *James Joyce Quarterly* 42–43 (Fall 2004–Summer 2006)): 269–296. Gold's source is A. C. Moorhouse, *The Triumph of the Alphabet: A History of Writing* (New York: Henry Schuman, 1953), although he also quotes Robert Graves, *The Greek Myths* (New York: George Braziller, 1957), who says something very similar (Gold, "Printing the Dragon's Bite," 277).

17. Alexander Humez and Nicholas Humez, *Alpha to Omega: The Life and Times of the Greek Alphabet* (Boston: David R. Godine, 1981), 6. They also wonder who Kadmos "chose to give the Greeks only sixteen of the twenty-two letters of the Phoenician proto-alphabet." Vincent Deane, Danis Rose, and more recently Scarlett Baron have discussed a book on the alphabet that Joyce bought in 1926: Clodd's *The Story of the Alphabet*. See Baron, "Joyce and the Rhythms of the Alphabet," 18l; Deane, "Claybook for *Finnegans Wake*"; Rose, "Clodd One and Two: Corrigenda and Agenda"; and Rose and Deane, "Clodd in VI.B.49.b," cited by Baron. The note that Baron refers to is in book 49 of the Buffalo Finnegans Wake Notebooks.

18. Johanna Drucker, *The Alphabetic Labyrinth: The Letters in History and Imagination* (London: Thames and Hudson, 1995), 22. Clodd also writes about Thoth, Cadmus, and letters (*The Story of the Alphabet*, 16–17).

19. Clodd uses the prevalence of spoken curses around the world to illustrate the persistence of a power that was once attributed to written signs as well, along with a power to protect. He references Jewish phylacteries and frontlets, the amulets of Abyssinians, and passages from the Koran hung in bags on Turkish and Arab horses for protection against the evil eye, etc. (*The Story of the Alphabet*, 17–19).

20. "Thoth," in *Encyclopedia Britannica*, last modified September 6, 2022, https://www.britannica.com/topic/Thoth.

21. Joyce echoes one of them: "The tasks above are as the flasks below" (*FW* 263.21) refers to the precept, "As below, so above; and as above, so below. With this knowledge

alone you may work miracles." From the Emerald Tablet of Hermes: https://sacred
-texts.com/alc/emerald.htm

22. See McHugh, *Annotations to Finnegans Wake,* 470. In *The Books at the Wake,* James
Atherton writes, "Thoth, the Egyptian god of letters, who plays a great part in the judgement in *The Book of the Dead,* is named very often and is probably intended in such
phrases as 'thother brother' (*FW* 224.33) as well as in the obvious references to ancient
Egyptian names as in 'thothfully' (*FW* 415.28)" (200).

23. Gold, "Printing the Dragon's Bite," 269–296.

24. Plato, *Phaedrus,* translated by R. Hackforth, in *The Collected Dialogues of Plato,
including the Letters,* edited by Edith Hamilton and Huntington Cairns (Princeton:
Princeton University Press, Bollingen Series LXXI, 1961, 274c–275b.

25. "Setne Khamwas and Naneferkaptah (Setne I)," in Miriam Lichtheim, *Ancient
Egyptian Literature: A Book of Readings,* vol. 3, *The Late Period* (Berkeley: University of
California Press, 1980), 127–137. See also Stuart Gilbert, *James Joyce's* Ulysses: *A Study*
(1930; New York: Vintage Books, 1952), 117–118.

26. The Book of Kells (probably dating from c. 800) was stolen from Kells Abbey
in 1007 and was found a few months later "under a sod," its golden, jeweled cover
ripped off.

27. According to Wikipedia, (Book of Thoth),Thoth's books were housed in libraries
called "Houses of Life" contained within temple complexes. According to one Egyptian
historian, Thoth was said to have written 36,525 books.

28. According to Drucker, the understanding that the alphabet was indebted to Egyptian hieroglyphs and not just Phoenicians and their Semitic precursors did not emerge
until the hieroglyphs were deciphered in the nineteenth century (*The Alphabetic Labyrinth,* 27).

29. Joyce, *Occasional, Critical, and Political Writing,* 110. Joyce identifies his source as
Charles Vallancey (1721–1812), *An Essay on the Antiquity of the Irish Language. Being
a collation of the Irish with the Punic Language* (1772); see Barry, p. 314, note 10. See also
Baron on Joyce's early interest in Rimbaud and Blake, especially their writings on the
importance of individual letters ("Joyce and the Rhythms of the Alphabet," 20–26).

30. *Letters of James Joyce,* ed. Stuart Gilbert (New York: Viking, 1957), 224. The idea was
the dominant one in Joyce's time, but more recent scholarship on Ogham letter names
suggests that this is a fiction. See Damian MacManus, "Irish Letter-Names and Their
Kennings," *Ériu* 39 (1988): 127–168 for another view.

31. See "Introduction," Ogham in 3D, last modified July 30, 2023, https://ogham.celt
.dias.ie/menu.php?lang=en.

32. Muiris O'Sullivan and Liam Downey, "Ogham Stones," *Archaeology Ireland* 28, no. 2
(Summer 2014): 27. Hereafter cited parenthetically in the text.

33. See Catherine Swift, "The Story of Ogham," *History Today* 65, no. 10 (October 2015):
4–5; and O'Sullivan and Downey, "Ogham Stones," 26–29.

34. John Sharkey, *Celtic Mysteries: The Ancient Religions* (London: Thames and Hudson,
1975), 90.

35. Nigel Pennick, *Celtic Sacred Landscapes* (London: Thames and Hudson, 1996), 57.
36. See "Alphabet," Ogham in 3D, last modified July 30, 2023, https://ogham.celt.dias.ie/menu.php?lang=en&menuitem=03. As noted on the website, and in Swift, the main manuscript sources are the *Lebor Ogaim* (The Book of Ogham), from the late fourteenth or early fifteenth century, and *Auraicept na n-Éces* (The Scholar's Primer), from the seventh century.
37. James Bonwick, *Irish Druids and Old Irish Religions* (1894; New York: Dorset Press, 1986), 312.
38. See Baron on Rimbaud's 1871–1872 sonnet "Voyelles" (Vowels), which Joyce knew by heart. The poem assigns colors, smells, sounds and symbols of each of the five vowels ("Joyce and the Rhythms of the Alphabet," 22–25).
39. According to Protagoras, as cited by Humez and Humez, *Alpha to Omega*, "Man is the measure of all things" (126).
40. "Gramma's grammar" also evokes "gamma," the third letter of the Greek alphabet. "Gramma" designates a letter of the alphabet, and "gamma" *is* one.
41. Humez and Humez provide evidence from a standard weights-and-measures table for English:
    "We speak of a *hand* when measuring the height of a horse; a *span* is the distance from the tip of the thumb to the tip of the little finger, conventionally reckoned at nine inches; a *foot* is a foot, and a *cubit*—from Latin *cubitum*, 'elbow'—is the distance from the tip of your middle finger to your elbow; a *fathom* is the length of a rope which a standard-issue-sailor stretches from one hand to the other across his back" (*Alpha to Omega*, 126).
42. For more on Joyce's use of numbers, see Eric Bulson, *Ulysses by Numbers* (New York: Columbia University Press, 2021).
43. See Elaine J. Horn, "Roman Numerals: Conversion, Meaning and Origin," *Live Science*, May 13, 2013, https://www.livescience.com/32052-roman-numerals.html.
44. One might speculate that the refusal to write vowels in early languages can be seen as an ancient instance of the suppression of the female!
45. See Clodd on the linear hieroglyphics found only in Crete, several of which correspond to one or more of Joyce's sigla for the characters of *Finnegans Wake* (*The Story of the Alphabet*, 174–175). Issy introduces the sigla as "the Doodles family" in *FW* 299n.4. Baron's discussion of the sigla is also relevant here ("Joyce and the Rhythms of the Alphabet," 42–43).
46. *A Fragment of Work in Progress* (The Hague: Servire Press, 1934). See also the letter "A" designed by Lucia Joyce in *Storiella as She Is Syung: A Section of "Work in Progress"* (London: Oxford University Press for the Corvinus Press, 1937).
47. Geoffrey Chaucer, *A Chaucer ABC, Being a Hymn to the Holy Virgin in an English Version by Geoffrey Chaucer, from the French of Guillaume de Guilleville*, initial letters designed and illuminated by Lucia Joyce, preface by Louis Gillet (Paris: Obelisk Press, 1936). Without Lucia's knowledge, Joyce paid to have these illustrations published in this volume.

CHAPTER 11   ON CLOSING AND OPENING

1. Jacques Derrida, *Given Time I: Counterfeit Money* (Chicago: University of Chicago Press, 1994). The classic work on the gift is that of Marcel Mauss, *The Gift: The Form and Reason for Exchange in Archaic Societies*, translated by W. D. Halls (New York: Norton, 2000).

2. In *Alpha to Omega*, Humez and Humez recount the mixed feelings that attended the innovation of the first new mechanical clocks in the Middle Ages, with their "rigid ticking away of the hours." They note that the Eastern Orthodox Church rejected clocks, proclaiming that "the mathematical division of time into hours, minutes, and seconds has no relationship with the eternity of time" (51–52).

3. Vicki Mahaffey, *Reauthorizing Joyce* (Cambridge: Cambridge University Press, 1988).

4. *Finnegans Wake* accents this "foreignness" within a "native" language by reversing what is dominant. Instead of seeming comprehensible with its foreign inflections being occluded, it uses words that seem foreign (or nonsensical) so that readers are tasked to link the jingles and jangles together.

5. For Stephen's ponderings about the reasons words might rhyme, see "Rhymes and Reasons" in the "Aeolus" episode of *Ulysses*. The poem Stephen began writing in "Proteus" contains the word "mouth," which prompts him to think, "Mouth, south. Is the mouth south someway? Or the south a mouth? Must be some" (*U* 7.714–715).

6. In a letter to Constantine Curran in 1904, Joyce wrote, "I am writing a series of epikleti—ten—for a paper. I have written one. I call the series *Dubliners* to betray the soul of that hemiplegia or paralysis which many consider a city." *The Letters of James Joyce*, ed. Stuart Gilbert (New York: Viking, 1957), 55. Joyce also told Stanislaus, "There is a certain resemblance between the mystery of the mass and what I am trying to do . . . to give people a kind of intellectual pleasure or spiritual enjoyment by converting the bread of everyday life into something that has a permanent artistic life of its own . . . for their mental, moral, and spiritual uplift." Cited in James Joyce, *Dubliners: Text, Criticism, and Notes*, ed. Robert Scholes and A. Walton Litz (New York: Viking, 1996), 253.

7. See Vicki Mahaffey, *Modernist Literature: Challenging Fictions* (Oxford: Blackwell, 2007), esp. 3–70.

EPILOGUE

1. Freud's *The Psychopathology of Everyday Life*, first published in 1901 (shortly after *The Interpretation of Dreams* [1899/1900]), seems to have come to Joyce's attention in 1910–1911, although he later bought a copy of the 1917 edition.

2. Sigmund Freud, *The Psychopathology of Everyday Life*, ed. and trans. James Strachey (1960; New York: W. W. Norton, 1965), 65.

3. Mary Sheehy (1884–1967) grew up to become a leading women's rights activist and a champion of social and economic justice, especially for women and children. She married Joyce's friend Thomas Kettle, who was killed in World War I. After his death in 1916

she worked to publish (and coauthor) his memoir, *The Ways of War*, which she assembled and for which she wrote a preface. Mary Sheehy Kettle, Thomas Kettle, *The Ways of War* (New York: Legare Street Press, 2022). See www.irishtimes.com/opinion/dear
-wife-and-comrade-an-irishwoman-s-diary-on-mary-sheehy-kettle-1.3347419.

4. Recounted in Ellmann, *James Joyce*, 52.

5. Henri Lefebvre, *Everyday Life in the Modern World*, trans. Sacha Rabinovitch (New York: Harper and Row, 1971). This use of the everyday should be distinguished from that of Michel de Certeau in *The Practice of Everyday Life*, trans. Steven Rendall (Berkeley: University of California Press, 1988). De Certeau's main interest is in the tension between institutional strategies for imposing rituals and representations upon a culture and the tactics deployed by individuals for reappropriating the everyday.

6. Lefebvre, citing Hermann Broch, *Dichten und Erkennen* (Zurich, 1955), 183–210, 237.

7. John Updike, *Hugging the Shore: Essays and Criticism* (1983; New York: Random House, 2013), 355.

8. It is worth noting that Joyce is not the only writer who was laboring to produce an epic of everyday life: his famous contemporary Marcel Proust was doing something analogous in *A La Recherche du Temps Perdu* (In Search of Lost Time), the first volume of which (*Du coté de chez Swann*, or Swann's Way) was published in 1913 (the first English translation appeared in 1922). Proust was also treating the everyday and the local with exquisite attention, as we can see just from one of the alternate titles he half-seriously proposed for *Swann's Way*: "Gardens in a Cup of Tea" (*Swann's Way*, trans. Lydia Davis [New York: Penguin, 2003], xv). Ollendorf, one of the publishers who rejected the book in 1913, complained, "I don't see why a man should take thirty pages to describe how he turns over in bed before he goes to sleep" (xiv).

9. Xavier de Maistre, *A Journey round My Room*, trans. and intro. Henry Attwell (London: Sisley's, 1908). First published in 1794.

10. See Joyce's reference to *Dubliners* as a "nicely polished looking glass," discussed in chapter 9, "On Glass." Jonathan Swift in the preface to *The Battle of the Books* describes satire as "a sort of glass, wherein beholders do generally discover everybody's face but their own." *The Battle of the Books* was published in 1704 as part of the prolegomena to *A Tale of a Tub*. It can be accessed here: https://www.gutenberg.org/files/623/623-h
/623-h.htm. or in print in *A Tale of a Tub and Other Works* (Oxford: Oxford University Press, 2008). De Maistre proffers the "moral mirror" as an alternative to the unrealistic images of the world he finds in his library: "If I go out of my way in search of unreal afflictions, I find in return such virtue, kindness, and disinterestedness in this imaginary world as I have never yet found united in the real world around me" (*A Journey round My Room*, 96).

11. One of my favorite exceptions is Jane Austen's Emma, who can be as embarrassing and irritating and Joyce's Stephen or Bloom.

12. It is interesting and important that Joyce called his modern epic *Ulysses* rather than *Odysseus*, because it calls attention to the fact that the figure that Homer celebrates as heroic is one that Dante places in Hell under the Latin version of the name, Ulysses.

13. Maurice Blanchot, "Everyday Speech," trans. Susan Hanson, *Yale French Studies*, no. 73 (1987): 17.

14. This description echoes something that is often said about reading Joyce: that his works cannot be read, only reread.

15. Blanchot quotes György Lukács, *Soul and Form* (1908) from Lucien Goldman, *Recherches dialectiques* (Paris: Gallimard, 1959).

16. It is also interesting to compare Joyce's treatment of the everyday with that of Wordsworth and Coleridge in their preface to the *Lyrical Ballads*. As Coleridge explained later, Wordsworth's goal was to give the charm of novelty to things of everyday, and to excite a feeling analogous to the supernatural by awakening the mind's attention from the lethargy of custom and directing it to the loveliness and wonders of the world before us.

BIBLIOGRAPHY

Adams, Robert M. "New Light on Joyce's *Exiles*? A New MS, a Curious Analogue, and Some Speculations." *Studies in Bibliography* 17 (1964): 83–105.

Adorno, Theodor W. *Aesthetic Theory*. Edited by Gretel Adorno and Rolf Tiedemann. Translated by Robert Hullot-Kentor. London: Continuum, 1997.

Alighieri, Dante. *The Divine Comedy: Inferno*. Translated by Charles S. Singleton. Princeton, NJ: Princeton University Press, 1970.

Ancient Egyptian Book of the Dead, The. Translated by Raymond O. Faulkner. Edited by Carol Andrews. Austin: University of Texas Press in Co-operation with British Museum Publications, 1972.

Aristotle. *Physics*. Translated by Robin Waterfield. Introduction and notes by David Bostock. Oxford: Oxford University Press, 1996.

Armstrong, Isobel. *Victorian Glassworlds: Glass Culture and the Victorian Imagination, 1830–1880*. Oxford: Oxford University Press, 2008.

Atherton, James. *The Books at the Wake: A Study of Literary Allusions in James Joyce's* Finnegans Wake. New York: Viking, 1960.

Attell, Kevin. "Of Questionable Character: The Construction of the Subject in *Ulysses*." *Joyce Studies Annual* 13 (Summer 2002): 103–128.

Attridge, Derek. *Peculiar Language: Literature as Difference from the Renaissance to James Joyce*. Ithaca, NY: Cornell University Press, 1988.

Baron, Scarlett. "Joyce and the Rhythms of the Alphabet." In *New Quotatoes: Joycean Exogenesis in the Digital Age*, edited by Ronan Crowley and Dirk Van Hulle, 18–44. Leiden: Brill/Rodopi, 2016.

———. *"Strandentwining Cable": Joyce, Flaubert, and Intertextuality*. Oxford: Oxford University Press, 2012.

Beckett, Samuel. *Waiting for Godot*. New York: Grove Press, 1954.

Bennett, Jane. *The Enchantment of Modern Life: Attachments, Crossings, and Ethics*. Princeton, NJ: Princeton University Press, 2001.

———. *Vibrant Matter: A Political Ecology of Things*. Durham, NC: Duke University Press, 2010.

Benstock, Shari. *Women of the Left Bank: Paris, 1900–1940*. Austin: University of Texas Press, 1986.

Bertonis, Gloria. *Stone Age Divas: Their Mystery and Their Magic*. Bloomington, Indiana: Author House, 2011.

Bevernage, Berber. "Time, Presence, and Historical Injustice." *History and Theory* 47 (May 2008): 149–167.

Bishop, John. *The Book of the Dark*: Finnegans Wake. Madison: University of Wisconsin Press, 1986.

Bishop, Rudine Sims. "Multicultural Literacy: Windows, Mirrors, and Sliding Glass Doors." *Perspectives: Choosing and Using Books for the Classroom* 6, no. 3 (Summer 1990).

Blanchot, Maurice. "Everyday Speech." Translated by Susan Hanson. *Yale French Studies*, no. 73 (1987): 12–20.

Bloch, Ernst. "Nonsynchronism and the Obligation to Its Dialectics." *New German Critique* 11 (1977): 22–38.

Boehme, Jacob. *Boehme's "Signatura Rerum" and Other Discourses.* Introduced by Clifford Bax. London: Dent, n.d.

Bonwick, James. *Irish Druids and Old Irish Religions.* 1894; New York: Dorset Press, 1986.

Brivic, Sheldon. *Joyce's Waking Women: An Introduction to* Finnegans Wake. Madison: University of Wisconsin Press, 1995.

Brooks, Cleanth. *Irony as a Principle of Structure.* PDF file. 1971. https://static1.squarespace .com/static/5441df7ee4b02f59465d2869/t/588e94e446c3c4023d8c80ae/148573923 6785/Irony+as+a+Principle+of+Structure.pdf.

Budgen, Frank. *James Joyce and the Making of* Ulysses. Bloomington: University of Indiana Press, 1961.

Bulson, Eric. Ulysses *by Numbers.* New York: Columbia University Press, 2021.

Burns, Robert. "To a Louse, upon Seeing One on a Lady's Bonnet at Church." https:// www.scottishpoetrylibrary.org.uk/poem/louse-seeing-one-ladys-bonnet-church/

Carroll, Lewis. *Doublets: A Word Puzzle.* London: Macmillan, 1879.

Carter, Angela. *The Sadeian Woman and the Ideology of Pornography.* New York: Penguin Books, 1979.

Chaucer, Geoffrey. *A Chaucer ABC: Being a Hymn to the Holy Virgin in an English Version by Geoffrey Chaucer, from the French of Guillaume de Deguilleville.* Initial letters designed and illuminated by Lucia Joyce, preface by Louis Gillet. Paris: Obelisk Press, 1936.

Clodd, Edward. *The Story of the Alphabet.* London: George Newnes, 1900.

Coleridge, Samuel Taylor. *Biographia Literaria.* Vol. 2, *1817.* London: Clarendon Press, 1907.

Crispi, Luca. "A First Foray into the National Library of Ireland's Joyce Manuscripts: Bloomsday 2011," in *Genetic Joyce Studies,* issue 11 (Spring 2011). https://www .geneticjoycestudies.org/articles/GJS11/GJS11_Crispi.

Crispi, Luca. "Storiella as She Was Wryt: Chapter II.2." In *How Joyce Wrote* Finnegans Wake: *A Chapter-by-Chapter Genetic Guide.* Ed. Luca Crispi and Sam Slote. Madison: University of Wisconsin Press, 2007.

Crispi, Luca, and Sam Slote, eds. *How Joyce Wrote* Finnegans Wake: *A Chapter-by-Chapter Genetic Guide.* Madison: University of Wisconsin Press, 2007.

Cross, Tom Peete, and Clark Harris Slover, eds. *Ancient Irish Tales.* New York: Henry Holt, 1936.

Curtin, Jeremiah. *Myths and Folk-Lore of Ireland.* 1890; New York: Weathervane Books, 1975.

Davis, Lydia. *Can't and Won't*. New York: Picador, 2014.

Davis, Tom. "Forged Handwriting." In *Fakes and Frauds: Varieties of Deception in Print and Manuscript*, edited by Robin Myers and Michael Harris, 125–137. Winchester, England: St. Paul's Bibliographies, 1989.

Deane, Vincent. "Claybook for *Finnegans Wake*." *A Finnegans Wake Circular* 3, no. 2 (Winter 1987): 21–39.

De Certeau, Michel. *The Practice of Everyday Life*. Translated by Steven Rendall. Berkeley: University of California Press, 1988.

De Kock, Paul. *Le Cocu*. Boston: Jefferson Press, 1903–1904.

De Maistre, Xavier. *A Journey round My Room*. Translated and introduced by Henry Attwell. 1794; London: Sisley's, 1908.

Derrida, Jacques. *Given Time I: Counterfeit Money*. Chicago: University of Chicago Press, 1994.

———. *Limited Inc*. Translated by Samuel Weber and Jeffrey Mehlman. Chicago: Northwestern University Press, 1988.

———. *Specters of Marx: The State of the Debt, the Work of Mourning, and the New International*, trans. Peggy Kamuf. New York: Routledge, 1994.

Devlin, Kimberly J. "'See Ourselves as Others See Us': Joyce's Look at the Eye of the Other." *PMLA* 104, no. 5 (October 1989): 882–893.

Dickinson, Emily. *The Complete Poems of Emily Dickinson*. Edited by Thomas H. Johnson. Cambridge, MA: Harvard University Press, 1983.

Donovan, Dick. *Jim the Penman*. 1901; London: George Newnes, n.d. [1917].

Drucker, Johanna. *The Alphabetic Labyrinth: The Letters in History and Imagination*. London: Thames and Hudson, 1995.

Duffy, Carol Ann. *The World's Wife*. London: Picador, 2000.

Ebury, Katherine. "Beyond the Rainbow: Spectroscopy in Finnegans Wake II.1." *Joyce Studies Annual* (2011): 97–121.

Eliot, T. S. *Four Quartets*. London: Faber and Faber, 1959.

Ellmann, Maud. *The Hunger Artists: Starving, Writing, and Imprisonment*. Cambridge, MA: Harvard University Press, 1993.

———. "Lotus Eaters." In *The Cambridge Centenary Ulysses: The 1922 Text with Essays and Notes*, edited by Catherine Flynn, 130–139. Cambridge: Cambridge University Press, 2022.

Ellmann, Richard. *The Consciousness of Joyce*. New York: Oxford University Press, 1977.

———. *James Joyce*. Oxford: Oxford University Press, 1982.

Flaubert, Gustave. *Madame Bovary*. Translated by Lydia Davis. New York: Penguin Books, 2010.

Fox, Brian. *James Joyce's America*. Oxford: Oxford University Press, 2019.

Freud, Sigmund. *The Interpretation of Dreams*. New York: Avon; reprint of Vols. IV and V of the Standard Edition. London: Hogarth Press and The Institute of Psychoanalysis, 1953.

———. *The Psychopathology of Everyday Life*. Edited and translated by James Strachey. 1960; New York: W. W. Norton, 1965.

Fried, Michael. *Menzel's Realism: Art and Embodiment in Nineteenth-Century Berlin*. New Haven, CT: Yale University Press, 2002.

Furbank, Philip Nicholas. *Italo Svevo: The Man and the Writer*. London: Secker and Warburg/British Film Institute, 1966.

Fuse, Mikio. "The Letter and the Groaning: Chapter I.5." In *How Joyce Wrote* Finnegans Wake*: A Chapter-by-Chapter Genetic Guide*, edited by Luca Crispi and Sam Slote, 98–123. Madison: University of Wisconsin Press, 2007.

Geheber, Philip Keel. "Assimilating Shem into the Plural Polity: Burrus, Caseous, and Irish Free State Dairy Production." In *European Joyce Studies* 24 (2016): 127–139.

Gilbert, Stuart. *James Joyce's* Ulysses: *A Study*. 1930; New York: Vintage, 1952.

Gold, Moshe. "Printing the Dragon's Bite: Joyce's Poetic History of Thoth, Cadmus, and Gutenberg in *Finnegans Wake*." *James Joyce Quarterly* 42–43 (Fall 2004–Summer 2006): 269–296.

Goldberg, Jonathan. *Writing Matters: From the Hands of the English Renaissance*. Stanford, CA: Stanford University Press, 1990.

Gorman, Herbert. *James Joyce*. New York: Rinehart and Company, 1939, 1948.

Gottfried, Roy. *Joyce's Misbelief*. Gainesville: University of Florida Press, 2008.

Greene, James, and David Lewis. *The Hidden Language of Your Handwriting*. London: Souvenir Press, 1980.

Gregory, Lady Augusta, and William Butler Yeats. *Gods and Fighting Men: The Story of the Tuatha de Danaan and the Fiana of Ireland*. 1904; London: Wentworth Press, 2016.

Groden, Michael, and Vicki Mahaffey. "Silence and Fractals in 'The Sisters.'" In *Collaborative Dubliners: Joyce in Dialogue*, edited by Vicki Mahaffey, 23–47. Syracuse, NY: Syracuse University Press, 2012.

Groom, Nick. *The Forger's Shadow: How Forgery Changed the Course of Literature*. London: Picador, 2002.

Hanaway-Oakley, Cleo. "'See Ourselves as Others See Us': Cinematic Ways of Being and Seeing in *Ulysses*." In *Roll Away the Reel World: James Joyce and Cinema*, edited by John McCourt, 122–136. Cork, Ireland: Cork University Press, 2010.

Hayman, David. *The "Wake" in Transit*. Ithaca, NY: Cornell University Press, 1990.

Homer. *Odyssey*. Translated by Stanley Lombardo. Introduced by Sheila Murnaghan. New York: Hackett Publishing, 2000.

Horn, Elaine J. "Roman Numerals: Conversion, Meaning and Origin." *Live Science*. May 13, 2013. https://www.livescience.com/32052-roman-numerals.html.

Humez, Alexander, and Nicholas Humez. *Alpha to Omega: The Life and Times of the Greek Alphabet*. Boston, MA: David R. Godine, 1981.

Jaurretche, Colleen. "Joyce's Common Reader: A Primer for Sensory Consciousness in I.5." In *Joyce's Allmaziful Plurabilities*, edited by Kimberly J. Devlin and Christine Smedley. Gainesville: University Press of Florida, 2015, 75–89.

"Jim the Penman." Life and Times of Actress EJ Phillips. Last modified August 25, 2020. https://www.maryglenchitty.com/jimthepenman.htm.

"John Andrews Informs Philadelphia of the Trouble with Tea in 1773." New England Historical Society. Accessed February 5, 2024, https://www.newenglandhistorical society.com/john-andrews-informs-philadelphia-of-trouble-tea-1773/.

Joyce, James. *Critical Writings*. Edited by Richard Ellmann and Ellsworth Mason. New York: Viking, 1959.

———. *Dubliners*. Edited by Terence Brown. New York: Penguin Books, 1993.

———. *Dubliners: Text, Criticism, and Notes*. Edited by Robert Scholes and A. Walton Litz. New York: Viking, 1996.

———. *Exiles: A Play in Three Acts, Including Hitherto Unpublished Notes by the Author, Discovered after His Death, and an Introduction by Padraic Colum*. New York: Viking, 1951.

———. *Finnegans Wake*. 1939; New York: Viking Press, 1967.

———. "From Work in Progress." *The Transatlantic Review* I, no. 4 (April 1924).

———.*Giacomo Joyce*. Introduction and Notes by Richard Ellmann. New York: Viking Press, 1968.

———. *James Joyce's Letters to Sylvia Beach, 1921–1940*. Edited by Melissa Banta and Oscar Silverman. Oxford: Plantin Publishers, 1987.

———. *Letters*. Volumes II and III. Edited by Richard Ellmann. New York: Viking, 1966.

———. *Letters of James Joyce*. Edited by Stuart Gilbert. New York: Viking, 1957.

———. *Occasional, Critical, and Political Writing*. Edited by Kevin Barry. New York: Oxford, 2000.

———. *A Portrait of the Artist as a Young Man*. Edited by Seamus Deane. New York: Penguin, 1992.

———. *Selected Letters*. Edited by Richard Ellmann. 1966; New York: Viking, 1975.

———. *Stephen Hero*. Edited by Theodore Spencer, John Slocum, and Herbert Cahoon. 1944; New York: New Directions, 1963.

———. *Ulysses: A Critical and Synoptic Edition*. Edited by Hans Walter Gabler with Wolfhard Steppe and Claus Melchior. New York: Random House, 1986.

Joyce, P. W. *A Social History of Ancient Ireland*. 3rd ed. Vol. 2. Dublin: M. H. Gill, 1920.

Kenner, Hugh. *Joyce's Voices*. McLean, IL: Dalkey Archive Press, 2007.

———. "The Portrait in Perspective." *Kenyon Review* 10, no. 3 (Summer 1948): 361–381.

Kettle, Mary Sheehy and Thomas Kettle. *The Ways of War*. New York: Legare Street Press, 2022.

Kiberd, Declan. Ulysses *and Us: The Art of Everyday Living*. London: Faber and Faber, 2009.

Kierkegaard, Søren. *Works of Love: Some Christian Reflections in the Form of Discourses*. Translated by Howard and Edna Hong. New York: Harper and Row, 1962.

Kristeva, Julia. "Stabat Mater." In *The Female Body in Western Culture: Contemporary Perspectives*, edited by Susan Suleiman, 99–118. Cambridge, MA: Harvard University Press, 1986.

Lacan, Jacques. "God and the *Jouissance* of the Woman." In *Feminine Sexuality: Jacques Lacan and the* école freudienne. Edited by Juliet Mitchell and Jaqueline Rose, translated by Jacqueline Rose. New York: Norton, 1982.

Langbauer, Laurie. *Novels of Everyday Life: The Series in English Fiction, 1850–1930.* Ithaca, NY: Cornell University Press, 1999.

Leckie, Barbara. *Culture and Adultery: The Novel, the Newspaper, and the Law, 1957–1914.* Philadelphia: University of Pennsylvania Press, 1999.

Lefebvre, Henri. *Everyday Life in the Modern World.* Translated by Sacha Rabinovitch. New York: Harper and Row, 1971.

Lehtonen, Heidi-Maria, Henri Penttinen, Jukka Rauhala, and Vesa Valimaki. "Analysis and Modeling of Sustain-Pedal Effects." *Journal of the Acoustical Society of America* 122, no. 3 (2007): 1787–1797.

Lernout, Geert. *Help my Unbelief: Joyce and Religion.* London: Continuum, 2010.

Lichtheim, Miriam. *Ancient Egyptian Literature: A Book of Readings.* Vol. 3, *The Late Period.* Berkeley: University of California Press, 1980.

Lowell, Robert. *Collected Poems.* Edited by Frank Bidart and David Gewanter. New York: Farrar, Straus and Giroux, 2007.

Lucy, Niall. *Debating Derrida.* Carlton South, Victoria: Melbourne University Press, 1995.

Lüdke, Alf. *The History of Everyday Life: Reconstructing Historical Experiences and Ways of Life.* Translated by William Templer. Princeton, NJ: Princeton University Press, 1995.

MacDonagh, Donagh. *The Hungry Grass.* London: Faber and Faber, 1947.

MacKillop, James. *Fionn mac Cumhaill: Celtic Myth in English Literature.* Syracuse, NY: Syracuse University Press, 1986.

MacManus, Damian. "Irish Letter-Names and Their Kennings." *Ériu* 39 (1988): 127–168.

MacManus, Seumas. *The Story of the Irish Race: A Popular History of Ireland.* Rev. ed. Old Greenwich, CT: Devin-Adair, 1921.

Maddox, Brenda. *Nora: A Biography of Nora Joyce.* New York: Fawcett Columbine, 1988.

Maeterlinck, Maurice. *Wisdom and Destiny.* Translated by Alfred Sutro. London: George Allen, 1898.

Mahaffey, Vicki. "Changing Perspective: Why Style and Structure Matter in *Ulysses*." In *Joycean Possibilities: A Margot Norris Legacy,* edited by Joseph Valente, Vicki Mahaffey, and Kezia Whiting, 189–204. New York: Anthem, 2023.

———. "Darkening Freedom: Yeats, Joyce, and Beckett." In *The Cambridge History of Modernism,* edited by Vincent Sherry, 646–661. Cambridge: Cambridge University Press, 2016.

———. "Irish Christian Comedy." In *The Edinburgh Companion to Irish Modernism,* edited by Maud Ellmann, Siân White, and Vicki Mahaffey, 284–298. Edinburgh: Edinburgh University Press, 2021.

———. "Love, Race, and *Exiles*: The Bleak Side of *Ulysses*." *Joyce Studies Annual* (2007): 92–108.

———. *Modernist Literature: Challenging Fictions.* Oxford: Blackwell, 2007.

———. "Nausicaa." In *The Cambridge Centenary Ulysses: The 1922 Text with Essays and Notes,* edited by Catherine Flynn, 473–483. Cambridge: Cambridge University Press, 2022.

———. *Reauthorizing Joyce.* Cambridge: Cambridge University Press, 1988.

———. "'Ricorso': The Flaming Door of IV." In *Joyce's Allmaziful Plurabilities: Polyvocal Explorations of Finnegans Wake,* edited by Kimberly J. Devlin and Christine Smedley. Gainesville: University Press of Florida, 2015.

———. "Wagner, Joyce, and Revolution." *James Joyce Quarterly* 25 (Winter 1988): 237–247.

———. "Who Resembles Molly Bloom?" *Joyce Studies Annual* (2022): 361–377.

———, ed. *Collaborative Dubliners: Joyce in Dialogue.* Syracuse, NY: Syracuse University Press, 2012.

Mauss, Marcel. *The Gift: The Form and Reason for Exchange in Archaic Societies.* Translated by W.D. Halls. New York: Norton, 2000.

McHugh, Roland. *Annotations to Finnegans Wake.* Baltimore, MD: Johns Hopkins University Press, 1991.

Molière. *The School for Husbands and The Imaginary Cuckold.* Translated by Richard Wilbur. New York: Theatre Communications Group, 2009.

Moore, Thomas. *The Re-Enchantment of Everyday Life.* New York: Harper Collins, 1996.

Niebuhr, Reinhold. *Discovering the Signs of the Times: Sermons for Today and Tomorrow.* New York: Charles Scribner's Sons, 1946.

Nietzsche, Friedrich. *The Portable Nietzsche,* edited by Walter Kaufmann. Harmondsworth, England: Penguin, 1976.

Norris, Margot. *Joyce's Web: The Social Unraveling of Modernism.* Austin: University of Texas Press, 1992.

Nussbaum, Martha. *Upheavals of Thought: The Intelligence of Emotions.* Cambridge: Cambridge University Press, 2001.

Odell, George C. D. *Annals of the New York Stage.* Vol. 13, *1885–1888.* New York: Columbia University Press, 1942.

Ostler, Nicholas. *Empires of the Word: A Language History of the World.* New York: Harper/Collins, 2005.

O'Sullivan, Muiris, and Liam Downey. "Ogham Stones." *Archaeology Ireland* 28, no. 2 (Summer 2014): 26–29.

The Oxford Dictionary of English Etymology. Ed. C. T. Onions with the assistance of G.W.S. Friedrichsen and R. W. Burchfield. Oxford: Clarendon Press, 1966.

Ovid. *The Metamorphoses.* Translated by Mary M. Innes. Harmondsworth, England: Penguin Books, 1955.

Partridge, Eric. *A Dictionary of Slang and Unconventional English,* 8th ed., edited by Paul Beale. 1937; London: Routledge, 2002.

Pelaschiar, Laura. "'My Story Being Done, / She Gave Me for My Pains a World of Sighs': Shakespeare's *Othello* and Joyce's *Ulysses.*" In *Joyce/Shakespeare,* edited by Laura Pelaschiar, 38–55. Syracuse, NY: Syracuse University Press, 2015.

Pennick, Nigel. *Celtic Sacred Landscapes*. London: Thames and Hudson, 1996.

Phillips, Siobhan. *The Poetics of the Everyday: Creative Repetition in Modern American Verse*. New York: Columbia University Press.

Plato, *Phaedrus*. Translated by R. Hackforth. In *The Collected Dialogues of Plato, including the Letters*, edited by Edith Hamilton and Huntington Cairns. Princeton: Princeton University Press, Bollingen Series LXXI, 1961.

Plato. *Republic*. Translated by Roblin Waterfield. Oxford: Oxford University Press, 1993.

Proust, Marcel. *Swann's Way*, translated by Lydia Davis. New York: Penguin, 2003.

Pulver, Morgan. "Folds of Nonsense: Explorations of Style in Joyce." MPhil thesis, University of Queensland, 2013.

Rasula, Jed. "*Finnegans Wake* and the Character of the Letter." *James Joyce Quarterly* 34, no. 4 (Summer 1997): 517–530.

Riepma, Siert F. *The Story of Margarine*. Washington, DC: Public Affairs Press, 1970.

Rose, Danis. "Clodd One and Two: Corrigenda and Agenda." *A Finnegans Wake Circular* 3, no. 3 (Spring 1988): 53–56.

Rose, Danis, and Vincent Deane. "Clodd in VI.B.49.b." *A Finnegans Wake Circular* 3, no. 3 (Spring 1988): 57–60.

Rose, Danis, and John O'Hanlon, "Finn MacCool and the Final Weeks of Work in Progress." *A Wake Newslitter* 17, no. 5 (October 1980): 69–87.

Saint-Amour, Paul K., and Karen R. Lawrence. "Reopening 'A Painful Case.'" In *Collaborative Dubliners: Joyce in Dialogue*, edited by Vicki Mahaffey, 238–260. Syracuse, NY: Syracuse University Press, 2012.

Sayeau, Michael. *Against the Event: The Everyday and the Evolution of Modernist Narrative*. Oxford: Oxford University Press, 2013.

Schlossman, Beryl. *Joyce's Catholic Comedy of Language*. Madison: University of Wisconsin Press, 1985.

Shakespeare, William. *The Riverside Shakespeare*. Boston: Houghton Mifflin, 1974.

Sharkey, John. *Celtic Mysteries: The Ancient Religions*. London: Thames and Hudson, 1975.

Shipley, Joseph T. *The Origins of English Words: A Discursive Dictionary of Indo-European Roots*. Baltimore: The Johns Hopkins University Press, 1984.

Smedley, Christine. "Shem's 'Strabismal Apologia': The Split Vision of the Famine in I.7." In *Joyce's Allmaziful Plurabilities: Polyvocal Explorations of* Finnegans Wake, edited by Kimberly J. Devlin and Christine Smedley, 114–132. Gainesville: University Press of Florida, 2015.

Smith, James M. *Ireland's Magdalene Laundries and the Nation's Architecture of Containment*. South Bend, IN: University of Notre Dame Press, 2007.

Swift, Catherine. "The Story of Ogham." *History Today* 65, no. 10 (October 2015): 4–5.

Swift, Jonathan. *A Tale of a Tub and Other Works*. Oxford: Oxford University Press, 2008.

Tanner, Tony. *Adultery and the Novel*. Baltimore, MD: Johns Hopkins University Press, 1979.

The Trial of Jim the Penman (James Townsend Saward). Edited by George Dilnot. London: Geoffrey Bles, 1930.

Twain, Mark. *Adventures of Huckleberry Finn*. Edited by Emory Elliott. Oxford: Oxford University Press, 1999.

Tweedy, Robert. *The Story of the Court Laundry*. Dublin: Wolfhound, 1999.

Updike, John. *Hugging the Shore: Essays and Criticism*.1983; New York: Random House, 2013.

Vaisey-Ginser, M. "Margarine: Types and Properties." In *Encyclopedia of Food Science and Nutrition*, 2nd ed., edited by Luiz Trugo and Paul M. Finglas, 3704–3709. Elsevier Science Ltd., 2003,.

Van Mierlo, Chrissie. *James Joyce and Catholicism: The Apostate's Wake*. London: Bloomsbury, 2017.

Visser, Margaret. *Much Depends on Dinner: The Extraordinary History and Mythology, Allure and Obsessions, Perils and Taboos of an Ordinary Meal*. New York: Collier Books, 1986.

The Walters Art Gallery. *Illuminated Books of the Middle Ages and Renaissance: An Exhibition Held at the Baltimore Museum of Art January 27–March 13*. Baltimore, MD: Trustees of the Walters Art Gallery, 1949.

Will, Emily J. "Theory: Handwriting and Signatures—Some Basic Facts and Theory." Emily J. Will, D-BFDE. Accessed February 4, 2024. https://qdewill.com/theory.html.

Wilde, Oscar. *The Picture of Dorian Gray: Authoritative Texts, Backgrounds, Reviews and Reactions, Criticism*. Edited by Donald L. Lawler. New York: Norton, 1988.

———. "The Truth of Masks." In *The Soul of Man Under Socialism and Selected Critical Prose*, edited by Linda Dowling, 280–304. London: Penguin, 2001.

Woolf, Virginia. *Between the Acts*. New York: Harcourt Brace Jovanovich, 1969.

Woolf, Virginia. *To the Lighthouse*. Foreword by Eudora Welty. New York: Harcourt Brace Jovanovich, 1966.

Yeats, William Butler. *The Collected Works of W. B. Yeats*. Vol. 1 *The Poems*. Revised and edited by Richard J. Finneran. New York: Macmillan, 1989.

———. *Mythologies*. New York: Collier Books, 1959.

INDEX

ABOUT THE AUTHOR

VICKI MAHAFFEY is a professor emerita at the University of Pennsylvania in Philadelphia and the University of Illinois, Urbana-Champaign. She is the author or editor of several books, including *Reauthorizing Joyce; States of Desire: Wilde, Yeats, Joyce, and the Irish Experiment; Modernist Literature: Challenging Fictions; Collaborative Dubliners: Joyce in Dialogue; Irish Modernism* (with Maud Ellmann and Sîan White); and *Joycean Possibilities: A Margot Norris Legacy* (with Joseph Valente and Kezia Whiting). A Guggenheim fellow, she has also published over forty articles.